Vera Watson was born in Atcham, Shropshire, and now lives in London. She has been an editor of technical and scientific journals for many years, and is a reviewer for *The Times Literary Supplement* and the *Daily Telegraph*. She has previously written a novel, a biography, and a study of Queen Victoria.

THE BRITISH MUSEUM

Its antiquities and civilizations from prehistory to the fall of the Roman Empire

Q

VERA WATSON

QUARTET BOOKS LONDON

First published in Great Britain by Quartet Books Limited 1973
27 Goodge Street, London W1P 1FD

ISBN 0 704 32029 0 *Casebound edition*
0 704 33023 7 *Large format paperback*

Printed in Great Britain by Acorn Litho Services Ltd, Feltham, Middlesex

Typesetting by Bedford Typesetters Ltd, Bedford

To Mary MacKenzie
in fulfilment of a promise made many years ago

Acknowledgements

I wish to express my gratitude to the Trustees for the unique facilities available in the Galleries and the Library for obtaining the material for this book. I have always considered it a privilege to work in the British Museum.

My debt is great to Sir Frank Francis KCB, Director and Principal Librarian, 1959–1968, and to Sir John Wolfenden CBE, the present Director. Sir Frank encouraged my attempt to describe the exhibits in their historical context, and Sir John's understanding of this aim has been my constant support during a task which has been formidable but infinitely fascinating.

I am under great obligation to the following Keepers of Departments and their staffs for reading the MS. and pointing out errors (those which remain are mine), and also for much help and advice at other times: Dr R. D. Barnett, Keeper of the Department of Western Asiatic Antiquities, and Mr T. C. Mitchell, Assistant Keeper; Mr J. W. Brailsford, Keeper of the Department of Prehistoric and Romano-British Antiquities, Dr I. A. Longworth, Assistant Keeper, Dr A. Rosenfeld, formerly Senior Research Assistant, and Miss Catherine Johns, Research Assistant; Dr I. E. S.

Edwards CMG, Keeper of the Egyptian Antiquities, and Mr D. E. L. Haynes, Keeper of the Greek and Roman Antiquities.

Thanks are also due to Mr E. J. Miller, Head of the State Paper Office for his constructive criticisms of chapter 1 on the history of the Museum, and likewise to Dr A. E. Werner, Keeper of the Research Laboratory, for help with the section on the work of his department. I have to thank Miss T. Molleson, British Museum (Natural History) for drawing Figure 1 after the chart in the exhibition illustrating Evolution at the British Museum (Natural History).

To Harry Slater, who gave me much assistance and wise advice, Aydua Scott-Elliot who drew the maps, Elsie M. Bryant who began the vast task of note-taking in the galleries and Neville Mapleston who helped me to complete it and undertook much invaluable work besides I am most deeply grateful. My thanks are also due to Betty Stephenson for her accurate typing of the MS.

The years spent in writing this book have been some of the most delightful and interesting of my life; and if I have been able to impart to my readers even a tithe of my own enthusiasm for the Museum and its splendid collections and for the ancient peoples they represent, I shall not have laboured in vain.

Vera Watson
Chelsea, 1973

The Author and Publishers wish to thank the following institutions for permission to publish the illustrations appearing in this book:

The Trustees of the British Museum, Fig. 2–6, 8, 9, 11–28 and 30–44; The Grosvenor Museum, Chester, Fig. 7; The Oriental Institute of Chicago, Fig. 10 and the Royal Ontario Museum, Fig. 29.

How to Use the Book

This book covers the period from Early Man to the end of Antiquity, that is, to the fall of Rome.

Each chapter consists of an historical summary of the civilization concerned which provides a background to the exhibits, and a list of books for further reading (p. 251) generally to be found in public libraries or in paperback editions.

Identification of exhibits

Exhibits are described in two different ways. First, under subject, indicated by a sub-heading such as 'The Temple, 'Agriculture', 'Siege of Lachish', when they are found under their case (bay or other location) and exhibit numbers, for example,

> [case 8, 1954 10–18 1. Bronze figure of a banqueteer, c. 520 BC]

Secondly, by the case when the title (and if available, the case number) are placed at the beginning of the relevant paragraph, for example,

> *Servants at work* [*cases 148–9*]. The objects described above were principally the . . .

This method is generally, but not invariably, used when the case is not numbered and also when its contents constitute a separate subject.

When an exhibit is mentioned as being on the [L] or [R], this means on the left or right of the viewer.

Dates

Many dates in this book are given in millennia and centuries BC, and this can sometimes be confusing. But if one remembers that there are 10 centuries to a millennium, that the beginning of the 1st millennium BC is 1000 BC, which figure decreases by 100 for every century to the beginning of the Christian era when BC becomes AD (there is no year 0). Early in the 1st millennium BC would be in about the 9th century BC, but early in the 1st millennium AD would be up to about 100 AD.

Itineraries

If it is desired to study a particular civilization, say that of Egypt, it is advisable to follow the suggested itineraries, for the Museum is large and time and energy will be wasted by random visits to galleries. If, however, the visitor wishes to see specific exhibits, such as the sculptures of the Parthenon (Elgin Marbles), the index will indicate where information on these subjects can be found.

Finally readers must bear in mind that the Museum, although enshrining so much of the past, is a live institution and that changes and improvements are taking place all the time. For instance, alterations are planned in the Department of Prehistoric and Romano-British Antiquities and a Palestine room is being arranged by the Department of Western Asiatic Antiquities. Moreover antiquities are lent to other institutions for exhibition, and are occasionally removed from the public rooms for cleaning, testing or repair, and for special exhibitions within the Museum.

Therefore although the text has been checked up to the time of going to press, if an object is mentioned in this book and cannot be found, the omission need not necessarily be due to the carelessness of the author, although she is far from claiming that this would never be the case.

Foreword by Sir John Wolfenden, C.B.E.

Who or what is the British Museum *for*? Is it for the scholar or for the general public? Is it for enjoyment or for education?

These are questions which I am asked almost every day. And my first answer is to deny the antitheses, the contrasts which are implied in the way the questions are expressed.

The British Museum is not for either the scholar or the general public to the exclusion of the other. In fact every day it serves a wide spectrum of interests, from the highly specialist scholar at one end, through private researchers, individual writers, radio producers, novelists, to the members of the general public (from Britain or from overseas) and schoolchildren.

Similarly, it provides both the relaxation which comes from the sheer enjoyment of beautiful things and the opportunity for serious educational study. Again, the two are not mutually exclusive. It would be a pity – and it is not the case – if we could not mix the two in the same activity. Nobody can fully enjoy the Elgin Marbles or the Lindisfarne Gospels without at the same time learning something: and nobody is going to learn much about clocks or Chinese ceramics unless he enjoys looking at them.

Perhaps this attitude could be made more explicit. Perhaps in the past we have taken too much for granted in the visitor's previous knowledge of what he sees. We have in preparation a wide-ranging development of our educational services. This does not necessarily mean that there will be more and more lectures for more and more school parties. What it does mean is a serious attempt to make teachers more familiar with what the Museum has to offer, so that its resources can be more deliberately related to syllabuses, curricula and projects, and so that youthful visitors may be better informed, before they come, about what they are going to see. This, properly done, will not diminish their enjoyment at the expense of improving their education: it will increase both. There is much to be said for 'education by stealth'.

Miss Watson's book is an embodiment of this attitude of mind. It would be difficult for anybody, scholar or schoolchild, to read it without learning a great deal in a very enjoyable way.

J. F. Wolfenden
Director and Principal Librarian

1 The British Museum

The British Museum

A Short Account of its Purposes, Foundation, Growth and Services

Introduction

The tradition of the British Museum is historical, and it aims to represent all periods. It is not primarily a museum of art although it contains some of the world's greatest treasures.

Its vast collections representative of the civilizations of antiquity and later and its magnificent library are housed under one roof, an inestimable boon to the scholar and to the non-specialist who, if he is sufficiently assiduous, can make himself well versed in the ways of the ancient world. On the other hand the overseas visitor, with only a short time to spare, has an unparalleled range of archaeological and artistic exhibits from which to make his choice.

A walk round the galleries is a humbling experience. It emphasizes how much the ancients achieved before the dawn of our era; how one civilization took over and expanded the ideas of an earlier; and how the vast technological and scientific structure of our times could not have come to pass without these basic achievements. Ancient man, indeed 'builded better than he knew'.

History

The British Museum owes its origin to Sir Hans Sloane, MD, FRS (1660–1753) who, in his will, offered his celebrated museum of natural history, antiquities, manuscripts and printed books (valued at £80,000) to the Crown for £20,000, in order that 'the same may be rendered as useful as possible, as well as towards satisfying the desire of the curious, as for the improvement, knowledge and information of all persons'.

King George II's response to the offer was that he doubted if there were sufficient funds in the Exchequer, whereupon Sloane's trustees, in accordance with his testamentary instructions, petitioned Parliament. The House, after considerable discussion, decided to acquire the collection, and to add to it the rare and valuable manuscripts of Robert and Edward Harley, 1st and 2nd Earls of Oxford of the second creation, for which £10,000 was offered, and the magnificent library of Sir Robert Cotton, scholar and antiquarian of the Elizabethan and Jacobean periods, already acquired for the nation in 1700 but since shamefully neglected and inadequately housed.

But Parliament, never a generous patron of the arts, was no more disposed than the King to provide the necessary funds. In the Act (26 Geo. II, c. 22) implementing its decisions, it was stipulated that a sum of money 'not exceeding Three Hundred Thousand Pounds in the Whole' was to be raised by a lottery supervised by the Trustees (nominated in the Act and headed by the Archbishop of Canterbury, the Lord Chancellor or Lord Keeper of the Great Seal, the Speaker of the House of Commons, various high officers of State and others) for the accommodation and purchase of these collections, which were not only to be available to the 'Learned and the Curious' but were also for the 'General Use and Benefit of the Publick'.

This lottery caused a scandal, even in those days of financial jobbery, for when the Lottery Office of the Exchequer opened for the sale of tickets at £3 each on 9 June, 1753, a corner was made in them by an unscrupulous lottery agent, Peter Leheup (in spite of a provision in the Act to prevent such a contingency), and the price rose immediately above par, at one time reaching £3 17s. 0d. However, before the draw, Leheup prudently unloaded on to other lottery agents (one of them appropriately named Hazard) and the price of tickets fell till it became as low as £2 10s. 0d. a few days before the draw.

The draw for the £200,000 prize money began on 26 November at the Guildhall and continued daily until the end of December, and within a few days a ticket sold by Messrs Hazard had won the largest prize of £10,000 (the prize winner was a stable keeper at the 'White Horse', London Wall). Both the lottery and the purpose for which it had been raised, the new Museum, aroused considerable interest among the public and were fully reported in the Press. Amid all the excitement of the draw at the Guildhall, the announcement in the *Public Advertiser* that the Trustees for the late Sir Hans Sloane's Museum had held their first meeting on 11 December at the 'Cockpit', Whitehall, to elect fifteen additional Trustees, would certainly not have passed without notice.

The Trustees' first task, as specified by the Act, was to erect or provide a suitable 'repository' for the collection within the cities of London or Westminster or their suburbs. There had been much speculation on the subject. In early May 1753 it was reported that the banqueting-house at Whitehall would be fitted up for the purpose, and a fortnight later that Buckingham House had been bought. The Trustees, however, eventually settled on Montagu House, Great Russell Street, a fine building in the French style on the site of the present building, for which they paid £10,250, and spent another £12,873 on repairing and fitting it up. On 15 January, 1759, the Museum was opened to the public.

But not in the modern sense of the term, for admission was by ticket for which a written application had to be made. Nor was the Museum anything but an embryo of the present vast establishment, for there were only three departments: Printed Books, Manuscripts, and Natural History and Artificial Productions, the latter consisting of Sloane's collections of natural history and antiquities.

The hours of opening were 9 a.m. to 3 p.m., Monday to Friday, except during the summer months of May to August when, on Mondays and Fridays, the hours were from 4 p.m. to 8 p.m. Visitors were escorted round in parties of five (only ten persons each hour being admitted to the Museum) and were allowed to spend one hour in each of the three departments. Those wishing to make use of the library facilities could only do so by permission of the Trustees which expired after six months when a fresh application had to be made.

The Museum's officers numbered seven, the chief being the Principal Librarian, Gowin Knight, MD, with a salary of £160 per annum, and £40 extra for exercising some supervision in financial matters. The officers were given free apartments and the hours were short, which compensated for the small salaries as they were able to undertake other paid work.

For the first 50 years of its existence the Museum stagnated, mainly through lack of money. The main part of the income available to the Trustees came from £30,000 invested in 1753 in the funds which, after paying for Montagu House and its furnishing, was all that remained from £100,000 which the Trustees obtained from the lottery. This with other small sums brought in some £1,150 per annum, which was insufficient to meet expenses. For any increase in the collections, therefore, the Trustees were mainly dependent on gifts.

With expenses perpetually exceeding income, the Trustees were obliged in 1762 to apply for financial assistance to Parliament, which provided £2,000 (less £107 17s. 0d. fees paid to the Exchequer and Treasury) every second year up to 1772 when, two years later, the grant was raised to £3,000.

At the turn of the century, however, the Museum, which had been mainly a resort of scholars, became a centre of public interest, a position it has held ever since. The immediate cause was the arrival of a ship in the Thames early in 1801 bearing Napoleon's collection of Egyptian antiquities, including the Rosetta Stone, captured after Sir Ralph Abercromby's victory at Alexandria in 1801, and subsequently presented to the Museum by George III. They were probably the first large Egyptian sculptures to reach this country. In the next few decades other large acquisitions were made: the Towneley collection of Greek and Roman sculptures in 1805, the Elgin marbles in 1816, and George III's fine library in 1823, all of which were fully reported in the Press.

A gallery had been built for the Egyptian antiquities in which the Towneley sculptures were also placed, but the other acquisitions could not be housed in the existing building. The Trustees therefore applied to the government for funds to construct a gallery for George III's magnificent library (the present beautiful King's Library) and to replace eventually Montagu House by a building with adequate accommodation. With Sir Robert Smirke as the architect this work was carried out in stages, and by 1847 the façade familiar to visitors today was completed, with the exception of the sculpture on the pediment which remained to be put into position. But even the rebuilding was only part of a series of constructional operations which began in 1804–5 and are still in progress today.

But there were other factors, besides spectacular antiquities, which brought the Museum into the public eye in the first half of the 19th century. The old order was changing and the oligarchical government of aristocratic Whigs and Tories was being assailed by the new and wealthy manufacturing class, demanding its place in the sun. Reform and progress were the watchwords, and an institution such as the Museum which provided educational facilities for even the humblest was very much in harmony with the prevailing ideas.

It so happened that during this period there were officers who were desirous of extending its facilities. The first was Joseph Planta, Principal Librarian from 1799 to 1827, who abolished the system of prior application for tickets and thus made the Museum easier of access, and who also simplified the Reading Room rules so that the number of readers increased considerably during his tenure of office. The second was Antonio Panizzi, who entered the Museum in 1831 as an extra assistant in the library, became Keeper of the Printed Books in 1837, and Principal Librarian in 1856.

Panizzi was a man of outstanding powers of mind and character, of whom it has been said that there was as much work in him as in any three average Englishmen. A brilliant organizer, he possessed sound judgement and enlightened views; but although kindly to those in lowly positions and senior staff who agreed with his views, he was intolerant of incompetence and did not allow any obstacles – human and otherwise – to interfere with his plans.

Panizzi was an Italian from the Austrian controlled duchy of Modena who had graduated in law at the University of Parma in 1818. When he entered the Museum at the age of 34 he had already been condemned to death as a member of the Italian revolutionary movement, but had escaped to England where he taught Italian for a livelihood in Liverpool. His marked abilities soon attracted attention, and an introduction to Brougham resulted in first, his obtaining the chair of Italian at the newly formed University College, London, and when that proved unremunerative and the new professor was faced with starvation, the post of extra assistant in the Library.

He therefore possessed worldly experience in a fuller measure than was customary among the majority of academic men, and had many contacts among foreign scholars as well as among international statesmen with a stake in Italian politics (with his friend, Prosper Merimée, the novelist and savant, he enjoyed for many years the friendship and hospitality of Napoleon III and the Empress Eugénie). Through Brougham he formed a connection with the Whig party which was to increase along the years, and was of inestimable value in ensuring a sympathetic understanding of his plans by ministers and men of high standing who were his personal friends. Indeed it was due to his friendship with the Whig bibliophile, Thomas Grenville, that the Museum received the bequest of the magnificent Grenville Library, now housed in the room on the right of the entrance hall.

With his dynamic qualities and his valuable personal connections, Panizzi was the right man in the right place at the right time. When he came to the Museum in 1831, it consisted of four departments (Manuscripts, Printed Books, Natural History and Antiquities) which were administered by sixteen officers with assistants and attendants. The total staff at that time was about seventy-nine, and the running expenses for the year £16,684. When he resigned in 1866, there were eleven departments and the estimated expenditure for 1866–7 was £102,744. Indeed the foundations had then been well and truly laid on which subsequent expansion was to take place.

But his greatest achievement was the creation of a comprehensive national library. In 1833 the collections of printed books amounted to some 218,957 volumes and although they contained valuable rarities, they were also notable for their deficiencies. Panizzi pointed out in 1836 to members of the Parliamentary Commission investigating the affairs of the Museum that these deficiencies had never been made good owing to lack of money, and pleaded for a generous parliamentary grant. Only when £100,000 had been spent over 10 or 12 years, he said, would there be the beginnings of a truly representative collection 'worthy of the British nation'.

This was indeed frank speaking. Nevertheless, it was not

until 10 years later that a grant of £10,000 was made, which had to be cut to £2,000 and then almost to nil owing to lack of space to house the books, and was not resumed until 1859. But there was no doubt that Panizzi's frank and lucid exposition of the plight of the department had made a profound impression, and when the Keepership became vacant in 1837, he was appointed to the post.

His Keepership was notable for a number of developments. He insisted on the fulfilment by publishers of the provisions of the Copyright Act of 1842, thereby adding a large number of modern books, and reprints of old books, to the Library. Furthermore, he evolved a system of cataloguing which was unique then but which embodied principles of library cataloguing as they are accepted today; and it was also his idea (although he was not the only one to think of it) that a glass-domed reading room, built on the principles of the Crystal Palace, should be erected, with adjacent storage space for books, in the courtyard of the Museum. This beautiful room is still in use today, but as admission is by ticket, the public do not have access to it. Indeed, his imaginative vision, combined with sound, practical methods of administration, laid the basis of what is today one of the principal libraries of the world.

In 1866, Panizzi finally resigned. His health had been deteriorating for some years and he suffered acutely from rheumatism, perhaps brought on by the strains and stresses of his tumultuous years at the Museum, combined with an injudicious diet, for he was an inveterate diner out. During his 35 years' service, he had refused all honours, but in 1869 the Queen made him a K C B. In his retirement he lived within sight and sound of his triumphs at 31 Bloomsbury Square where, on 8 April, 1879, he died at the age of 82.

From Panizzi's retirement to the turn of the century, the Museum made steady progress, as witnessed by the number of visitors. In 1864, the figure was 432,339 which, by 1882, had risen to 767,402. However, the removal of the natural history departments to South Kensington in 1880–83 caused a serious drop in the number of visitors to Bloomsbury, and the position was not restored until 1913. The highest attendance recorded in the 19th century was 2,524,154 in 1851, the year of the Great Exhibition in Hyde Park, and the highest in the present century so far is 4,540,786 in 1972, the year of the Tutankhamun exhibition, which accounted for 1,656,300 of the total.

Conditions of entry to the public had become progressively easier, but it was not until 1878 that the Museum was open every day, except Sunday. Although the Reading Room had been lighted by electricity in 1879, there was no lighting system in the galleries, and visiting hours varied with the season; but when electric light was installed in 1890, the Museum was open in the evening from 8–10 p.m. This evening experiment had only an initial success and was abandoned in 1897; far more popular was Sunday afternoon opening, inaugurated in 1896, and still in operation at the present time. Other experiments which have stood the test of time were a refreshment room opened in 1866 (a plate of beef, roast or boiled, cost 6d., and bottled beers and stouts were sold) and on a rather higher level, the introduction in 1911 of a guide-lecturer to conduct parties round the Museum and lecture on specific classes of objects, as well as a bookstall a year later for the sale of the Museum's own publications and postcards.

Throughout the 19th century there had scarcely been a time when building operations were not either in contemplation or actually taking place, and the same situation prevails in the present century. To relieve pressure on space in the library, a newspaper store was built at Hendon and opened in 1905, which was later enlarged and opened as a newspaper library in 1932; and from 1906–13, a new north wing was erected which included the Edward VII gallery and the galleries and students' room of the Department of Prints and Drawings, as well as Maps, Music and since 1931, the State Paper Office. Incorporated in this scheme, and paid for partly by a benefactor's legacy, was the North Library which joined the new wing to the old building. Between the two wars other improvements were carried out, mainly connected with increasing the storage space in the library, but a new gallery for the sculptures from the Parthenon was also completed in 1939 through the generosity of Lord Duveen.

In the 1914–18 war little damage was done to the Museum in the German raids on London, although it was thought necessary to store valuable objects in the tube and to close the galleries as a measure of economy in 1916 (the Reading Room and the Department of Manuscripts were never closed). Exhibitions of casts and lesser sculpture, however, and a display of manuscripts and printed books were later put on view.

But the situation was very different in World War II when high explosive, oil, and incendiary bombs fell on the building. Fortunately, three high explosive bombs did not detonate and two more fell in the forecourt, but damage was done to the King's Library and the Duveen Gallery. The greatest destruction, however, was caused by the fire raid of 10 May, 1941, when dozens of incendiaries set alight the roofs of the main staircase and seven exhibition rooms which were completely burnt out. Bookstacks outside the Reading Room were also set on fire and about a quarter of a million books destroyed.

The losses would have been infinitely greater had it not been for the large-scale evacuation of books, manuscripts and antiquities planned in detail in the years before the war. The Museum had several repositories, country houses, the National Library of Wales, Aberystwyth, and an air-conditioned rock tunnel under that building which it shared with the National Library, a stone quarry near Bristol also used by other institutions, the new Bodleian building which took 65,000, books and a disused tube tunnel in London. The latter protected the frieze of the Parthenon throughout the war, for the galleries, with the exception of sculptures too heavy to move and most of the Assyrian low reliefs which were fixed to the wall, were completely cleared. But the service of the Reading Room, although curtailed and transferred to the North Library, was maintained through the war, except when the antiquities were being moved or bomb damage required the attention of the staff.

When peace came books, manuscripts and antiquities had to be brought back to London from their various repositories and bomb damage repaired before the Museum's services could be restored. So far as the library departments were concerned the Reading Room (which had had an oil bomb through the roof) was reopened on 3 June, 1946, and the Department of Manuscripts on 2 December of the same year. But repairs to the galleries, where damage was extensive, was a vast task which is not yet wholly completed.

In the meantime, however, far-reaching changes in the constitution of the Museum have come into operation through the passing of the British Museum Act, 1963, which alters the composition of the Trustee body, reduces its numbers, limits the number of years each member may serve, and includes other clauses to facilitate the government of the Museum.

Before these changes, plans had been drawn up for considerable constructional and organizational developments. For reasons beyond the control of the Trustees, only some of them have been carried out, those recently concluded being the reconstruction of the Greek and Roman rooms on the ground floor, the Assyrian Saloon complex and the exhibition areas of the Departments of Prints and Drawings and Oriental Antiquities. On the first floor the Prehistoric and Roman-British rooms have been rebuilt.

The former gallery (first floor) of the Ethnographical Department (now installed at 6 Burlington Gardens under the title of the Museum of Mankind) will be remodelled for occupation by the Departments of Western Asiatic Antiquities and Coins and Medals and to provide space for temporary exhibitions. The former Oriental Rooms and Iron Age Gallery on this floor are now being prepared for the Department of Medieval and Later Antiquities which has now vacated the Edward VII Gallery in favour of the Department of Oriental Antiquities.

The current building programme incorporates an extension at the south west corner of the Museum which will contain galleries for special exhibitions, workshops and preparation areas, restaurants for the public and staff and facilities for the British Museum Society.

* * *

There are several matters which could not be dealt with in the above short narrative as they merit more detailed treatment, but on which readers nevertheless may care for some information.

Acquisitions

The Museum possesses one of the largest collections of antiquities in the world and it may well be asked, as one gazes round the galleries, 'Where do they all come from?

How were they obtained?' The answer is: by means of excavations, by purchase, and by gift and bequest, statements which require, however, some elaboration.

Excavations

The Museum has undertaken excavations at many sites in the Ancient World. It also contributes financially to the expeditions of universities and various archaeological organizations and schools (such as the British School of Archaeology in Iraq). In this way it has qualified for a share in the finds on digs, for in some of the countries of the Middle East a proportion of the finds is allocated to the excavators by the host country, the latter taking the first choice. In this way the excavators receive some return for their work other than the knowledge gained (this is only fair for excavation is a very costly business, and when the dig lasts several seasons, the expense runs into many thousands of pounds), and the host country obtains valuable antiquities at little cost to itself.

But this arrangement is of comparatively recent origin and when the Museum began operations in northern Mesopotamia (Iraq) in 1846 (which were continued intermittently throughout the latter part of the 19th and early 20th century) under the direction of the eminent explorer, Sir Henry Layard, all these countries formed part of the Turkish empire (as did Greece up to 1830), and a permit from the government at Constantinople not only enabled excavations to take place but also the antiquities discovered to be removed to England. The Turks, being Moslems, then had no interest in the peoples of the past whom they regarded as infidels.

However, the sensational discoveries made by Layard and his successors aroused such world-wide interest that the news eventually reached both the Turkish government and the inhabitants of Mesopotamia. The government enacted laws forbidding the dealing in, and export of, antiquities; but the population of Mesopotamia, who knew well that the inefficient and corrupt Ottoman administration would never be able to enforce its laws, dug furiously in the ancient sites. Several of the sites which suffered depredations in this manner were those licensed by the Turkish government to the Museum. The spoils, mainly clay tablets engraved with cuneiform script (which were the records of the ancient civilizations), eventually reached dealers in Baghdad and Mosul, where the Museum was obliged to buy them back, in several instances from the very watchmen who had been paid to guard the sites.

The same anarchical state of affairs existed in Egypt where excavations by Europeans had started the natives on a hunt for antiquarian objects. It is, therefore, satisfactory that, after the First World War and the creation of independent states out of the erstwhile territories of the Ottoman Empire, the situation was eventually regulated in a way equitable to all concerned. It should, however, be pointed out that until Europeans investigated the ancient civilizations of the Middle East (and thus created a market for antiquities) the indigenous populations of those regions merely regarded their ancient cities as sources of building materials, bricks and stone, and also of fertilizer for agricultural purposes.

Gifts and bequests

'It is often supposed that the Museum is supported by Parliament', wrote Sir Frederic Kenyon, Director and Principal Librarian (1909–31), 'and so in great measure it is: but the grants which Parliament is able to make for the acquisition of objects would not nearly suffice to maintain the Museum in the position which it has acquired among the museums of the world. . . . The Trustees are indebted, to an extent which few but themselves realize, to a continual flow of gifts from private benefactors.'

Ample confirmation of this last statement is to be found in the number of labels on exhibits in the galleries which bear the words 'Presented by . . .'. The Museum has indeed been the recipient of many magnificent bequests from enlightened collectors, too numerous to mention here. In 1836 Panizzi pointed out that over half the books in the Library came from bequests and that they accounted for two-thirds of the Library's value. But not all gifts come from persons who have amassed large collections. Many are family heirlooms or prized possessions which the public-spirited owners prefer to present to the Museum rather than send them to the sale room.

However, owing to fiscal policy, it seems probable that large bequests will be much fewer in future; and it is to be hoped that government, which spends so much on education, will bear this point in mind when funds are being allocated for the purchases of the various departments.

Purchases

The departments of the Museum make their purchases at the sale rooms, through agents and dealers, foreign and British, and from private individuals. In the latter category is the discerning collector who is unable, for financial or other reasons, to make a gift of his collection to the Museum but who nevertheless does not wish it to be dispersed after his death. In such cases, he will often offer it to the Museum at considerably less than the sum at which it has been valued.

However, it cannot be too strongly stressed that, in spite of the objects obtained through excavations; in spite of the many splendid bequests, the majority of the items seen in the galleries have been purchased through the normal trade channels.

The Research Laboratory

In World War II objects were safely stored underground in controlled conditions (p. 22); but in the 1914–18 conflict, when little was known about the effects of temperature and humidity on antiquities, considerable damage was done by subterranean storage.

At that time there was no laboratory in the Museum and, the limited facilities in the workshops were wholly inadequate to deal with the effects of decay. In 1919, therefore, the Trustees applied to the Department of Scientific and Industrial Research for assistance, and as a result a room in the Department of Prints and Drawings was equipped in 1920 for scientific investigation.

The new Research Laboratory was under the direction of Dr Alexander Scott, FRS, a former president of the Chemical Society and a man with antiquarian tastes. Dr Scott took up his labours with the Museum at an age when most men give them up (he was 85 when he retired in 1938). Nevertheless, within a short period DSIR Reports on the methods of preservation devised by the new Laboratory made their appearance and attracted much attention in the museum world, for at that period there was no other laboratory of this type functioning in the country, and the only one elsewhere, which had been established at Berlin, had ceased to function after the 1914–18 war.

Indeed the Laboratory, initially regarded only as a temporary experiment, was so successful that in 1931 it was incorporated as an independent department of the Museum. But long before then larger premises had become imperative and a move was made in 1922 to 39 Russell Square, a Georgian house which was adapted as a Laboratory. Owing to bomb damage the Laboratory was moved after the war to another Georgian house at 1 Montague Place. Finally it was considered necessary to build a properly designed laboratory and in 1962, on the site of 39 and 40 Russell Square, behind the Georgian façades which had to be retained to harmonize with the other houses, a new building arose. In it were incorporated a series of laboratories for the scientific examination of antiquities and a conservation laboratory beneath which, in a concrete basement, is a radio-carbon dating laboratory.

In the early days the Laboratory was mainly concerned with the preservation of objects and the treatment and restoration of stone and metal which had suffered deterioration. Now, however, due to the availability of such techniques as X-radiography, ultra-violet and infra-red radiations, X-ray diffraction, spectroscopy, metallography and micro-chemical analysis, it has been able to extend the scope of its activities and to concentrate on two particular aspects.

The first was the devising of scientific techniques to discover from what materials an ancient object was made and the technical means whereby the ancient craftsman made it, which in turn resulted in the knowledge so gained being applied to problems concerned with the authenticity of antiquities. This service is essential in an establishment where the majority of acquisitions are purchased.

The second line of investigation was the development of reliable methods of conservation using modern materials, many of which have proved of value for such purposes as the consolidation of fragile silver and bronze objects, the stabilization of waterlogged wood and leather, and the removal of soluble salts from pottery and stone (under museum conditions, salt deposits can cause deterioration).

Another important service, offered free to archaeologists all over the world, is the dating of organic matter by the radiocarbon method (Appendix 1). In the past there has often been difficulty in deciding how long any given civilization may have lasted, and this method of radiocarbon dating can provide the answer within certain limits.

2 The department of Prehistoric and Romano-British Antiquities

The department of Prehistoric and Romano-British Antiquities

First Floor:
Early Man Gallery (Mezzanine), Central Saloon, First Bronze Age Room, Second Bronze Age Room, Iron Age Room, Roman Britain Gallery

Prehistoric Antiquities

Introduction
The prehistory of man, as covered by the Early Man exhibit of the Prehistoric Department, comprises the period from the emergence of early forms of man to the appearance of *Homo sapiens sapiens* (modern man) up to the stage before he becomes a settled farmer. It is represented here by man's works, that is, mainly stone tools for they are the only objects to survive in quantity during the immensely long period of human development. But the biological evolution of man can be studied in the British Museum (Natural History), South Kensington, where the subject is covered by a most comprehensive exhibition.

Before we proceed, one point must be clarified: the prehistory of man is a comparatively new study, and evidence is still sparse, with many gaps. Research, however, is increasing and new discoveries coming to light. Therefore, although the broad outlines are considered known, modifications will take place, and statements made here must be considered in this light. These remarks apply to prehistory all over the world.

To understand the account which follows it is necessary to know that man and the modern great apes (chimpanzee, gorilla, gibbon and orang-outang) are descended from a

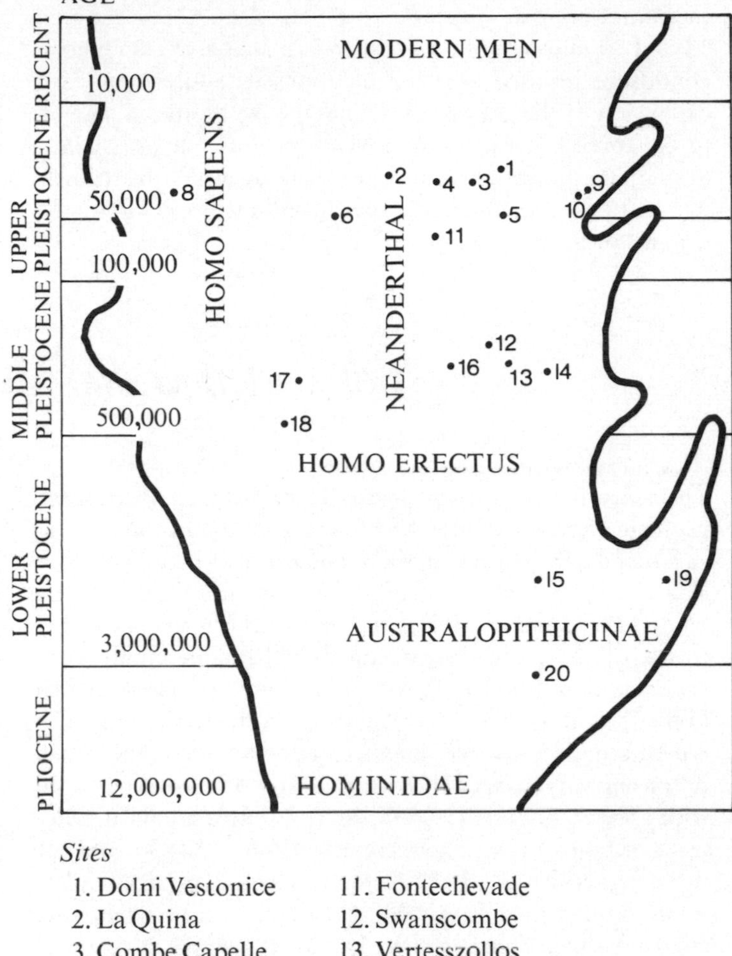

Sites

1. Dolni Vestonice	11. Fontechevade
2. La Quina	12. Swanscombe
3. Combe Capelle	13. Vertesszollos
4. Gibraltar	14. Ternifine (*H. erectus*)
5. Haua Fteah	15. Olduvai (*H. Habilis*)
6. Mount Carmel	16. Arago (Tautavel)
7. Ehringsdorf	17. Peking (*H. erectus*)
8. Niah	18. Lantian (H. modjokertensis)
9. Broken Hill	19. Olduvai (A. boisei)
10. Saldanha	20. East Rudolf

Fig. 1. The descent of man, after the chart in the exhibition illustrating Evolution at the British Museum (Natural History)

common ancestor, and that the two lines, hominids (proto-men) and pongids (proto-apes) diverged in Africa between 15 and 30 million years ago when increasingly arid climatic conditions resulted in a contraction of the forests, and an expansion of the grasslands. While the proto-apes remained in the forests, the proto-men ventured into the grasslands, developing an upright stance for walking which freed their hands for tool-making and other purposes. Fig. 1 shows the descent of man (see Appendix 2).

Early Man Gallery

Australopithecus

The majority of hominid fossils belong to the Pleistocene geological epoch, and the first found was in a Bechuanaland cave-deposit by Professor Raymond Dart in 1924, who considered that it was a link between the apes and man, and who named the genus *Australopithecus* (southern ape). Further fossils of these early members of the human family were found in South and East Africa, and now in North Africa (Tchad) and possibly in Palestine (Tell Ubaidiya). The Australopithecines had massive, ape-like jaws and small brain capacity (within the range 400–800 c^3 as compared with 1700 c^3 for *Homo sapiens sapiens*, that is, modern man), teeth of human type, and were about 4 ft in height. But the recent discovery at Lake Rudolf, Kenya, of a complete fossil skull nearly 3,000,000 years old, with a brain case similar to that of *H. sapiens*, has upset current theories of man's descent.

Homo

Olduvai Gorge, Tanzania. Early Stone Age. Olduvai Gorge in the Serengeti Plain is a site of impressive grandeur [see exhibition photograph]. About 300 ft deep and with a narrow floor it was formed by erosion in post-Pleistocene times when a river cut its way through to the bed of a lake about 20 miles long, formed in the Lower Pleistocene period. It is also one of the most prolific sites for hominid remains.

Here in 1960 Dr Louis Leakey and his wife, Dr Mary Leakey, discovered a skull [Diagram, skull no. 1] with a brain size of about 680 c³ and also hand and foot bones closely similar to those of man. It was considered that these finds differed sufficiently from *Australopithecus* to constitute a species of the genus *Homo*, which was named *H. habilis* (Fig. 1).

Later in bed II the fossil of a more advanced species was found with a brain capacity of 1000 c³, *Homo erectus* [skull no. 3]. Similar fossils have been discovered in Europe and Asia dated to this period, Fig. 1.

The species described above were associated with stone industries. Bed I contained mainly flaked tools, represented here [see exhibits] by choppers made from a stone core and flaked on one or both sides to make a cutting edge. In bed II a long series of hand-axes began with primitive implements, and culminated in the finely worked Acheulean hand-axes (named after St Acheul, near Amiens, where the type was first located) and cleavers of bed IV [for tool-making, see wall panel 'Stone Artefacts']. These are not the only tools made at this period but are the most representative.

Primitive man camped near water where the vegetation served as a source of food and concealment from carnivorous animals. His living site was small and probably occupied by two or three families of mothers and their children and three or four males. They could communicate, but elementary speech probably did not evolve before the Middle Pleistocene.

Mount Carmel Caves, Israel. Lower and Middle Paleolithic. In the numerous caves in the coastal areas and ranges of Syria, Lebanon and Palestine, prehistoric remains abound. In four caves of Mount Carmel, the north-western extremity of which forms the southern arm of the Bay of Acre, is a comprehensive sequence of Lower and Middle Paleolithic cultures.

Three of the caves, Mugharet el-Wad, Mugharet et-Tabun and Mugharet es-Skhul are situated in the Wady el-Mugharah (Valley of the Caves) on the western side of Mount Carmel, and the fourth, Mugharet et-Kebarah, lies further to the south.

LOWER PALEOLITHIC. Among the Lower Paleolithic

tools from Tabun are pointed or pear-shaped Acheulean hand-axes [rows FG 1; ECD 1, 2], scrapers and cores [FG 3; ECD 3, 4] and blade tools [EAB 5–6] usually associated with the Upper Paleolithic.

MIDDLE PALEOLITHIC. This period is represented in Tabun by the Levalloiso-Mousterian culture, that is, by flakes struck from prepared cores, such as points [C 5, 6; B 4, 5] and scrapers [B 1–3].

Both the Mousterian culture and its associated Neanderthal man were widespread, for in addition to Western Asia and North Africa, they have also been found throughout Europe (type site, Le Moustier, southern France), northern Iran and in Russia. The cave was both the Neanderthals' dwelling and their burial ground, and in Tabun and Skhul eleven individuals were interred whose skeletal features were intermediate between Neanderthal and modern man, those in Tabun being much earlier than the Skhul fossils. Were these people undergoing evolutionary changes from Neanderthal to modern man, or were they the offspring of intercourse between the two species? Unfortunately, these questions cannot be answered until reliable dates are obtained from the caves, and more is known about the origin of modern man (see Fig. 1).

Mount Carmel Caves. Upper Paleolithic. At present all we know is that modern man appeared suddenly in Europe about 40,000 years ago and that the Neanderthals vanished from the scene. *H. s. sapiens* was first identified in 1868 at Cro-magnon, Les Eyzies, and later at Combe Capelle, in the Dordogne (Fig. 1). In the late Upper Pleistocene these remarkable people began their world-wide expansion, and today all men, even if their culture is Stone Age, belong to the same species. They produced the world's first art, decorating their caves with splendid paintings of the animals they hunted [see dais: reproduction of Spanish cave paintings of a later (Mesolithic) period], and carving female figures in stone, bone and ivory, etc., and tools and animals in bone.

But the Upper Paleolithic cultures at Mount Carmel (caves of el-Wad and et-Kebarah) are represented only by a diverse range of hunting tools: burins (engraving or chiselling tools) and scrapers [C 1, 2], points, probably spear heads

[E 6; F 1], bladelets [E 3–5], and finely worked blades and bladelets of the Kebaran culture [top 2–7] (the cutting components of composite tools).

Mount Carmel Caves, Mesolithic period. The Natufian culture (type-site: the cave of Shukba, Wady en-Natuf) is one of the microlith-using cultures of south-west Asia, and is represented in the caves of el-Wad and et-Kebarah. Here blades and lunates [lowest row] were found for mounting in a wooden or bone haft used as a sickle to reap wild wheat and other grasses, and to tip arrows [see exhibits]. Fish hooks and barbed spear points were also made, the Natufians being experienced fishermen, as well as bone needles and awls [see exhibits]. Natufians also built small villages of round stone houses (Aïn Mallaha, Palestine).

Almost unaffected by the profound climatic changes caused by the retreat of the ice in Europe at this time, except for a slightly increased aridity, the Natufians zealously hunted the gazelle, and there is no evidence that, although on the verge of farming, they domesticated animals, but perhaps the reaping of wild cereals ultimately led to the collection of seed and its subsequent sowing.

There is, however, evidence of a more settled life in the house [see photograph] at Jericho's first settlement, c. 7800 BC, and the burial of 87 persons in el-Wad, some of whom were adorned with headdresses of shells and bone heads [see exhibits]. Small figures were also carved, as represented by the cast.

Kalambo Falls, Tanzania, Middle Stone Age. A world-wide lowering of temperatures about 70,000 years ago signalled the start of the last glaciation in the temperate zones; and although Africa had no 'Ice Age', within 20,000 years mean temperatures had dropped 5–6°C below today's in tropical and semi-tropical regions, rainfall had increased, also surface water supplies. These and other changes caused the mountain forests and their associated animals to spread to parts of the central African plateau, while the northern and central areas of the Sahara and the south-western deserts became habitable.

Tool kits were developed to meet the new, diversified local and regional conditions, and examples are displayed from the deposits of a lake which, in Upper Pleistocene times, was situated above Kalambo Falls at the south-eastern end of Lake Tanganyika.

They cover the relatively rapid change-over from the final hand-axe tradition [bottom row] to that suited to a forest environment [centre and top], including new types, such as the heavy duty pick [centre, no. 1] probably for breaking ground and digging up roots, and small scraping and cutting tools [top] used, among other things, for fashioning artefacts from raw materials other than stone.

These new developments were the work of an early form of *Homo sapiens*, *H. sapiens rhodesiensis*.

Haua Fteah, Cyrenaica, North Africa. Middle and Upper Paleolithic. Man occupied the cave at Haua Fteah [see photograph] almost continuously for 100,000 years. In such a long sequence, cultural traditions were much diversified.

For instance, the Pre-Aurignacian culture (so named because of its affinities with the Upper Paleolithic Aurignacian which, some 50,000 years later was associated with *H. s. sapiens*, is found in some Mediterranean lands, and is a blade-using culture [below 4–7]. It is followed by the local Levalloiso-Mousterian characterized by thin flakes struck from prepared cores [see exhibits]. This culture belongs to *H. sapiens neanderthalensis* (Fig. 1), whose fossils were found in the Haua. The Upper Paleolithic industries of the Dabban, Oranian and Capsian cultures emphasize hunting tools: blades (some for hunting), points and microliths.

The Haua is situated in a vegetation belt of light woodland and semi-arid scrub and steppe, bordered in the south by desert. In the 45 ft of occupation debris were the bones of wild animals, ox, sheep and gazelle, and their relative frequencies indicate the climatic and vegetational fluctuations over the period [see notes].

In Pre-Aurignacian times, the climate was warm with steppe vegetation, and the gazelle predominated. In the Levalloiso-Mousterian period with present-day temperatures, vegetation was open woodland suitable to the wild ox; but the increase in sheep in Dabban and early Oranian times indicates a cool, moist climate. A reversion to less dense woodland in late Oranian and Capsian times is testified by the return of the ox.

Before studying the first exhibit from Europe, we must digress to the 'Ice Age' which covered intermittently the northern hemisphere from the Lower to the Upper Pleistocene. Within this period there were at least four glaciations, three interglacials and many interstadials or oscillations of climate, the former being warm periods between the glaciations when the temperature was as warm as or warmer than today, and others less warm. These fluctuations of temperature profoundly affected the vegetation and animal population which, near the ice sheets consisted of tundra and Arctic species, such as reindeer, while during the interglacials and interstadials temperate and warm-temperate plants and animals flourished.

Vértesszöllös, nr. Budapest, Hungary. Lower Paleolithic. One of the earliest industries of Europe, a variant of the chopper tool industry, is dated to the interstadial of the second glaciation, and was found at Vértesszöllös in the Danube basin [see map] during quarrying operations on travertine rock.

Travertine is a pale coloured freshwater limestone formed during periods of great spring activity. Embedded in it were many plants [see leaf] and leaves of tree species which today are found in Mediterranean latitudes, indicating a higher temperature than the present day. Furthermore, blackened bone and reddened stone from hearths on the living floors provide the earliest evidence for the use of fire. The tools have affinities with Olduvai except that they are made from river pebbles not more than 2–3 cm long, which makes them unique among Lower Paleolithic industries.

Associated with the site is a very early form of *H. sapiens*, Fig. 1.

Dolni Vestonice, Czecho-Slovakia. Upper Paleolithic. In the Upper Pleistocene, we find in central Europe that the supply of game in the 4th glacial period was abundant and that the hunters became specialized and tended to concentrate on one species.

At Dolni Vestonice in Moravia [see exhibition map], there was a camp of mammoth hunters whose skill, judging from the quantity of bones found there (in which mammoth preponderated) [see photograph], must have contributed greatly to that animal's extinction.

These hunters lived in circular huts with a central hearth, a low circular stone wall, storage pits, and holes for posts to support the roof [see diagram]. The floors were sunk below the level of the ground, and some form of covering was supported on the interior and held down against Arctic winds by mammoth bones and boulders on the exterior.

Star Carr, Yorkshire, Mesolithic period. The people of northern Europe known as Maglemosians (from the big bog, *magle mose*, at Mullerup, Denmark) adapted themselves to the changed environment at the end of the 4th glaciation, when the sea rose and began to cover the land bridge between northern Europe and Britain, by beach-combing added to a hunting economy. When, much later, owing to the rise in temperature, the deciduous forest had replaced the Arctic park-tundra, they hunted the wild ox, elk, red and roe deer instead of the reindeer and other Arctic species. Another important feature of Maglemosian life was inland fishing and fowling to supplement hunting.

At Star Carr, near Scarborough, their camp was on a birch and brushwood platform over the reedy marshes edging a lake, from which they took water birds. They hunted game, preferably red deer, in the forest, and their tool kit included stone and barbed antler points for spears, and microliths as barbs for arrows [top row]. It also included a hafted adze (a type of axe) with which they felled trees and fashioned canoes, and from the latter they fished with wood and antler harpoons [see exhibits].

* * *

This short and selective account of Early Man finishes with the Mesolithic period. The next stage can be seen in the Department of Western Asiatic Antiquities (p. 82 ff.) where, in the exhibits from Mesopotamia (Iraq) can be followed the establishment of farming, building of cities, practice of arts and crafts, religion, and above all the invention of writing: in short man's approach to civilization.

The adjacent Prehistoric rooms cover the European Bronze Age and the Iron Age from about 2500 BC to about AD 50. Thus while Europe was still illiterate and barbarian, the arts of civilization had been practised in Mesopotamia and Egypt for about 2,000 years.

First Bronze Age Room

Introduction

Western Asiatic farming practices reached Greece about the 8th millennium BC (p. 179) and spread to the Bulgarian plain, western Ukraine, and along the Danube and Rhine to Belgium. Immigrant farmers, probably from the Levant, travelled westwards along the islands and coastline of the Mediterranean to Italy and Sicily, southern France and Spain. From there they went inland to France, Switzerland, the Atlantic coasts, and Britain, where settlement took place in the south-west between 4000–3700 BC [for the locations of European Neolithic farming cultures, see case 5, map]. In the late Neolithic period in Europe, local farming cultures were disturbed by the arrival from east and west of peoples bringing a knowledge of metallurgy and other innovations.

Late Neolithic period

European Bell Beaker and the Globular Amphorae – Corded ware – Battle-axe complex, c. 2500–1500 BC. One of these new groups was the Bell Beaker people who left their homeland, believed to be around the Lion Gulf in southern France and north-east Spain, and spread up the Atlantic coast to Brittany and North-Western Europe, including Britain. Other Beaker folk migrated to central Europe via the Rhône and Danube valleys, and as far east as Hungary and southern Poland. They were small farmers, growing crops and rearing cattle, pigs and sheep, as well as traders with an elementary knowledge of gold and copper working, and their characteristic vessel was the bell beaker [76 10–12 14, from nr. Erd, Hungary].

In central and northern Europe they met other groups who came from the Pontic region north of the Black Sea but whose origins lay ultimately in the steppe country to the north and north-east. These people may have spoken Indo-

European dialects (from which most modern European languages are derived) and are sometimes referred to as Kurgans because the dead were buried under a barrow (*kurgan* in Russian). When they first arrived in central and northern Europe, they brought with them the horse and wheeled vehicle and a knowledge of copper-working; but although growing crops they were essentially stockbreeders.

The newcomers mixed with the indigenous farming groups, and by 2500 BC hybrid cultures had evolved in which Kurgan features predominated: a ruling warrior caste, fortified villages, stockbreeding, and burials generally under mounds, containing vessels with impressed cord decoration [68 12–28 224. Spittwitz], and in male graves, stone battle-axes [GER 101, Saxony].

The Bell Beaker and Corded Ware people met in central and northern Europe, and although the former soon disappeared corded vessels appeared in a variety of new shapes greatly influenced by the beakers.

The British Beaker culture, c. 2000–1500 BC. Beaker people (see above) arrived in Britain between 2000 and 1700 BC in two main waves, but infiltration by smaller groups was continuous throughout this period.

The first wave crossed over about 2000 BC in canoes loaded with livestock, cereal seed and equipment, and settled in groups of about 100 in the upper Thames valley, the areas of the Wash and Humber, and in north-east Scotland. They came from the Rhine Delta and the Drenthe peninsula (Holland) and were makers of early bronze implements and All-over-cord beakers [1909 5–18 14. From Thames, Mortlake]. About the same time the European Bell Beaker people [93 4–26 8] settled on the East Anglian coast and the Wessex plain.

Between 1800 and 1700 BC the second stage of Beaker settlement took place in several groups, one of which included wealthy chieftains from the Middle Rhine around Mainz and Coblentz who settled in Wessex [Top R; 90 6–22 1–3] from which they effected contact with Ireland. They brought over craftsmen trained in Únětice [see below] metallurgical techniques and introduced more elaborate weapons. Their rich graves were in the north-west of Wessex around Stonehenge, and the contents indicated the wealth they obtained by acting as middlemen in the trade of Irish gold and copper for Germany. Eventually all the Beaker groups coalesced into three long-enduring British cultures: a northern, with territory north of the Wash [3rd shelf: 79 12–9 1841–4; 84 5–20 1, with archer's stone wrist guard, amber beads and knife. Driffield, Yorks.]; a southern, concentrated south of the Wash [lower shelf WG2282. Denton, Lincs.]; and an East Anglian, covering the coastal areas and the Thames estuary [2nd shelf R].

The Bronze Age, c. 1800–500 BC

The Beaker and Corded ware peoples both possessed a knowledge of simple metallurgy which they had spread throughout Europe. But it was in central Europe with its abundant supplies of copper ores and tin in the western Carpathians, Bohemia and central Germany that Near Eastern gold and bronze objects, mainly jewellery, were first copied by the central European metalsmiths, the Únětice people.

The Únětice culture, 1800–1450 BC. The Early Bronze Age. The opportunities for trade in raw materials and manufactured goods were most brilliantly exploited by the Únětice people (named after a cemetery near Prague), heirs to the Kurgans, whose cultural area at its greatest extent was bounded by the middle Rhine and middle Danube in the south, in the north by Brandenburg and Poznan, and included Saxo-Thuringia, Bohemia, Moravia and Slovakia.

The Úněticians were stockbreeders and cereal cultivators, and they lived in small, timber-built houses. But their territory lay in the centre of Europe, and they developed the trade in copper, gold and amber and manufactured goods between the British Isles, the Baltic, and Mycenaean Greece, growing rich in the process. Copper was traded in the form of ingot torcs, such as the pair from Beitzsch with dagger [68 12–28 249–51] as well as such weapons and implements as axes, halberds [see blade and circular handle], daggers, some with metal hilts, and double-ended picks. They obtained gold from Ireland via Britain, mainly for objects of personal adornment, for example the gold hair ring [68 12–28 362]. The double spiral bronze pendant

[1929 10–14 1] was probably ultimately copied from one made in the Levant in the 18th century BC. The rich burials of the Únětician chieftains are evidence of prosperity [illustration], and suggest a warrior aristocracy.

Wessex culture, 1600–1400 BC. In Britain, the disparate elements of the Wessex region's population evolved into a homogeneous culture which spread over an area comprising most of Wiltshire, Hampshire, Dorset, east Somerset, and the chalk ridge of Berkshire. Its riverine system, the Christchurch Avon to the Channel, the Kennet to its junction with the Thames, and thence to the North Sea, and the Bristol Avon to the Bristol Channel, south Wales and Ireland, made it the principal British centre for overseas trade, while overland routes spread Wessex culture to Devon and Cornwall, Sussex and, by the Icknield Way, to Norfolk and east Yorkshire. The early Beaker people built the first stone erections at Stonehenge, and the Wessex chieftains were responsible for the monument of which we see the ruins today.

Confirmation of Wessex's prosperity comes from objects recovered from hoards and chieftains' burials: flanged axes [Arreton Down, Isle of Wight; Plymstock, Devon], tanged and socketed spearheads [Arreton Down; Snowshill, Glos.], and daggers, some grooved and riveted [Plymstock; Snowshill; Arreton Down].

Objects of personal adornment figured prominently, many covered with sheet gold, such as the two decorated gold cones, accompanied by eleven cylindrical beads [Upton Lovell], the cover for a conical shale button and gold bound amber discs [Wilsford G8], decorated covers for lozenge shaped plates and a gold cover for belt hook [Bush Barrow, Wilsford G5] and the beautiful gold fluted cup from Rillaton, Cornwall, of beaker shape and made by a craftsman who copied a Mycenaean technique (Fig. 2). Gold neck ornaments, such as the crescent-shaped lunula made in Ireland and found in north Wales [Central Saloon, Gold case: 69 6–19 1] were popular at this period, and basket-shaped ear-rings [1940 4–4 1, 2] in Beaker times; but the most beautiful gold object is the ceremonial embossed cape found at Mold, Flintshire.

In Wessex both inhumation and cremation were practised, and in the cremation from Stockbridge Down a collared urn was inverted over the cremated bones and associated grave goods, a bronze awl, and a necklace of calcite, faience, jet, lignite and shale beads [1939 5–6 2–11]. Occasionally small cups were present among the grave goods [79 12–9 1818] [scc also *British Bronze Age pottery, 1600–1000 BC* for vessels for cremation and other purposes].

Second Bronze Age Room

Southern Britain, 1400–900 BC: Pottery. By 1400 BC the majority of the Bronze Age population of Britain practised cremation. While the collard urn popular in Wessex culture times [1st B.A. Rm, Brit. B.A. Pottery] was still in use in most parts of Britain, the bucket urn [83 6–12 2, from Acton, Middx], which in Suffolk was heavily decorated with fingertip impressions [1914 7–20 1, Brantham, Suffolk] was now fashionable from Dorset to Lincoln.

This type was also found on a farmstead at Itford Hill, Beddingham, Sussex [see illustration] where it was used for storage, probably of grain. In the south-east of England in the earlier Bronze Age, almost no dwelling places are known, but a number of farmsteads have been excavated dated to the later Bronze Age.

At Itford Hill the main farmstead consisted of circular living huts, a weaving shed and storage hut, an area set aside for cooking, and huts which were used as barns, byres and workshops. Sheep and cattle were raised and barley grown, and potsherds representing 96 Bucket- Barrel- [1927 7–4 2] and Bag-shaped urns were found in the farmstead.

Throughout barbarian times and into the Roman era, the dwellings of the native peasants were usually circular huts. At Itford Hill these were timber framed and thatched with straw, but on Dartmoor and Bodmin Moor not only the circular walls of the pastoralists' huts but also the enclosure walls of their settlements were built of the plentiful stone. Arable settlements were generally open, the hut being placed in a yard or on the edge of a field, the latter edged with stone. The huts were often large and divided into working and living quarters.

Britain, 1400–900 BC: Bronze. Although dwellings yielded domestic objects, a large percentage of prehistoric antiquities emanated from burial sites, barrows, cairns and cemeteries. It is their contents which constitute many of the exhibits in this case and indeed throughout the Bronze and Iron Age Rooms.

At this time there were regional bronze industries which functioned with imported supplies of metals and itinerant bronzesmiths. New types of weapons and tools were evolved: the thrusting rapier [92 9–1 303, from Shapwick Down] and later the slashing sword with two cutting edges [62 2–12 1, from the River Lea], socketed spearheads [WG 2033, from Mawbray, Cumberland] with loops on socket for attachment by thong or cord to the shaft, and haft- and later winged-flanged axes [WG 1826, from Brackley, Nairn; WG 1830, Rougham, Norfolk] which were developed in northern Britain. In addition there was the palstave, a narrow form of the early flat axe given wide side flanges and stop ridge designed to facilitate the fixing of the head to the handle of the implement [shelf L, from Hollingbury Hill, Sussex].

Jewellery was fashionable, and some ornaments, although made in Britain, are derived from north German forms, such as necklets (torcs) of twisted bronze [92 9–1 321–5], and the bracelets from Ramsgate [1900 7–19 7; 1916 10–4 2–3]. On the other hand the quoit-headed pins and Sussex loops are a British development [1937 7–16 1–5. East Dean, Sussex, Fig. 3]. The bronze cauldron [centre case: 61 3–9 1] preserved by the waters and mud of the Thames from bacterial action, must not be overlooked, nor the two beautiful shields from Welsh bogs [73 2–10 1–2].

The Dowris Hoard, Ireland, 650 BC. Another source of antiquities is the buried hoard which safeguarded the objects concealed but not, it would seem, the life of their owner as so many were never reclaimed. In the Late Bronze Age

Fig. 2. Fluted gold cup from Rillaton, Cornwall, see page 42
Fig. 3. Sussex loop, a British prehistoric ornament, see page 44
Fig. 4. Bronze collar incorporating the human face, a typically Celtic feature, see page 51

supplies of metal were comparatively plentiful, and the itinerant craftsman who must have carried some of his stock from place to place, provided a tempting target for the predatory.

The owner of the Dowris hoard from Co. Offaly perhaps belonged to this category. He was certainly prosperous, for the hoard consisted originally of about 200 objects, many broken, scrap metal to be melted down and reused [see heap]. The variety is astonishing: large end-blow horns and a string of graded crotals, bells or rattles, which probably emitted different sounds when struck or swung; bifid razors, bronze vessels much patched to prolong their use; socketed hammers, gouges and spearheads, leaf-shaped swords and tanged and socketed knives.

Many of these exhibits have been influenced by British, northern central European and eastern Mediterranean forms which have been modified to suit Irish taste.

Heathery Burn Cave, Co. Durham, 700–600 BC. The splendid bronzes and other objects, probably deposited at different times, in the Heathery Burn cave, were intermingled with animal bones and traces of fires which indicate that it had been inhabited. Indeed human bones were found in the locality, including a complete skeleton.

The occupants were probably bronzeworkers in a good way of business because they used horse-drawn vehicles, as is suggested by the bone and antler cheek pieces [R panel] and the bronze nave bands [R panel below]. The amber, stone and shell beads and pendants also indicate affluence.

Evidence of the bronzesmith's craft is provided by the valve of a two-valve bronze mould for socketed axes [L panel], bronze casting jet, fragment of bronze or copper ingot [below] and, possibly, metalworkers' bronze tongs [L below].

The cave was situated in a ravine near Stanhope, and was destroyed by quarrying.

* * *

We must now return to central Europe dominated by the Úněticians at the end of the Early Bronze Age. They were followed by the Tumulus people, so called because they, too, were buried under mounds, who occupied Únětice cultural areas, and in addition spread into western Hungary, Austria, Switzerland, the Rhine basin and eastern France. Their successors were the Urnfield people (c. 1250–750 BC) who intermingled with the Tumulus people, practising the rite of cremation and burial in flat cemeteries, although other cultural features were similar to those of the Tumulus period.

Indeed it has been suggested that the Únětice-Tumulus-Urnfield cultures evolved one from the other, with local variations, and no new people were involved, and that the Urnfield people in the 13th and 12th centuries BC expanded into Italy, the Balkans and southern Greece, overthrew the Hittites in Anatolia and raided the eastern Mediterranean and Egypt (pp. 76 , 132 , 181). They also expanded in the West.

The Lusatian culture, 1400–700 BC. Middle and Late Bronze Age. The Lusatian culture originated during the Tumulus period in eastern Germany and western Poland, and later was to be found in northern Czecho-Slovakia, eastern Poland and farther into Moravia, Bohemia and Slovakia.

The exhibits of this vigorous culture are here mainly confined to the early pottery decorated with the characteristic breast-shaped bosses, and vessels found in the large cremation cemeteries with which smaller pots are often associated [68 12–28 2, 58, 153, 199, 201. From the Lubenau grave], and more rarely bronze objects, such as the two pins and ring [from the Frankenhain grave].

The Zsujta hoard, 1200–1000 BC. Late Bronze Age. In Urnfield times bronze swords were manufactured in the region between the Tatra mountains and the upper basin of the River Tisza which joins the Danube near Belgrade. Here hoards of fine swords and other objects have been found.

That found at Zsujta, near Abauj [88 1–10 1–21], consists of eight swords, seven with decorated hilts, eight bracelets in whole or part, four socketed spearheads, and a mount possibly for a ceremonial wagon in the form of a duck. Since about 1200 BC the water bird had become increasingly popular as a decorative motif [centre case, 56 12–22 1. Flesh fork from N. Ireland].

Northern Europe, 1100–650 BC. The remaining regional Bronze Age culture of Europe represented in this room is that of the north European province, which comprised Denmark and its islands, southern Sweden, northern Germany and part of western Poland. The Bronze Age there was at first concerned with imported metal goods, the entire area, except on the periphery in northern Germany, being devoid of metal ores. But from 1100 BC a thriving bronze-working industry developed, displaying superb craftsmanship.

With cremation prevailing at this period, only those objects which could fit inside an urn were placed in burials. Hence the survival of small razors [L, below: 69 7–24 55], some engraved [R: 69 7–24 57. Small boat] and which with tweezers [R: WG 1500] and a sword [back L: 74 3–13 8] were associated with the cremation. The latter was sometimes in miniature, not represented here, although there is an engraved miniature knife [R: 1916 6–5 176].

Besides hoards and burials, votive offerings provided a source of bronze objects, particularly those worn by women, for example belt boxes [electrotype] containing toilet articles, neck rings [69 7–24 69], spectacle brooches [74 3–13 44, Denmark], and bracelets [1921 11–1 14. Hemse, Gotland, Sweden]. Later it became fashionable to wear heavy ornaments, perhaps to emphasize wealth and position, for instance the neck ornament from Vigstrupguarde [90 11–13 20] and the brooch from Glostrup, Zealand, Denmark [WG 1474].

The Iron Age, 700–450 BC

The Hallstatt culture, 7th century BC. Iron was known in central Europe from the end of the 2nd millennium BC but was not worked extensively till about 400 years later when the Hallstatt culture evolved out of the north Alpine culture.

It was first located in a vast cemetery near the town of Hallstatt in Austria where a prehistoric settlement had grown rich exploiting the local salt and copper mines; and it spread over south Germany, Switzerland and eastern France, and down the Danube to Yugoslavia [see map and illustrations]. There was no change in population except a small number of intruders from the Russian steppes who eventually formed part of the aristocracy and perhaps brought a knowledge of iron-working. When the Hallstatt people entered into history through the writing of their literate classical contemporaries, we learn that they were the Celts.

Brave and savage barbarians who delighted in war, the Celts were vain of their personal appearance, witness the ornaments exhibited here: brooches, fibula [back of case] and spectacle type, dress pins, anklets and bracelets, and imported amber necklaces. As warriors, they had developed many types of bronze and iron swords and exhibited here is an addition to the range, a short antenna sword with a fishtail chape (covering for point), as well as an iron (socketed) palstave and a celt with trunnions. The ribbed bronze bucket with repoussé decoration of water birds and wheel motifs is probably a cult object, but the splendid polychrome pottery with incised and painted geometric patterns may have been developed in the late Bronze Age.

The Iron Age Room

About 450 BC the Celtic centre of power moved to the west. This was indicated by discoveries made at La Tène on Lake Neuchâtel where numerous votive (dedicated) objects were found which, though undeniably Celtic in style, displayed new and exotic cultural influences. These trends were confirmed by further finds of earlier date in graves on the Middle Rhine and in the Marne, but there were no signs of any invaders who might have brought this new La Tène art style.

The catalyst which created it was undoubtedly the opening of communications down the Rhône valley with the Greeks in Marseilles (p. 183), contacts with the Scythians, invaders from the steppes and neighbours of the Celts in central Europe, and trade with the Etruscans in central Italy. The results can be seen in the opulent grave goods of the Celtic nobles, of which the Department has many examples, Continental [left-hand side coming from Second Bronze Age Room] and British [centre]. We will begin with the former as, chronologically, they are the first.

Rich graves in north-east France, c. 500 BC to end 1st century BC. Inhumation was the custom, though not invariably, throughout Hallstatt and La Tène times, and the objects placed in the grave were those necessary to uphold the occupant's rank and to sustain the inner man in the next world.

For instance, the sword of the warrior buried at Montfercaut [illustration and exhibit, R], c. 250–100 BC, his inverted spear (the shaft of which has perished), were placed on his right side [next to sword], while an iron knife and pair of shears [not exhibited] lay below his left elbow. At his feet was an incised and painted pedestal bowl which may have contained wine [extreme R], a product of civilization much appreciated by the Celts.

An aristocratic woman buried at Courtisols, river Vesle (Marne), c. 475–250 BC, was accompanied by a twisted bronze torc [1st panel, back], a pendant with glass beads which, with the bronze and ivory rings, had been worn as a diadem, a pair of bronze bracelets, two brooches (fibulae) and a pin, the latter not exhibited.

The Somme-Bionne chariot burial, c. 4th century BC. The most magnificent Continental burial represented in the Department is the chariot burial at Somme-Bionne (Marne).

The Hallstatt Celts had been buried with a cart or wagon, generally four-wheeled, encased in a timber structure covered by a barrow (mound), a burial rite of the Russian steppes, but the La Tène nobles replaced the wagon by a light two-wheeled chariot.

In the Somme-Bionne burial the chariot and harness were dismantled, the wheels with iron tyres being placed on either side of the warrior's body [see illustration] and the harness trappings in a trench at his feet. As can be seen, his sword [ML 1349] was on his right side in a decorated scabbard. Three spears lay on his left side [ML 1490 89–92] and an iron knife [exhibited] at his waist.

Only a few pieces of harness can be identified, such as the two bridle bits and the pole bindings. The beautiful circular bronze [see photo and original] may have been a breastpiece or perhaps a side piece for a bridle bit. Foreign contacts are manifest in the Greek red figure drinking cup (athlete throwing the discus), dated c. 525 BC, and the Etruscan bronze flagon, both of which had been placed at the warrior's feet. The Celts drank prodigious quantities of wine from Italy and the Marseilles region.

Early Celtic art in north-west Europe. The highly individualistic art styles developed by the Celts were fundamentally decorative, original and strikingly effective. But Celtic art was not great art, being far too limited in scope; nevertheless motifs borrowed from foreign sources were effectively transformed into art forms unmistakably Celtic.

Early Celtic art (La Tène style) has been divided into four major art styles. The Early style (c. 450–350 BC) in which classical and oriental features predominated [89 5–7 28. Ornament between bosses of cheek piece derived from the classical palmette], as well as Hallstatt elements [1957 7–15 1. Handle from a flagon]; the Waldalgesheim style (c. 350–200 BC), the fully developed La Tène style (named after a great find) and characterized by lively free-running patterns [see illustration; the Plastic style (2nd century BC) characterized by three-dimensional relief [see illustration], and the sword style (2nd century BC) exemplified by diagonally running designs on sword scabbards [see illustration].

The two bronze collars with human faces worked into the pattern [ML 1711. From Courtisols (Marne) Fig. 4; ML 1709. From Avon-Fontenay (Aube)] are works partly in the Waldalgesheim and partly in the Plastic styles; but the upper of the two coral and bronze bracelets [L, back] is in the Early style.

But these are Continental art styles which, it is considered, are not so aesthetically satisfying as the more austere insular style of Great Britain and Ireland, examples of which we will now examine.

Insular art (centre display)

Crossing to the opposite side of the room, we see in the first side case of the centre display two bronze shield bosses [58 11–16 2, 3, c. 200 BC]. The design on the round boss is asymmetric and the birds' bodies have been dislocated to fit the design, both features of Celtic art. Birds' heads in profile also appear in the centre of the long boss, an early example of British La Tène art, and at each end were two gloomy human faces (one now missing), for Celtic artists lost no opportunity of incorporating the human face among their designs.

In contrast, the design of the beautiful Desborough mirror [1924 1–9] is symmetrical, and is of a precision which is astounding. Its effect is obtained by the use of curvilinear blank spaces combined with a curvilinear design.

It is difficult to believe that the six gold torcs (c. 1 BC) in the next case when found in 1968 and 1970 at Ipswich had been buried for nearly 2,000 years, but gold, unlike other metals, does not corrode in the earth. All these lovely torcs have different designs on the terminals.

On the left are two decorated bronze helmets, one with horns (c. 1 BC, from the Thames) and the other with a peak [72 12–13 2, c. 1 AD. From north Britain] almost certainly for ceremonial use: they are too fragile to give protection in battle.

The adjacent shield [72 12–13 1, c. 200 BC. From river Witham, Lincs.] originally carried a blazon (heraldic device) of a stylized boar on a thin bronze sheet, nailed to the background, traces of which can be seen. Later, the present lovely boss was substituted in which, beneath the end roundels, are staring animal faces (Fig. 5).

The end case contains the spectacular electrum (gold and silver) torc [1951 4–2, c. 50 BC] found in a hoard at Ken Hill, Snettisham, Norfolk, and believed to have belonged either to a royal house or to a priestly association. It was made from strands of twisted wire, and the relief decoration of the terminals was cast and the detail chased.

In the second case on the next long side is the brilliant Battersea shield [57 7–15 1, c. 1st century AD], found in the Thames and preserved from bacterial action by the water and mud. A ceremonial piece, with a symmetrical design incorporating two ox-heads on the central boss, it was originally gilded and decorated with red glass set in cloisons (mountings).

The final case is devoted to weapons, and the very beautiful chased scroll ornament on the scabbard from Lisnacroghera, Co. Antrim [80 8–2 115, 4th century BC], and the incised tendril design on that from Bugthorpe, Yorks.

Fig. 5. The Witham shield. Note the staring animal faces beneath the roundels

[1905 7–17 1, 1st century BC] should be noted.

Iron Age Britain

Evidence for early Celtic settlement in Britain is sparse, and even less is known of the coming of the Celts to Ireland. However, present knowledge is summarized below within the framework of three main cultural traditions, A, B and C. In Iron Age A (6th–4th century BC), immigrants brought late Hallstatt equipment and pottery, and practised simple farming. They came from north Germany and settled in north-east Scotland and Yorkshire. During Iron Age B, 4th–2nd century, small bands of chieftains and warriors of La Tène Celts made extensive settlements in the 3rd and 2nd centuries BC in Yorkshire and on the south coast, introducing fine metallurgical techniques and pottery, and the war chariot. Iron Age C, late 2nd century BC–AD 43, saw the arrival of the warlike Belgic tribes of mixed Celtic and German stock, who spread over south-east England and brought advanced metalworking and enamelling techniques.

Iron Age sites in Britain can be seen on the other side of the room. We will start with one of the hill forts, those distinctive features of Celtic life, which from Sussex to Dorset dominate the high points of the Downs and high places elsewhere in Britain. They functioned as tribal centres and refuges in troublous times.

Hod Hill, nr. Blandford, Dorset, 400 BC–AD 43. Situated above the river Stour, Hod Hill was defended from 400–200 BC by a rampart and ditch [Diagram: Stage I], occupied, probably intermittently, by occasional campers, judging by the pottery (A type) which was strewn over the interior. A very different state of affairs pertained from 200 BC to 100/50 BC, when a major reconstruction of defences was undertaken [Diagram: Stage IIa] by different occupants using the pottery 'Southern B' [see exhibits]. Occupational debris abounded, but as only one hut was built, the inhabitants probably camped in the fort.

Activity decreased from 100–50 to the end of the century, although the current occupants, users of Southern 3rd B pottery [see exhibits] doubled an existing rampart [Diagram:

Stage IIb]. But from the beginning of our era to AD 43 a vast reorganization of the defences was carried out (Stage III) by the powerful tribe of the Durotriges, in whose territory the fort lay, and who also minted their own coins [see exhibits]. Numerous huts were also built at the east end, suggesting prolonged residence. All these extensive preparations were undertaken under the threat of Roman invasion, but they proved abortive. The Roman army, under Vespasian, the future emperor, during its drive to the west sacked Hod Hill, killed and ejected the tribesmen and established a Roman garrison within its confines.

The Lady's Barrow, Arras, Yorkshire. Late 2nd or early 1st century BC. The burial of a notable La Tène woman in a circular grave covered by a mound was discovered in an important La Tène cemetery, now a farm in the parish of Market Weighton in the Wolds.

The exhibits from it are arranged as far as possible in the same relation to one another as they were found in the grave: an iron mirror beneath the head, the iron tyres and nave bands of the wheels of a two-wheeled vehicle, a cart or a chariot [see illustration below], behind the skeleton and two bridle bits and a rein ring (terret) in front of the body. To sustain the lady, two joints of pork had been laid by her head.

The Aylesford cemetery, Kent, 50–10 BC. When Caesar invaded Britain in 55 and 54 BC, he came into contact with the Belgic tribes of the Catuvellauni of Hertfordshire and the Trinovantes of Essex, whose culture was similar to that found in the Aylesford cemetery, objects from which are exhibited here.

The finest is the stave-built bucket bound with embossed hoops, with the arresting human masks and their great crested helmets on the handle mounts [86 11–12 3–5]. The rim is decorated with opposed horses of fantastical shape. From the same grave comes the bronze jug [86 11–12 2], patella (pan) [86 11–12 1] and brooches which resemble types found in a Celtic cemetery at Ornavasso, north Italy.

From another grave comes the bronze plated tankard with finely wrought handles. The cremation urns from both graves, one with pedestal, and other pottery, are characteristic of this culture [see Central Saloon, Welwyn Garden City graves].

Camulodunum, Essex. During the century which intervened between Caesar's expeditions and the Roman invasion of AD 43, the Catuvellauni of Hertfordshire annexed adjacent areas, including Essex. In 10 BC their king, Tasciovanus, minted his coins at the Trinovantian capital of Camulodunum (Colchester) inscribed CAMV(lodunum) [coins, 1, 2], but subsequently the site changed hands several times. By 10 AD it was the seat of power of Cunobelinus [see coins 3–14] (Shakespeare's Cymbeline and Tasciovanus's son) who, by the time of his death in AD 41, had gained control of south-east England.

Camulodunum was a large fort defended by earthworks and containing the royal residence and other official buildings which, it must be realized, were merely primitive wattle and daub huts. Its real significance, however, was as a port of entry for Continental goods, among which pottery was predominant.

Some vessels imported [see exhibits] were designed and made by Belgic tribesmen in Gaul [2nd shelf], who also copied Italian red ware [top shelf, R]. Indeed so great was demand that branches of Continental industries were set up, as well as a native industry [see native British copies of Gallo-Belgic ware]. In return Britain's principal export was probably slaves. This exchange of goods was facilitated by coinage which was based on classical designs adapted to suit Celtic taste [see coins and moulds for blanks, perhaps from Cunobelinus' mint].

The end of Iron Age Camulodunum came when the Romans invaded Britain in AD 43, captured the fort and destroyed most of its buildings.

The display in the Roman Britain Room illustrates events in Britain from AD 43 when Europe south of the Rhine and the Danube was already part of the Roman empire, which encircled the Mediterranean.

Roman Britain Room

Introduction

Britain was conquered by the Romans to prevent its being used as a base for operations against Rome, for its mineral wealth and corn surplus, and its manpower which could be recruited as auxiliaries for the Roman army.

In addition there was the question of prestige. In AD 40, the emperor Gaius (Caligula) had assembled an army at Boulogne for the invasion of Britain which had mutinied, thus convincing the Britons that they were invincible. The emperor Claudius (AD 41–54) was determined to restore the army's good name and to make his own illustrious, and plans for an invasion were once more put into operation.

The rôle of the Roman army during it and for some 400 years afterwards can be studied upstairs on the gallery, which should be visited first.

The Gallery

Conquest of Britain, AD 43–c. AD 120. In the spring of AD 43, the Roman army under Aulus Plautius landed at Richborough in Kent. The Britons, led by Caractacus and Togodumnus, sons of Cunobelinus (p. 56), who had inherited the Catuvellauni kingdom, were no match for the legions, and were decisively defeated at the Medway, nor could they prevent the Roman crossing of the Thames where Togodumnus was killed. Here Aulus Plautius awaited the arrival of the emperor, after which the legions pressed forward and captured Camulodunum (Colchester) when numerous tribes made their submission. The emperor ordered the advance to be resumed and then returned to Rome. His visit had lasted 16 days.

By AD 47 the lowland zone, east of the Severn and the Trent, was under Roman control. During the advance to the west Vespasian, the legate (divisional commander) of the 2nd legion, captured the Iron Age fort at Hod Hill near Blandford. A Roman fort was later built in one corner where numerous objects accumulated in the debris during its occupation (AD 43–60): [1st case] iron spear head [L], catapult dart [top row L], iron dagger [centre], buckle [3rd row L nr. dagger], legionary's cheek piece [top row, 2nd from R], cuirass hinges [4th row L nr. dagger; 2nd row L], and spur [2nd row R].

Also exhibited are an iron sword and scabbard [83 4–7 1, 1st century AD, from the Thames, Fulham], standard equipment of this time, but the bronze helmet with vizor mask from Ribchester, Lancs. (late 1st century AD) was too fragile for anything but ceremonial use.

The emperor considered that the lowland zone could be held successfully with the assistance of friendly protectorates beyond its boundaries; but this proved impossible and a stable frontier was not achieved until Hadrian's Wall was built.

Meanwhile although Wales had been subdued by AD 78, the hitherto friendly Brigantes who controlled the north had turned hostile about AD 69, and six campaigns were undertaken by Julius Agricola (governor, 78–84), before they and their lowland Scottish allies and the Caledonian highland tribes, were mastered. Indeed Agricola, by his victory at Mons Graupius (probably near Inverness) was only prevented from conquering all Britain by his recall to Rome by the emperor Domitian in AD 84.

Establishment of Hadrian's Wall: northern frontier AD 121–c. AD 190. Little is known about the next 40 years except that southern Scotland seems to have been held on the Clyde-Forth isthmus, although by about AD 105 a withdrawal had taken place to the Tyne-Solway line. In AD 121 the emperor Hadrian (Fig. 6) [2nd case, 48 11–3, 1, from the Thames at London Bridge] visited Britain and ordered that a fortified wall should be built on the Tyne-Solway line, probably to separate the rebellious Brigantes from their turbulent allies of southern Scotland.

This fortification was constructed by the legions, some of whom left relics of their sojourn, such as the stone relief representing the standard with capricorn and goat, badges of the 2nd legion Augusta [OA 250, 2nd century AD] from the legionary fortress at Caerleon and found on the wall near Benwell, Northumberland. From the Tyne and therefore from a soldier serving on the wall, comes the bronze shield boss [93 12–13, 1, 2nd century AD] on which is depicted the Roman eagle against a niello (black composi-

Fig. 6. Head of Hadrian (117–138 AD), the only certain bronze portrait of the emperor still in existence

tion) background, as are the figures in the eight panels on the surround which include two standards and a bull, the badges of the 8th legion Augusta. The shield must have been used for ceremonial parades, being too light for battle use. An inscription tells us that it belonged to Junius Dubitatus of Julius Magnus's company.

The bronze helmet from Hawkedon, Suffolk (1st century AD) may have been that of a gladiator. If so, it is the only piece of gladiatorial armour so far known in this country.

Antoninus Pius succeeded Hadrian in AD 138, and shortly afterwards a fortified turf wall was built on the Forth-Clyde isthmus which remained the frontier, although breached, rebuilt and used in combination with the earlier wall, until the reign of Commodus (180–192) when it was destroyed and the frontier finally withdrawn to Hadrian's Wall. This barrier was restored under Septimius Severus (193–211), and he and his son, Caracalla, campaigned so successfully against the Scottish tribes that peace reigned in the north until 296.

Pirates, pretenders and the withdrawal of the army c. AD 200–AD 450. From 235 to the last decade of the 3rd century imperial anarchy prevailed (p. 190f) which encouraged almost continuous barbarian invasions on Roman frontiers in Europe and Asia. Britain at first escaped these ravages but as the result of incursions by Saxon pirates towards the end of the 3rd century on the south and east coasts, the defences of the Saxon shore were strengthened. For example, alterations were made to the fort at Richborough [1950 4–2 1. Bronze goose head, perhaps from a piece of furniture. Late 1st–3rd century], and a coastal fort was built at Burgh Castle, Suffolk, where about AD 400, the green glass vessels exhibited [3rd case] were in use.

The instability of the imperial throne had also encouraged usurpers. In AD 287 Carausius, admiral of the British fleet [56 7–1 5027. Fragment of a roofing tile stamped 'BR CL' (classis Britannicae), 2nd or 3rd century AD] proclaimed himself emperor of Britain and North Gaul. But by now the emperor Diocletian (284–305) was sufficiently powerful to deal with both usurpers and barbarians. He appointed three experienced soldiers as co-emperor and caesars (heirs apparent) who successfully drove back the barbarians in Europe and Asia, and Constantius, the caesar in charge of the western provinces, defeated Carausius' successor in 296 and also re-established the northern frontier in Britain which seems to have been depleted of troops (to fight for the usurper) and to have required extensive restoration. Constantius became emperor of the western provinces at Diocletian's abdication (305) but died in York in 306, when the legionaries proclaimed his son, Constantine (the Great) as his successor (306–337).

But in AD 342 barbarian attacks were resumed, and Britain's northern frontier was raided by Picts (from Scotland) and probably the Scots (from Ireland). This was the first of a series of incursions which, in 367, culminated in a combined operation: the Picts and Scots with the savage Attacotti (probably from Ireland) overwhelmed (or turned) Hadrian's Wall and western coastal districts, while the Franks (of the Lower Rhine) and the Saxons (from Jutland and north Germany) descended on the coasts of northern Gaul and probably also on the east coast of England.

Britain was unable to withstand this attack and in 368 the emperor sent his distinguished general, Count Theodosius, with reinforcements. He rounded up the armed bands who were pillaging the country and reorganized its defences in the towns and on the coasts, where he built a number of signal stations in Yorkshire and Durham [1933 4–3 1, 1912 6–30 1. Two pieces of woollen cloth found at the bottom of a well in the signal station at Huntcliff, nr. Saltburn, Yorkshire, AD 369–370, which was destroyed by raiders in c. AD 395]. His work was so effective that the last quarter of the century was both peaceful and prosperous.

During the 5th century the western empire was destroyed by the great German migrations, in particular by the Goths, who were themselves under pressure from the Mongolian Huns and the Vandals. Britain's connection with Rome virtually ended when the emperor Honorius (395–423) sent a letter to the cities telling them to undertake their own defence. Thereafter the raiders had to be faced alone.

On the wall at the top of the stairs is a most attractive mosaic panel [Dep. p. 27, 4th century] part of a large floor from a villa at Horkstow, Lincs., representing a chariot race, and as we descend to the lower floor on our right is a Hadrianic milestone [83 7–25 1, 10–9 Dec, 121] found on a farm one mile south of Llanfairfechan, Caernarvonshire, and nearly 7 miles west of the Roman fort at Caerhun (Kanovium). The inscription reads:

> The Emperor Caesar Trajan Hadrian Augustus, pontifex maximus, in his fifth year of tribunician power, father of his country, thrice consul: from Kanovium, 8 miles.

The exhibits here are concerned with aspects of life in Roman Britain, and those in the first free-standing case by the lift entrance come from London.

Town and country

London. At the time of the invasion (AD 43) there was no settlement of any importance at London; but some 60 years later it had become a thriving commercial port with a population of possibly 30,000 souls, frequented by Continental merchants. Merchandise arriving by sea was dispersed by the Roman road system radiating all over the province.

The central office of the procurator, who was in charge of the province's finances and responsible only to the emperor, was situated in London. A tile [56 7–1 717, 1st or 2nd century AD] bears the stamp 'P.P. BR. LON.', that is 'Publicani (tax gatherers) of London in the province of Britain', and is a witness to one of the office's least popular activities. Its records and correspondence were written in ink [1950 2–6, 1, ink pot, from Cannon Street, London] with a split bronze pen such as is still used [65, 12–20, 21] on papyrus, parchment (4th century) or waxed boards [1934 12–10, 98, 1st–2nd century AD from the Walbrook], sometimes in a cursive script [see mirror, 1953 10–2, 1, 2, 3] with a stylus [1934 12–10 78].

The model prow of a galley [56 7–1 29, 1st century AD] with the inscription on one side in reverse is a votive offering or perhaps a mount for a piece of furniture. But the three figures of deities found in the Thames at London Bridge [56 7–1 14–16] are almost certainly votives. The splendid archer [82 5–18 1, 2nd century AD] found in Queen Street, Cheapside, is in the finest classical tradition, and was probably made in Italy or Gaul in the reign of Hadrian or Antoninus Pius. Another interesting exhibit is the bronze helmet [1950 7–6 1] which was standard equipment for a legionary of the 1st century AD (Fig. 7).

Lincoln and Colchester. The left wall case contains exhibits from two Roman *coloniae*, chartered settlements inhabited

Fig. 7. Life-size model of a Roman legionary

by time-expired soldiers who were granted land outside the town and would render military services in emergencies. The Colchester *colonia*, founded in AD 49, bore the brunt of the opening stages of Queen Boudicca's rebellion in AD 60. The town was sacked (as were London and St Albans), and the bronze head of the emperor Claudius [see exhibit, 1st century AD] found near Saxmundham, was probably looted from a temple. Brutal reprisals against the rebels were taken by the governor, Paulinus, of which the procurator, Julius Classicianus, disapproved. His intercession with Nero on behalf of the Britons resulted in Paulinus' recall. Classicianus was buried in Britain, c. 65, and his tomb is in the Museum.

Lincoln (Lindum) was a legionary fortress before it became a *colonia* in about AD 90. By that time there were no immediate internal or external dangers to be feared, and the exhibits from the site denote peaceful occupations, such as the homely money-box [97 9–13 1], the face-urn [66 12–3 47] with a painted dedication to Mercury, and the stone relief of the three Mother Goddesses with bowls on their laps signifying plenty [56 5–7 1, 2nd or 3rd century], who were much worshipped in the imperial provinces of north-west Europe.

Industry and Commerce

Pewter from Appleshaw, nr. Andover. While wealthy citizens throughout the empire possessed silver tableware [see wall case, Mildenhall Treasure, late 4th or early 5th century AD], the less prosperous in Britain in the 3rd and 4th centuries used pewter ware made in the Bath region [2nd case] in their houses and villas. This period was the heyday of the Roman villa, a large or medium size stone or timber house owned generally by a Romanized Briton, and the hub of an estate devoted to farming or industry. The large villas were well appointed with central heating and mosaic floors, such as those displayed on the walls, and the early Christian pavement from Hinton St Mary with the male head and the Christian chi-rho monogram behind it.

The Romans used very great quantities of pottery, both British-made and imported. In the second case are a few examples of vessels from the important pottery industry of the Nene Valley, near Peterborough, including two fine decorated colour-coated vessels which were popular in the 3rd century [1962 4–4 1, jar with hunting scene of dogs and horses; 75 6–5 5, hunting scene. Both 3rd century AD].

Pottery: glass. Part of this case [3rd] is devoted to samian ware, a superior glossy-surfaced red ware made in Gaul and exported throughout the Roman empire during the 1st and 2nd centuries AD. Samian is standardized in form and decoration, and can be closely dated; the case contains a representative selection of vessels.

So far as is known elaborate glassware was not made in Britain. Imports came from the Cologne factories (early 1st century) and other Rhenish sources and later from north Gallic and Belgic factories (2nd century). They were often of fine workmanship, such as the elegant blue pillar moulded bowl with white marbling [1923 6–5 1, mid-1st century, from Radnage, Bucks], the ribbed blue-green flagon [S264, 50–75 AD, from Barnwell, Cambs.], and the green circus beaker, decorated in three registers [70 2–24 3, mid-1st century AD, from Colchester].

Silver and bronze plate. Ritual vessels, show pieces, toilet articles and decorative furniture fittings as well as tableware were made from silver and also bronze, such as the bronze jugs used in sacrificial rites where the figure decoration was usually concentrated on the handle [4th case], and the heavily decorated silver dish [40 11–11 1, 4th century, from Mileham] which may have adorned some Romanized establishment. [For minerals found in Great Britain and their method of working, see wall case: *Mining and metal-working*.]

Burial

Under Roman law, no burial could take place within a town's boundary: consequently the roads near populous centres were lined with tombs, for example, the Appian Way. Both cremation and interment were practised. In cremations the ashes were often inserted in pottery jars or glass vessels [1st case, Dep. p. 6] which were inserted in lead cannisters [1st case, Dep. p. 7. Late 1st century]. In interment the body was placed in a coffin, which in the case of a boy buried outside the Roman walls of London and found near Minories, was made of lead [centre display, top: lid, 53 6–20 2, 4th century A D] and subsequently encased in a stone coffin [53 6–20 1, 4th century], decorated on the side by a youthful head in relief.

It was customary to erect a tombstone inscribed with a few biographical details of the individual commemorated with, in some cases, the name of the person setting it up and a sculptured representation of the deceased. An example is the tombstone of Volusia Faustina [62 4–23 1, 1st or 2nd century A D] who can be seen side by side with her husband. The inscription reads: 'to the spirits of the departed: Volusia Faustina, a citizen of Lindum (Lincoln), lived 26 years, 1 month, 26 days. Aurelius Senecio, a councillor, set this up to his well deserving wife.'

But tombstones were expensive (in Britain there were burial clubs for the less wealthy to which members paid regular subscriptions, elected officers and attended club dinners) and later Volusia's tombstone was also used by Claudius Catiotus, perhaps a relative, who, the inscription tells us, 'lived 60 (or more) years'.

The very rich had large and impressive funerary monuments, decorated with stone sculpture, such as the arresting head [10, 200–300 A D, from Towcester, Northants.], probably representing a native deity, which was found on top of a Roman monumental tomb.

Religion

Temples, shrines and priests. The Romans worshipped their state gods, for example Minerva [1925 6–10 2, 3rd century A D, from a hoard found at Felmingham Hall, Norfolk], Mars [OA 248, 2nd or 3rd century A D, from Torksey, Lincs.], as well as some foreign deities, and in Britain these included Celtic and northern deities. In addition there were the household gods represented in each home in the family shrine, for example the young Lar [1925 6–10 4, 3rd century A D] wearing a short tunic, boots, and holding aloft a drinking horn in his right hand and a libation vessel in his left, found in a hoard, probably votive, at Felmingham Hall, Norfolk. Here too, is the statuette of the emperor Nero in the guise of Alexander the Great, wearing imperial dress, which was probably connected with emperor worship [13 2–13 1, 1st century A D, from Baylham Mill, Suffolk]. The crowns were probably part of priestly regalia when celebrating the imperial or other cults.

The silver and bronze votive plaques from Barkway and Stony Stratford probably come from a shrine or temple. They are in the same category as the 2nd century A D Roman plaques of floral and plant form [Greek and Roman Life Room: *Religion*], but of inferior workmanship and design.

All these cult objects are pagan but in the 4th century Christianity and paganism flourished concurrently. Christian paintings have been found in a villa at Lullingstone, Kent (the only early Christian paintings so far found in Britain) which, with the paintings from Verulamium (St Albans) [see exhibits] give a good idea of the interior decoration of rich Roman dwellings.

Lullingstone has also provided other memorable exhibits in the portrait busts of two men. The least damaged depicts a man in semi-military dress, and is dated c. 125–35 A D, while the other portrait is represented in civilian dress of a toga and tunic, and assigned to c. 155–65 A D. Both portraits represent aristocrats of Mediterranean origin and may be the ancestors of a high Roman official who occupied the villa at the end of the 2nd century when it was rebuilt on more luxurious lines.

3 The department of Western Asiatic Antiquities

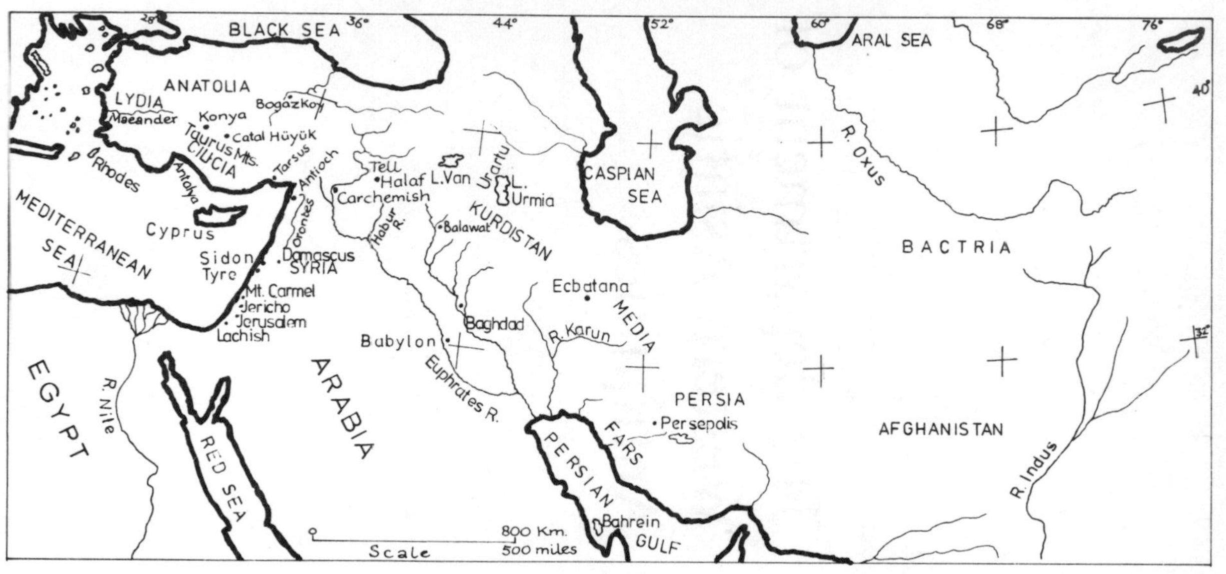

Map 1. Western Asia

The department of Western Asiatic Antiquities

Historical Summary

Western Asia

Introduction

Western Asia comprises the modern states of Turkey, Iraq, and Iran to the Afghan frontier, and Syria, Lebanon, Israel, Arabia and the States of the Persian Gulf to Aden. With the exception of Syria, Palestine and the Ionic (Greek) cities of the west coast of Turkey, its history is not nearly so well known as that of Greece and Rome because the principal source lay buried for many centuries and was only rediscovered in the middle of the 19th century.

Yet it was in the southern part of the country known today as Iraq and formerly as Mesopotamia (a name still retained by archaeologists and historians) that civilization arose. Here writing was invented and large cities built in which were the amenities of civilized life: vast temples and public buildings, irrigation systems, organized government, education and the arts. But perhaps the finest achievement of all was that this civilization was the first and owed nothing to any other source.

Prehistory

Those who have already visited the Early Man Gallery in the

Department of Prehistoric Antiquities will have seen in the Natufian (Mesolithic) culture of the Mount Carmel (Israel) caves of el-Wad and et-Kebarah the last stage in Western Asia before the introduction of farming (p. 35).

From 9000–7000 BC radical changes took place in man's way of life. From hunting and food gathering, and living in a cave or some primitive shelter, he learned the arts of crop cultivation and stock breeding. We do not know what caused him to do so, but it may have been that the increasing aridity of the climate forced him to seek new ways of obtaining food. That he was able to do so was due to the wild grasses from which wheat and barley are descended and the wild ancestors of the domestic animals, sheep, goat, cattle and pig, which were all to be found in Western Asia.

Neolithic, Chalcolithic and early part of Early Bronze Age, 7000–2800 BC

Thus it was that from about 7000 BC onwards settlements were established in the valleys and on the slopes of the western Zagros mountains, in the foothills of Iraqi Kurdistan, the northern Mesopotamian plain, southern Anatolia, north Syria, the Syrian coast and south-west of Damascus, Palestine and the Iranian plateau.

Some were small farming villages, such as Jarmo in Iraqi Kurdistan which, about 6750 BC, consisted of about twenty houses with probably a population of about 150; while in Palestine at Jericho, c. 7000 BC, the settlement covered 10 acres with an estimated population of 2,000, and was enclosed by a massive defensive wall against which, on the inside, was a round tower. Jericho was a well-watered oasis and with irrigation its population could therefore have easily been supported by agriculture. To the north in the fertile Konya plain, southern Anatolia, the site of Catal Hüyük covered in 6700 BC 32 acres and probably housed 10,000 souls, all supported by agriculture. Pottery was not made there, nor at Jarmo and Jericho at the dates given above.

These are just a few of the numerous farming settlements known in Western Asia. Archaeologists can tell us about the material circumstances of their inhabitants, their food, dwellings, tools and weapons, but nothing about their personalities, moral codes or, more important, who they were, for such knowledge is only available when the art of writing

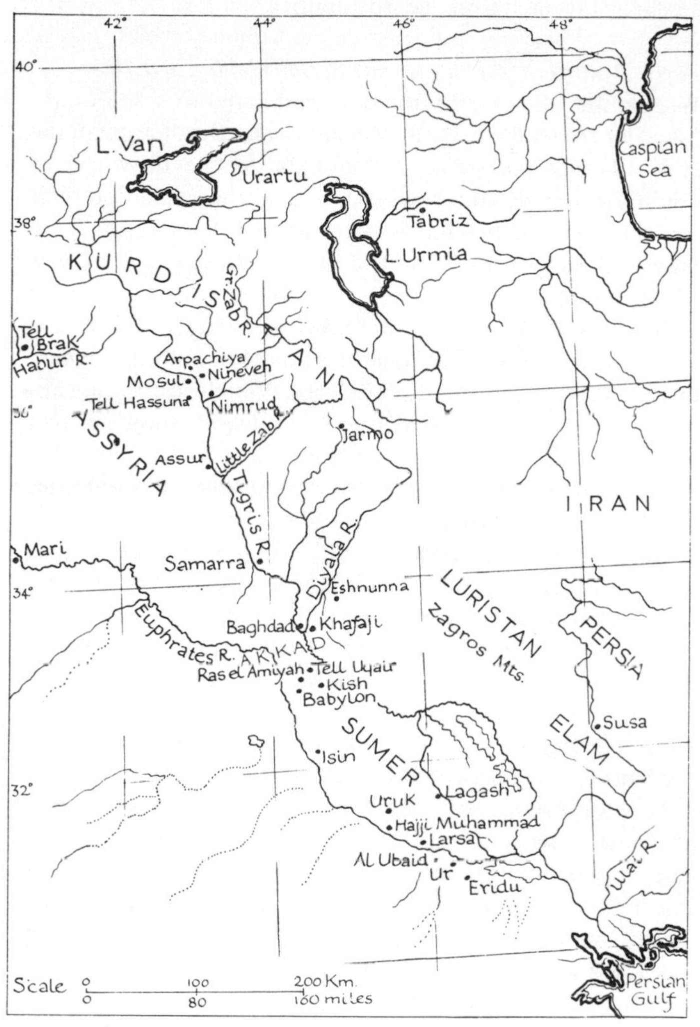

Map 2. Mesopotamia

has been invented and records kept.

Early Dynastic (Old Sumerian) Period, 2800–2370 BC

Writing was invented by the Sumerians, and was well established by about 2800 BC in Mesopotamia. Originating in the later 4th millennium as pictographs (simple drawings of objects), the signs had, by this period, already achieved their characteristic wedge-shapes, of which the later script, now known as cuneiform (from the Latin *cuneus*, a wedge), was wholly composed.

Geographically, the region known as Sumer extends from the southern end of that area of Iraq (Mesopotamia) where the great rivers Euphrates and Tigris flow closest to one another, down to the Persian Gulf, but Sumerian influence had spread northwards through Mesopotamia by the early 3rd millennium, as towns such as Mari on the middle Euphrates and Brak in the Habur valley testify (Map 2).

The Sumerian King List attributes fantastically long reigns to the early rulers, but some of these legendary figures are known to have been actual rulers. The inhabitants of southern Mesopotamia in the Old Sumerian period were a mixed stock of Sumerians and others who had settled in the area, including speakers of the Semitic languages known as Akkadian and other as yet unidentified groups. Nevertheless, the Sumerians constituted one civilization.

They were not, however, a nation in the modern sense, i.e., possessing a central government with authority over cities, towns and villages within its boundaries. Their unit was the city-state, the walled and fortified stronghold which drew its supplies from its farming villages in the vicinity and was ruled over by its king or governor. The citizens were highly skilled in metal-working, architecture and agriculture; and they also developed an extensive system of trade over wide areas of western Asia, Afghanistan, Arabia and the Indus valley.

The Sumerian city-state was the germ of the modern state. Becoming powerful, it conquered its neighbours, and its ruler established a hegemony over other cities. Inevitably, however, a ruler arose who was sufficiently powerful to unite all Sumer under a centralized control.

Akkadian Period, c. 2370–2113 BC; New Sumerian Period, c.2113–2006 BC

Such a man was Sargon, a Semite in the service of the King of Kish, who established a kingdom in Akkad (the site of its capital, Agade, has not yet been located) in the north of Sumer about 2370 BC. Sargon conquered not only the Sumerian city-states but also Assyria (northern Mesopotamia), northern Syria and Elam, in south-west Persia.

But these early Western Asiatic dynasties did not last long; they were frequently brought to an end by the incursions of barbaric tribes or the migrations of peoples from distant regions who overwhelmed the original populations. This was the fate of the Sargonic dynasty which, after about 100 years, was overrun by a tribe of Persian hill folk, the Guti.

But not all the cities of Sumer were overwhelmed, and when the Gutians were finally expelled in the 21st century BC the city of Ur, which had already been politically prominent in the Old Sumerian period, established control over the whole of Mesopotamia, including Assyria, for about a century under the 3rd dynasty of Ur. But once again barbaric tribes were attracted by Sumer's wealth. Semitic Amorites from the Syrian desert first infiltrated and finally came to rule several Mesopotamian cities, while the Elamites, whose destiny was inextricably intermingled with that of Mesopotamia, sacked Ur and carried off its last king to their capital, Susa, in southern Persia. Lacking centralized control, Sumer reverted to independent city states and two, Isin and Larsa, jockeyed for supremacy. But Sumer's political power was finished, and control eventually passed to the Semites of Babylon in central Mesopotamia and, after vicissitudes, to Assyria in the north.

1st Dynasty of Babylon, 1894–1595 BC; Kassite Dynasty, c. 1600–1157 BC

Babylon, at the end of the 3rd millennium during the ascendancy of Ur, was a small city on the middle Euphrates ruled by a governor. But by the 19th century BC it had become a kingdom which, in the time of its sixth king, the Amorite Hammurabi, was sufficiently powerful to conquer Sumer (Sumer and Akkad are from now on known as Babylonia) and to extend its boundaries in other regions.

But here again a highly civilized state (Hammurabi had initiated great civil reforms and regularized commercial practice) was supplanted by an inferior one. The Kassites, a non-Semitic warrior tribe, raided Babylonian territory under Hammurabi's successors while peaceful infiltration also occurred. When, therefore, in 1595 BC Babylon was sacked by a sudden descent of the Hittites from Anatolia (who returned to Asia Minor as swiftly as they had come), the Kassites were able to occupy Babylon's territory which their kings ruled until 1157 BC.

The Hittites, 19th–13th century BC; Mitanni, 16th–13th century BC

The Hittites, who spoke an Indo-European language and came from beyond the Caucasus, infiltrated into central Anatolia (Turkey) in the 19th century BC, and by the 15th century had welded the indigenous population into a powerful empire which eventually included northern Syria. The state of Mitanni, in northern Mesopotamia (including Assyria and parts of Syria) was also formed by a warrior caste of Indo-European ancestry. In addition, from 1500–1450 BC, Egypt controlled Palestine and Syria as far as the Euphrates. Three centuries later, however, all three states were a factor no longer to be reckoned with in Western Asia. The state of Mitanni foundered under the blows of the Hittites, civil wars, and a resurgent Assyria. The Hittites, after a struggle with Egypt for the mastery of Syria, were overwhelmed partly by a mass migration of peoples coming, it is believed, from eastern Thrace and the eastern Mediterranean, and hordes of immigrants, including natives of Asia Minor dispossessed by the European invaders, marched and sailed down the Mediterranean coast for an attack on Egypt which was only stemmed on its border by the energetic measures of its pharaoh, Ramesses III (1198–1166 BC). This invasion brought the Phrygians to Asia Minor and the Philistines to Palestine.

The Assyrian Empire, 9th–7th century BC

Although there were settlements at Nineveh from the Hassuna period onwards, not a great deal is known of Assyria's early history. As mentioned above she was subject to the control of the kings of Ur and Agade (23rd–21st century BC) (p.75) although Shamsi-Adad I (1813–1781 BC) seems to have been independent, it was not until the fall of Mitanni in the 13th century that Assyria's rise to power began.

A period of consolidation (1200–1000 BC), however, was first necessary, when local and regional gains were made and great expeditions launched into foreign lands. Then, slowly at first, but later with increasing momentum, under a series of exceptionally able kings (from Ashurnasirpal, 883–859 BC, to Ashurbanipal, 668–627 BC), the Assyrian armies invaded the greater part of the Near East including southern Mesopotamia to the Persian Gulf, the regions east of the Tigris, Elam in south-west Persia, the mountainous districts of Urartu, eastern Turkey, Syria, Palestine, Arabia and Egypt (as far as Thebes).

But there came a time when the drain on manpower and materials was too great and the territory too extensive to be properly defended, and this provided the opportunity for Assyria's enemies. An alliance of the Medes, an Iranian people, and Scythians from the north-east, with Nabopolassar, an Aramaean general who had revolted against his sovereign, Sin-shar-ishkun, and seized the throne of Babylon in 625 BC, invaded Assyria in 612 BC, and, after a siege of two and a half months, sacked the capital, Nineveh, when according to a Greek tradition, the king perished in the flames. The cities of the homeland were reduced to ruins and the mighty Assyrian empire, after a last stand in the west, lay crumbling in the dust.

The New Babylonian Empire, 625–539 BC

Nabopolassar, the new king of Babylon, considered himself the heir to the Assyrian empire, but Egypt thought otherwise. This seemed, indeed, the moment to recover the lost Asiatic provinces. The Egyptian army invaded Palestine, and after vainly attempting to aid the remnants of the Assyrian army after the fall of Nineveh, occupied Carchemish (Jerablus) in northern Syria on the Euphrates. Nabopolassar's son, the Crown Prince Nebuchadnezzar, was sent to dislodge it. In 605 BC, a bitter battle was fought when the Egyptians were utterly routed, the fleeing remnants being pursued by Nebuchadnezzar as far as Pelusium in Egypt.

This brilliant military campaign warned the petty states

of Syria and Palestine that they had exchanged Assyrian domination for Babylonian and they remained quiescent, all but the state of Judah which twice revolted. It paid a severe penalty. In 597 and 587 BC, Nebuchadnezzar attacked Jerusalem, deporting on each occasion sections of the population to Babylon, by the waters of which, the Psalmist assures us 'they sat down and wept'.

Nebuchadnezzar reigned for 40 years but after his death the empire collapsed within 25 years. The last king, Nabonidus, attempted religious and economic reforms which made him unpopular. When, therefore, in 539 BC Babylon was attacked by the great power which had arisen in the east, the empire of the Medes and Persians, it surrendered with scarcely a struggle to Cyrus the Great, an ignominious end to Mesopotamian pre-eminence, which had endured for over 2,000 years.

The Persian Empire, 539–331 BC

Little is known of the Persians until the military prowess of their king, Cyrus the Great the Achaemenid brought them into prominence in the 6th century BC.

But it seems that Iranian emigration from the north (by way of the Caucusus) into northern Persia east of the Zagros mountains began late in the 2nd millennium, and that the Medes, kinsmen of the Persians, filtered into the northern and central Zagros ranges before the 9th century BC with increasing momentum from the 7th century. They were opposed by the Assyrians, whose opposition was terminated when the Medes, Scythians and Babylonians sacked Nineveh (612 BC). The Persians probably arrived in the province of Fars, their homeland, before the 6th century BC.

Cyrus the Great, who was a vassal of the Median king, revolted and defeated his overlord in 549 BC, annexing the Median kingdom. Campaigning in Asia Minor, he overcame Croesus of Lydia in 546 BC, who had attempted to block Persian expansion, and also became overlord of the Ionic (Greek) cities on the Aegean coast. His final triumph was the capture of Babylon in 539 BC which opened the route through Syria and Palestine to Egypt, conquered after his death by his son and successor, Cambyses, in 525 BC.

But Cambyses died in 522 BC and the throne passed to

Darius I (522–486 BC) and his successors, a collateral branch of the Achaemenids, who extended the Persian empire in the east to the Indus, and in the south to the shores of the Indian Ocean. But as will be seen later, they were not so successful when they invaded Europe.

Western Asiatic Antiquities

First Floor:
Prehistoric Room, Babylonian Room, Room of Writing, Syrian Room, Hittite Room and Persian Landing

Ground Floor:
Assyrian Transept, Nimrud Gallery, Assyrian Saloon, Assyrian Basement, Assyrian Entrance, Nimrud Central Saloon, Nineveh Gallery

Prehistory

Introduction

The sites of early settlements in Western Asia can be seen in Maps 1 and 2. Some of these developed into towns with a long history, while others reached the farming village stage and progressed no further. Settlement over the area occurred at different times, and the progress of these small communities varied from place to place.

It is generally conceded that a community is civilized when writing is used to transmit language and not just to indicate objects or ideas, as is the case with pictographs and ideographs. This point was first reached in southern Mesopotamia at the end of the Late Prehistoric Period, c. 2800 BC, and its advent there is all the more surprising since the first known settlement in the south at Eridu in the early 6th millennium is considerably later than that, say, at Jarmo in the north (6750 BC), although in the south excavation may not have reached the bottom yet, which is probably below the water table.

The Prehistoric Room

The Prehistoric Room is arranged to demonstrate the successive stages of man's material progress to civilization in the key area of Mesopotamia, north and south [cases 7–10] during the Neolithic period, and the areas which it influenced, Syria [cases 5 and 6], Palestine [case 4] and Persia [cases 1 and 2].

The walls are divided into four bands which represent periods of time, as in Fig. 8 [taken from the chart in case 7], and the names given – Hassuna, Eridu, Halaf, Hajji

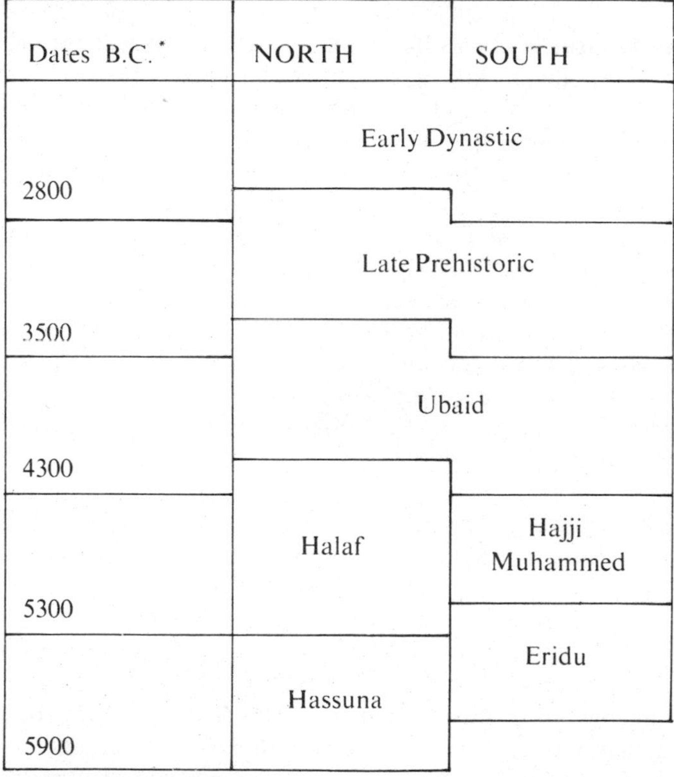

*Cambridge Ancient History volumes 1 & 2

Fig. 8. Mesopotamia, 5900–2800 BC

Muhammad, 'Ubaid and Late Prehistoric – represent the cultures [Appendix 2] in those periods in the north and south of Mesopotamia.

Prehistoric Mesopotamia

5900–5300 BC. Bearing these points in mind and also that each culture represents a material advance, it can be seen that in the north, when the Hassuna culture flourished (the settlement at Tell Hassuna is the earliest known in the northern plain of Mesopotamia), the design of the farmhouse [see case 8, reconstruction], about half-way through the site's existence, was quite advanced. The fabric was built of sun-dried bricks and consisted of rectangular rooms round or beside an open courtyard in which animals, cattle and sheep, could be kept at night, and the roof was gabled. These early farmers also cultivated crops. Pottery was decorated with simple incised and painted linear designs [case 7, potsherds north] and the characteristic vessels were bowls and jars [case 10].

From Eridu (mod. Abu Shahrain), 6th millennium BC, the first known southern settlement, there are no exhibits. Nevertheless the Eridu people, who may have come from southern Persia in the early 6th millennium, brought with them a well-developed culture. Their settlement, founded on a lagoon but now in the desert 150 miles from the Persian Gulf, was then probably connected with the sea by a series of lakes in the delta region, thus serving as a port which greatly facilitated its growth and eventual commercial prosperity.

5300–4300 BC. The Halaf culture takes its name from Tell Halaf in north Syria but its type site is Arpachiyah near Mosul, Iraq. The culture covered a large area from the Zagros foothills to Carchemish on the Euphrates and the foothills of the Taurus mountains of Turkey. The bull's head was a characteristic motif for pottery decoration [case 7, 4th row, no. 2; 6th row, no. 1]. In the middle Halaf period houses were circular with domed roofs, and the buildings were on stone foundations [case 8, reconstruction] although gabled houses were still built. Clay figurines, probably connected with fertility (fertility of man, beast and crop was vital at this period; without it man faced annihilation), stamp seals to identify property, and in middle Halaf times [case 9] amulets in the form of a double axe (a motif persisting throughout antiquity), as well as tools and implements of bone, obsidian and stone, were all made throughout the period, as were characteristic vessels of buff or pinkish clay [case 10] in the form of bowls and plates.

In the south, however, in the latter part of the 6th millennium, the Eridu culture developed locally into that discovered at Hajji Muhammad, near modern Warka (Uruk), which is found at many other southern sites. From this culture was derived the first homogeneous Mesopotamian way of life, the 'Ubaid culture which, beginning in the south, spread northwards.

4300–3500 BC. During the 800 or so years of the 'Ubaid period (type site at Al-'Ubaid on the banks of an ancient canal 4 miles west of the city of Ur) important developments took place. At the beginning of the period primitive methods of irrigation were practised in southern Mesopotamia which, by its end, was carried on by a large network of canals. As a result food production increased; there was a rise in population and towns sprang up in the delta region. The inhabitants were housed in mudbrick dwellings and reed huts, and the latter can be seen on the gypsum trough [centre case: 120000, from Uruk, 3300–3000 BC] which, although of later date, depicts a type of hut which is still in use by the marsh Arabs today.

Furthermore this vigorous culture spread and has been found at Ur, Eridu, which by now was a market town of about 4,000 inhabitants, Uruk, the Old Testament Erech (mod. Warka), Lagash (mod. El-Hibbeh) and other southern sites; at Tell 'Uqair and Ras el-'Amiya in central Mesopotamia where the Euphrates and the Tigris flow closest to each other; at Nineveh and other Assyrian sites; and indeed in northern Mesopotamia. Thus Mesopotamia had a unified culture which was to be the case for the next 3,000 years.

The most typical small object of the 'Ubaid culture was its pottery with a light ground and generally decorated in a dark paint with simple designs [case 7]. Characteristic shapes are plates, bowls, dishes and spouted cups [case 10]. Representative, too, are baked clay nails [case 8] used for hanging reed matting inside the walls of a mud hut (from

Eridu), and slender, terracotta figurines with lizard heads, one suckling a child [case 8], depicting the mother-goddess, which were placed in graves. Clay models of implements have been found in abundance [case 9], the axe, adze, hammer-axe and clay sickle, which may have been copies of copper originals or, as some authorities think, for actual use, for Mesopotamian clay, when baked hard, is almost indestructible. The obsidian knife, point and scraper [127324–26] should also be noted for this material is not indigenous to Mesopotamia and had to be imported. In the model boat with curved ends we see a craft which is still plying on the Euphrates today [123614]. But in spite of all these developments, the 'Ubaid people were still a race of peasant farmers.

3500–2800 BC. But now, towards the end of the Late Prehistoric period, come startling developments which brought about an urban civilization with architecture, art, much improved technology, and later the use of metals. These innovations are best represented at Uruk (mod. Warka), but they are also to be seen in contemporary occupation levels in other cities of the south, and as far north as Tell Brak in the Habur Valley.

The most outstanding achievement of this period is monumental architecture represented by the temples. There had been shrines and small temples on platforms from very early times in the south, and the platform or terrace in the course of time developed into the stepped tower, known as the ziggurat, a feature which could be seen for miles across the plain. At Uruk one of the ziggurats was 40 ft high (in historic times they rose to as much as 300 ft) and was ascended by a stairway. On top stood the 'White Temple', built about 3200–3100 BC [case 8, reconstruction], so-called because it was covered with white plaster. The façades, walls and columns of temples were decorated with mosaic cones, that is clay nails [case 8] with heads painted in different colours. On the opposite wall of this room this form of decoration can be seen. It was first found at Uruk [see inset: four cones fixed in plaster], but the columns exhibited are reconstructed from cones found at Ur.

Uruk pottery is a monochrome ware, red or grey [case 7, row 4; first sherd of rows 1, 2 and 3] and is found in both north and south, but later the wares diverged. Jamdat Nasr painted ware [Babylonia, top row] was found in the south while in the north at Nineveh about 3000 BC was a gaily painted polychrome pottery which was probably introduced from northern Iran.

In this last phase, too, fine sculpture was produced, as can be seen from the three carved limestone sherds of bowls [case 8], from the beautiful head of a ewe (Fig. 9) and the sculptured vase [case by opening, 132092, 118465, both c. 3000 BC], as well as cylinder seals [case 8], introduced at this time. Metal, which appeared at the end of the 'Ubaid period, was worked on a greater scale.

Above all, the earliest known writing is dated to the middle of the Late Prehistoric period, and the first large collection was found at Uruk, inscribed with pictographs which recorded economic data as, for instance, the tablet displayed in case 8, an early agricultural record. By 2800 BC writing had so far advanced beyond the pictograph stage that it became decipherable, and we now know that the language written was that of the Sumerians. When did they arrive? It is not known for certain, but one opinion is that they may have been there from the beginning, while another

Fig. 9. Clay head of a ewe, c. 3000 BC

is that they arrived at the beginning of the Uruk (Late Prehistoric) period.

Life had indeed become swiftly diversified in the closing centuries of the period, and instead of a man spending his whole life in the production of necessities, there was now sufficient time and labour for the production of luxuries.

The Peripheral Regions

Western Asia, in addition to the countries mentioned above, also includes Iran where the majority of settlements were not so advanced in the Late Prehistoric period as in Mesopotamia, although its painted pottery is superb, as shown by vessels from Susa, a considerable town in southern Iran [case 1], and Bakun in Fars [case 2. Bowl decorated with demon motif]. Furthermore exhibits from the previous period demonstrate that fine painted pottery was traditional.

In Palestine a most interesting exhibit is the skull [case 4] found with six others under the floor of a house in Jericho (c. 6200 BC) at a time before pottery was made, although the inhabitants of the town were food producers.

The skulls, with one exception, lacked a lower jaw. The facial flesh had been reproduced in plaster and bivalve shells inserted for eyes. The missing jaw was modelled over the upper teeth, giving a foreshortened appearance to the head, the top of which was left bare (except in one example which was painted with black bands), while the cheeks were originally coloured. The intention was probably to produce a portrait for the heads were almost certainly connected with ancestor worship.

Syria was much influenced by Mesopotamia on the coast and in the east during the 'Ubaid and the Late Prehistoric periods respectively. At Tell Brak a temple was built which, in spite of local variations, contained the basic features of the Sumerian temple [case 6, plan]. This is known as the Eye Temple, and in the accumulated remains of a former temple on the site were thousands of eye idols in black and white alabaster. Metal was in use [copper tools], and the Halaf and Hassuna periods are represented by fertility type figurines (Mother Goddess). Asia Minor, too, was subjected to Mesopotamian influence, but in the later phases, that of the West predominated, as is demonstrated by the pottery exhibits.

The Mesopotamian exhibits in the Prehistoric Room cover the transition from small farming settlements to great cities. They should indeed be regarded with awe, for they are material witnesses of the advance to the world's first civilization. And this is all the more remarkable because this civilization was not brought about by contact with other civilized peoples for there were none, but arose wholly spontaneously.

We do not know why, but only that it was so; and now we will see in the Babylonian and adjacent rooms how these first civilized people lived and some of their astonishing achievements.

The Babylonian Room

The swift progress of architecture during the Late Prehistoric period was followed by many fine buildings and large cities in the next, the Early Dynastic period (2800–2370 BC). These developments occurred mainly in Babylonia, which is that part of Mesopotamia from Baghdad in the north down to the Persian Gulf in the south. Here flourished the Sumerian city states, the kingdom of Akkad, the First Dynasty of Babylon, and the New Babylonian kingdom.

How did these Babylonian cities appear to a traveller as he made his way in the heat and dust across the Mesopotamian plain? We are concerned here with a period of about 2,500 years, from the Sumerian city states down to the Persian conquest of Babylon, and during this long time one would expect radical changes. But Babylonian civilization was fixed by the Sumerian, and architectural features which the Sumerians evolved to meet their religious and secular needs remained more or less constant, except for local variations, throughout this period. Therefore, our traveller, as he approached his journey's end, would have seen a city similar in appearance to that shown in Fig. 10, which is a reconstruction of Babylon under Nebuchadnezzar in the 6th century.

The Babylonian city

Here can be seen many of the principal features of the Babylonian fortified city: the crenellated walls with buttress towers and inset city gate (facing bridge); the ziggurat or staged tower (left) with the small temple on the summit; the temple of the city's god (right), and the buildings concerned with temple affairs, quarters for the priests, priestesses and other personnel, workshops, storehouses, all of which, with the ziggurat, were surrounded by a substantial wall to form the main sanctuary of the city. In addition, the principal thoroughfare (left to right), the canal (flanked by trees), the quays and part of the new city, and the narrow, irregular streets of the residential areas, can be clearly distinguished.

Many representations of fortified cities will be seen later in the Assyrian Galleries (ground floor), but in this room there is a bronze model [case 16, 91177, 91250, c. 700 BC] of a city of Urartu, eastern Turkey, a country whose armies constituted a menace to Assyria (northern Mesopotamia) from the 9th–7th century BC. Public buildings in that mountainous country were built of stone.

Bricks

However, in Babylonia, owing to an almost total lack of stone, clay bricks, sun-dried or baked, were used, the latter sparingly in early times owing to the shortage of fuel to fire them. In Sumer, in Early Dynastic times, the building unit was the plano-convex brick [case 16, below, brick with ancient thumb impression]. Furthermore, buildings of consequence carried foundation deposits: tablets [case 16, 91013], figures of gods [102613] or the ruler who always moulded the first brick of a temple [90865. King Ashurbanipal of Assyria, 668–627 BC, depicted as a building labourer], or clay cones [91071]. These were placed under the building in the angles of the outside walls, and were inscribed with the name of the king [see Room of Writing for further examples of foundation deposits].

Burial

Although the Babylonian Room contains exhibits from different periods, many are of Early Dynastic date and come from the 'Royal' tombs in the Sumerian city of Ur 'of the Chaldees', Abraham's native city (mod. Tell Mukaiyar). They are breathtakingly beautiful and beyond price, and were found in tombs which had been dug in a cemetery out-

Fig. 10. The city of Babylon. In the foreground is the Euphrates which flowed between the old and new parts of the city, 6th century BC

side the wall of the main sanctuary in about 2500 BC.

Two of the best known tombs are assumed to belong to a king and his queen, Pu-abi. The king's domed tomb, which had been robbed in antiquity, was built at the end of a long and deep subterranean shaft or passage entered by a ramp in which were the skeletons of 63 men and women, including six copper helmeted guards [centre case D, 121414, crushed skull and helmet], who had probably led in six oxen drawing two carts.

After the king's burial, the shaft was filled in but reopened later on a higher level where a second tomb was constructed for Queen Pu-abi, whose skeleton and that of an attendant were unearthed. The shaft contained a sledge [centre case C, 121200] drawn by oxen with copper collars [121480] and reins threaded through a silver rein ring decorated with an electrum onager (wild ass) [121348]. There was also a lyre and harp [centre case B, 121198 A, B]. The sounding box of the lyre is decorated with a bull's head of gold sheet hammered over a wooden core, and beard and mane of lapis lazuli (probably from Afghanistan), and edged with lapis lazuli, red limestone and shell. Each end was decorated with shell plaques depicting lively scenes of human figures and mythological animals. The silver lyre [121199] was found in the Great Death Pit (see below).

In the queen's grave, too, were the gold goblet [centre case D, 121345], the lovely fluted feeding cup [121346], two boat-shaped bowls, one gold with the original gold wire handle [121344] and the other of obsidian (volcanic glass) [121690], and a gold strainer [121347].

In a tomb known as the Great Death Pit 74 persons were immolated, 6 men and 68 women, the latter in court regalia [centre case A] with head-dresses made of gold bands ornamented with gold beech leaves, necklaces consisting mainly of lapis lazuli, carnelian and gold beads, and large gold lunate ear-rings. An adjacent case displays the skull of a female courtier crushed by the weight of earth above it [attachment to A, 122294]. Another exhibit is the superbly beautiful billy-goat [case D, 122200, Fig. 11] standing on its hind legs with its forelegs resting on a tree, symbolic of the fertility gods, and itself vibrant with power. Its body was originally made of wood, sheet gold and silver being hammered over the head, legs and belly. The thick coat

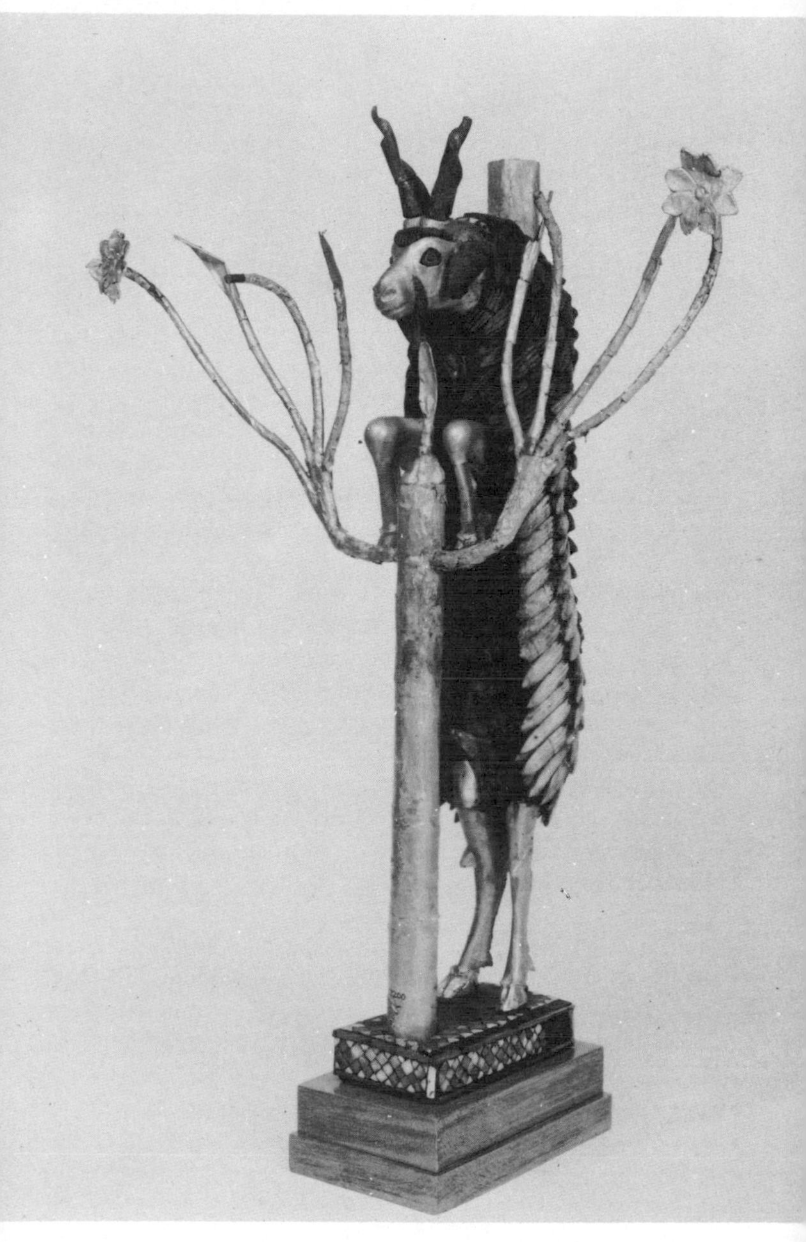

Fig. 11. Billy-goat from the Royal cemetery, Ur, c. 2500 BC

is rendered by carved pieces of shell and lapis lazuli set in bitumen.

Other lovely objects from the Royal cemetery can be seen in cases 8 and 9. The former contains electrotypes of exhibits in the Baghdad museum, in particular the electrum wig-helmet which belonged to 'Mes-kalam-du, king' of Ur. But perhaps the most informative exhibit is the so-called 'Royal Standard' of Ur [centre, 121201] representing on the two long sides in mosaic the king in war and peace. In war [lowest register] we see four-wheel chariots drawn by asses or onagers charging the enemy. Next [mid. register] the infantry wearing cloaks and helmets and armed with short spears marshal the prisoners; and [top] the king inspects the captives. In peace [lower reg.] servants lead onagers and carry heavy bundles; and [mid. reg.] lead bullocks and thick-coated rams, perhaps for the banquet [above] where the king (largest figure) drinks with his courtiers while listening to music.

The graves mentioned above were not the only royal burials to contain the bodies of retainers who, it would seem, were sacrificed so as to be able to serve their royal masters in the afterlife, although such practices were almost unknown in Babylonia. However, the majority of Babylonians were not buried in such state. In this cemetery, which had been in use for a long time (more than 2,500 graves were investigated, many robbed), bodies were generally placed in coffins of terracotta, wicker-work or wood, wrapped in matting, or placed straight into the earth.

The Ziggurat

But to turn to another feature of Babylonian life, the Ziggurat, which at Ur had been built by Ur-Nammu, the first king of the Third Dynasty (c. 2113–2006 BC), and rebuilt by subsequent Babylonian kings, one of whom was Nabonidus (554–539 BC) [Bay 15, 90837], the last king of the New Babylonian dynasty (p. 78). He restored the temple on the tower's summit, decorating it with blue glazed bricks [116981], probably on the outside, for the coloured brick was much employed for exterior decoration at this time.

The Temple

The temple was the focal point of the Babylonian's religion.

To understand the significance of religion in his life it must be realized that, although so skilled technologically, he lacked that body of knowledge which enables us to attribute the processes of nature, that is to say, the germinating and maturing of crops, the fecundity of animals and such phenomena as storms, eclipses and earthquakes, to the action of natural laws. He was aware, however, that he could not control these processes himself, and believed that they must be controlled by divinities with powers more extensive than his own. But as the processes of nature represented life, and as the gods controlled nature – in fact were immanent in it for there was a sun god, a moon god, a god who nurtured the crops, a storm god and other deities – human existence lay at the mercy of the gods. This was not a comforting thought, for they were obviously capricious and often allowed man to be overwhelmed by disaster. Fortunately, the Babylonian believed that the human mind was not capable of fathoming the divine mental processes, and so he did not question the manifestations of the divine will; but it is not surprising that he spent a good deal of his time trying to propitiate the deities. It is perhaps for this that the temple absorbed so much of the decorative and architectural talents of this gifted people: it was, after all, the home of the god.

The Al-'Ubaid temple

Vast temples were built in Early Dynastic and later times, but the temple exhibits in this room [see dais] come from a small shrine at Al-'Ubaid [see east end of room]. The inscription on the foundation tablet [116982] tells us that A-ane-pada, king of Ur, son of Mes-ane-pada, king of Ur, had built a temple for Nin-hur-sag, the Lady of the Mountain, goddess of life and fertility: Mes-ane-pada was known as the first king of the First Dynasty of Ur which, until this tablet was discovered, was thought to be mythical. However, now it is possible to date both the dynasty and the temple and its contents to some time after 2600 BC.

The building, which stood on a platform and was approached by a central stairway, had been wrecked, and the objects it contained lay buried on either side of the stairway. One of the most magnificent finds was the copper panel [top back, 114308] above the two mosaic columns [115328, 116760] representing Imdugud, the mythical lion-headed eagle of the god Ningirsu (Babylonian religion was so intermingled with natural forces that the gods not only represented aspects of them – Ningirsu was the Storm God – but were also symbolized by animals, often in hybrid form) gripping two stags by the claw. Two other superb metal pieces were the copper figures of calves [case 10, 116743, 116744–5] and copper standing bull [116740]. In addition there were limestone and shell friezes set in bitumen in a copper frame of doves on the temple [left, 116742], cows [right, 116741], a milking scene [centre], the latter being a reproduction of the original frieze in the Baghdad Museum, as well as a frieze of petalled rosettes or flowers [top].

The position of these objects on the building is not known and the reconstruction we see of the interior of the temple is only conjectural. Nevertheless, it would seem probable that the two lions' heads [114317, 114318] were placed on either side of the entrance. One has pieces of the original beaten copper in place, whereas only the bitumen core of the second has survived. But each beast had eyes made from red jasper (iris), shell (white eyeballs), and blue schist (eyelids), teeth of white shell and a red jasper tongue.

These splendid relics are witness to the outstanding mastery of the skills of inlay and metal-working, which are all the more remarkable when one realizes that these beautiful objects were made by men who lived about 4,500 years ago.

Temple furnishings and rites

All temples, from the earliest times, had two constant features, a niche for the appearance of the god (later filled by his statue) and an offering table. Subsequently an altar was added [case 13, 1930 5–8 218], and as temples increased in size, statuary representing rulers and high officials. Into this category come the very fine diorite (a black rock) statue of Gudea, ruler of Lagash (mod. El-Hibbeh) [centre of room, 122910], and the limestone figure of Kur-lil [Temple dais, 114207], Keeper of the Granary at Uruk (mod. Warka), who had contributed to the Al-'Ubaid temple's restoration. There were also vessels for the pouring of libations [Temple. Two vessels on floor].

The temple was the house of the city's god and represented the official religion. In early times its purificatory rites were performed by naked priests [case 13, 118561, limestone plaque; case 9, 120850] assisted by temple attendants [see case 13, R: bronze statuettes of temple assistants c. 1800 BC] in the presence of the king and perhaps the crown prince. But the ordinary Babylonian citizen, who may never have penetrated farther than the temple courtyard, needed something more personal, and there was a host of minor deities under whose protection ordinary folk could live. They were usually represented by rough statues or reliefs on small terracotta plaques [case 13, collection of plaques] which were pressed out from moulds [case 3, collection of moulds and matching plaques] in large numbers and were bought at famous shrines and local temples for use in the home. For the traveller and those without the amenity of a family chapel, there were small shrines containing cult statues and plaques in residential areas set up by pious private citizens where a passer-by, such as the female worshipper [case 13, 122933, early 2nd millennium], could pray.

If we have dwelt at length on the various aspects of religion, it is because of the overwhelming part it played in Babylonian life; but it is now time to examine more mundane matters.

Houses

Babylonian houses were mainly of one storey, and consisted of a series of rooms leading one from the other, with the entrance in the street. Some had an open central court, off which were the rooms, while in others there was a roofless passageway behind the street entrance. In Ur, however, about 2000 BC, there was a fair proportion of two-storeyed houses, built round an open courtyard from which a staircase led up to a second floor wooden balcony which gave access to the rooms. But whatever the type of house, the furniture was sparse: built-in brick benches and hearths, matting on the floor, stools, slatted wooden beds and perhaps high-back chairs [see case 16 for models and reliefs], although the latter were probably confined to the palace. Every household would also possess a quern and pestle [case 17, 127828, 127833] for milling grain, pots for cooking [case 14] and storage [case 9, 121691]; bowls, cups, spouted jars for eating and drinking; and, to while away the leisure hours, a gaming board and dice [case 9, 120834, from the Great Death Pit at Ur].

Dress

The customary dress of Sumerian men was a tufted garment reminiscent of a kilt, sometimes called kaunakes [case 3, 22470, 104729, 115031]. The king and his guests at the banquet on the Standard of Ur are clad in it. Sometimes cloth garments were worn. Men were both clean shaven [cf. brass razors] and bearded, and with shaven heads, although the latter custom might have been confined to priests.

Women were not so lightly clad, as shown by the six exhibits in case 3. One wears a choker and ear-rings with full kaunakes dress, and another sports a tunic and fringed gown (late Early Dynastic or Neo-Sumerian times). In the lower row [1st figure L] a slim goddess (identified by her horned head-dress) is clad in an elegant flounced gown.

The Semitic Assyrians and Babylonians wore their hair long and favoured beards. The robes of kings and the upper classes were beautifully embroidered [case 16, 90865; case 14, 90922], and some fine examples will be seen in the Assyrian galleries downstairs. Both sexes at all periods bedecked themselves with jewellery.

Agriculture

The inhabitants of Babylonian cities never became divorced from the land as are modern city dwellers, and the majority must always have gained their living from it. At Ur, c. 2000 BC, there were vegetable gardens and palm groves outside the city walls. Farther out in the surrounding plain were the farming villages and arable land, interspersed with canals for irrigation, where crops, mainly wheat and barley, were grown. On a man's land a boundary stone might be erected on which would be inscribed the deed of entitlement and engraved figures of the gods as witnesses to the deed. Boundary stones were used in early times, but the greatest number have survived from Kassite and Neo-Babylonian periods [case 6, 90829, Kassite period].

In prehistoric times harvesting was by means of clay and denticulated flint sickles [case 17, 115345], later made in metal, and in the 3rd millennium and probably earlier, the wooden plough was in use. Stock, too, was raised [case 17], sheep, goats and pigs, also cattle, as we have seen from the 'Ubaid temple decorations. Some domestic animals were probably housed in the towns, while in the villages they would be herded into compounds and yards to prevent their falling prey to the wild animals which lurked in the countryside. Fish, too, was a staple food, and as Babylonian cities were situated on the two great rivers or on canals, it was in good supply [case 17, fish-hooks and harpoons].

Trade

The waterways were also extensively used for the transport of goods. For instance, wood from the cedar forests of Lebanon was dragged overland to the Euphrates and floated down to its destination in Babylonia, while manufactured products were loaded from the quays of Babylonian cities into ships which sailed to Bahrain, Oman and even, it is thought, north-west India, returning laden with copper, semi-precious stones and ivory. The ships which made these hazardous voyages were incredibly small (see Fig. 10, p. 89 , for sea-going ships moored at Babylon). Inter-city trade, on the other hand, was carried in the coracle, or round boat (see Fig. 10), made of wattle and pitch, or flat-bottomed boats with pointed prow and stern [case 12, 133043–4]; and goods were also floated down the rivers on rafts supported on inflated skins. It was by this means that the huge Assyrian lions and bulls from Nimrud [Assyrian Transept and Nimrud Central Saloon] made the first stage of their journey to the British Museum.

Goods were transported on land by caravans of donkeys. Control of the trade routes was, therefore, of vital importance and many military campaigns were undertaken for this purpose. Commercial transactions were meticulously recorded [Room of Writing, case 7] and contracts enforced by law. Large numbers of business documents have been found, evidence of that commercial pre-eminence for which in antiquity Babylonia was renowned. But the most significant evidence is the gold and silver cups, the copper and bronze weapons, the ivory ornaments and the beads already mentioned, the raw materials of which were transported many hundreds of miles by land and sea to be fashioned by Babylonian craftsmen into the form in which we see them in the Museum.

The Room of Writing

Writing is one of the world's most momentous inventions. It stores the learned experience of mankind which confers an intellectual superiority on man above all other species. Without it, to give a pertinent example, the objects in this Museum would be meaningless or subject to the distortions of folk memory. The Room of Writing, therefore, is one of the most important in the Museum, for it demonstrates the development of the cuneiform script, the first form of writing, and also the evolution of the alphabet.

Development of the cuneiform script, case 2. The first attempt at recording information was by the Sumerians with pictures (pictographs) of objects [case 2, 116630, cast of one of the very earliest specimens of Sumerian writing, from Kish, c. 3100; 86260–61, implements engraved with the oldest characters on stone, c. 3000 BC]. This method was clumsy owing to the complicated forms of the pictographs and the large number required. The number was reduced, however, when certain signs which represented mainly monosyllabic words, were used for their sounds (syllables) rather than their meanings in the writing of other words. The signs were also conventionalized so that they no longer resembled the original pictographs (above). But even after this simplification, it was necessary to memorize between at least several hundred signs, a considerable feat compared with the 26 letters of our alphabet. Nevertheless, the advantages derived from written information were so manifest that by the 2nd millennium cuneiform was current throughout the Middle East and continued in use into the Christian era, though by that time Aramaic and Greek had replaced it for most purposes.

To write cuneiform correctly required a long training, restricted mainly to the sons of the wealthy owing to the expense. Boys were sent to school at an early age and on attaining the necessary proficiency entered government service as scribes in which they could rise to high posts. In the central case are circular clay tablets: on one [78260] a Babylonian schoolmaster has written an exercise for his pupil to copy, and on the other [78262] is an exercise in writing syllables, both dated to the 19th century BC. Above is a reed stylus (modern) for engraving the wet, ruled clay.

Historical texts, case 4. Returning to the wall cases we see the Babylonian chronicle for the years 616–609 BC [21901] which records the destruction of Nineveh, the Assyrian capital, by the Medes, Scythians and Babylonians (p. 78). Its importance lies in the fact that until the discovery of this tablet by C. J. Gadd of the British Museum and its publication in 1923, the date of this historic event, August 612 BC, was not definitely known.

In the ancient world there was little respite from war. Some years later the Babylonian chronicle for 605–595 BC [21946] records the defeat of Necho II of Egypt at Carchemish (mod. Jerablus) by Nebuchadnezzar II, and the latter's siege and capture of Jerusalem in March 597 BC, the Babylonian chronicle for the first time giving the exact date, namely 2nd Adar (15/16 March).

Epics and religion, case 5. The account of the Flood or Universal Deluge is of far greater antiquity than the *Book of Genesis*, being known to the Babylonians in the 18th century BC, and before them to the Sumerians. The tablet exhibited here records a late Assyrian version [K3375, 7th century BC], and was found in the Royal Library at Nineveh. It forms part of the well-known (to the ancients) literary work, the *Epic of Gilgamesh*.

Gilgamesh was a Sumerian priest-king in the heroic tradition who nevertheless ruled at Uruk (mod. Warka) about 2600 BC. But after the death of his boon companion, Enkidu, he realized that he, too, would ultimately die. In an attempt to avoid this fate, he undertook a long journey to consult Uta-napishtim, who possessed the secret of eternal life.

Uta-napishtim said he had been warned by Ea, god of wisdom, that Enlil, the Storm God, was angry with mankind and was determined to destroy it by a Universal Deluge. He had therefore built a boat (ark), and taken aboard his family, livestock and craftsmen. The next morning the rains came and lasted six days and six nights, after which the waters subsided (the third bird he sent out, a raven, did not return), the ark grounded, and he landed and sacrificed. The gods were furious at his escape, but Ea persuaded them to grant him eternal life. There was, however, no Ea to intervene on Gilgamesh's behalf, so the young ruler returned to Uruk and became reconciled to his fate.

There can be no doubt that the authors of *Genesis* were familiar with this story which originated in Sumer.

Letters; the Nineveh Library, case 8. The letters exhibited, a small fraction of the Museum's great collection of tablets, are extremely varied in subject matter, but our selection must unfortunately be confined to a few examples.

The first [23144] shows how the king meticulously supervised every aspect of administration, for we find the great Hammurabi of Babylon (1792–1750) (p. 75) ordering Sin-iddinam, perhaps an official or merchant, to ship corn for cattle food, presumably to Babylon on the Euphrates, that great commercial highway. Another letter, despatched in a clay envelope and sealed by the writer, gives an insight into the methods of the civil service in Assyria, c. 650 BC. Assur-risua (81 7–27 199) complains to an official that he has received no reply to his three previous letters. It must indeed have been a disadvantage that, when dealing with dilatory officials, there was no room to enclose an addressed clay envelope for a reply.

Here, also, are examples from the important diplomatic correspondence (Amarna letters) between Amenophis III and Amenophis IV (Akhenaten) of Egypt and the King of Mitanni [37645], the Hittite king, and the loyal Egyptian governors, tribal chiefs, and vassals of Syria and Palestine [29840]. Due to neglect of the latter's appeals for help, Egypt lost her Asiatic empire (p. 132).

The Royal Library at Nineveh, found in the palaces of Sennacherib and Ashurbanipal, was expanded to something approaching the requirements of a modern library by Ashurbanipal (668–627 BC). A man of scholarly tastes who could both read and write (a rare accomplishment outside the scribal profession), he gave orders that ancient Babylonian and Akkadian works should be copied and translated (hence the *Epic of Gilgamesh*) for the library [K821. *Report on the legends and other literary compositions to be inscribed for the Royal Library*, c. 650 BC], together with syllabaries, vocabularies, classified commentaries and lists of words

[K251. *Words and phrases used in legal documents in Sumer with Akkadian translation*, c. 650 BC] on every branch of learning and science then known.

Nearly every important tablet was inscribed with Ashurbanipal's colophon (the ancient equivalent of a book plate): 'Whosoever shall carry off this tablet, or shall inscribe his name upon it side by side with mine name, may Ashur and Bêlit (Assyrian gods) overthrow him in wrath and anger, and may they destroy his name and posterity in the land.' This minatory inscription proves that the non-returning book borrower is a very ancient species.

* * *

Having just examined a few of the documents written in the cuneiform script, the alphabetic scripts must now be considered [L of entrance to Prehistoric Room].

Development of an alphabet. The idea of an alphabet probably evolved between 2000–1500 BC in the Syria-Palestine region. It was devised by isolating the basic consonant of each syllable and representing it by a sign, a method particularly suited to the structure of the north-west Semitic languages (Hebrew, Phoenician, Aramaic) (cf. Fig. 12 a, b, col. V) which resulted in the North Semitic alphabet. The method was probably inspired by the Egyptian hieroglyphic script (col. I) which also sometimes used signs to represent single consonants [case 1, 52881, c. 1750 BC]. For Egyptian scripts see Fourth Egyptian Room, cases J and K.

The earliest known examples of a Semitic alphabet are the early Canaanite inscription on a dagger from Lachish, southern Palestine (16th century BC; see photo) and on the sphinx [case 1, 41748, 15th century BC] from the turquoise mines at Serabit el-Hadem in the Sinai desert, which is inscribed in a Semitic language and written in an alphabet based on Egyptian hieroglyphs (col. III) probably by a Semitic slave drafted to the mines by the Egyptians.

In the 9th or early 8th century the North Semitic alphabet [see cast of Moabite stele, L of door, for example of the North Semitic alphabet in the 9th century BC] was taken over by the Greeks who adapted certain symbols of consonants that they did not require to represent vowels which

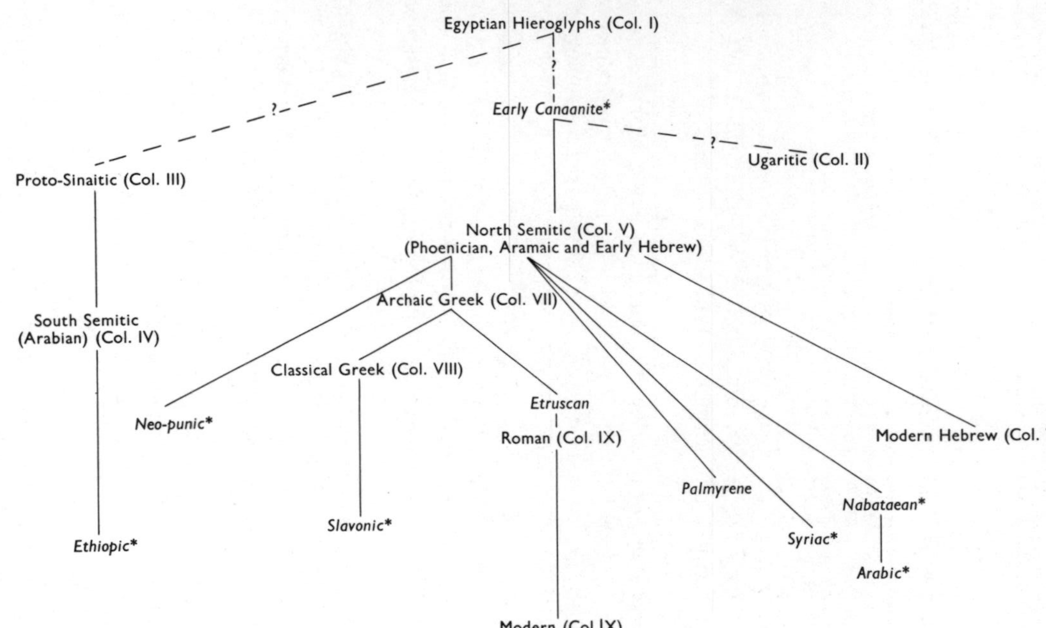

Fig. 12a. Ancestry of the alphabet

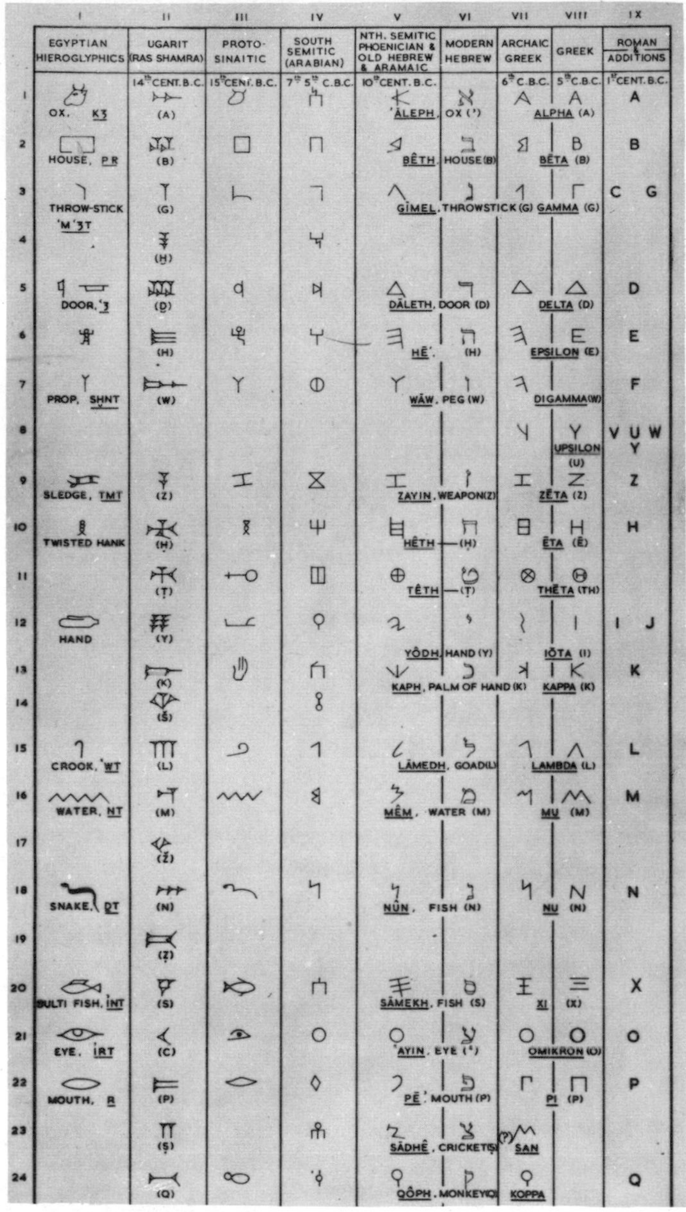

Fig. 12b. Development of the alphabet. Compare col. V, lines 2, 3, 5, 6 with their archaic and classical Greek equivalents, col. VII, VIII, for examples of similarities

they had isolated correctly for the first time [see Greek and Roman Life Room: *Writing*]. From this early Greek alphabet (col. VII), the Classical (Ionic) Greek alphabet (col. VIII) and ultimately those of the Slavonic languages were derived and it also influenced the Etruscan alphabet. From the latter descends the Latin alphabet of the Romans (col. IX), and with little change, our western alphabet from the Latin.

Seals.

Before writing was invented the seal was used to identify a man's property, and by far the most beautiful and interesting as to subject are the cylinder seals [wall cases], introduced in the Uruk period and carried round the neck or suspended from the wrist. They illustrate religious, mythological and legendary subjects, and had a definite influence on Mesopotamian metalwork and textiles.

The Department has a magnificent collection, but here we can only point out a few outstanding examples, such as the fantastic world of men and animals depicted in the Early Dynastic period [89538], the religious scenes of the Third Dynasty of Ur [89126] and the Akkadian period [89115], and the heroic subjects of the Middle Assyrian period, [89140, Fig. 13], the hero represented here being, perhaps Gilgamesh.

* * *

Leaving aside Assyria (the Assyrian exhibits, owing to their weight, are on the ground floor and in the basement) and passing through the Sixth Egyptian Room, we must take a quick look in the next room (Syrian) at the ivories [cases 9, 10 and 11] which decorated Assyrian palace furniture, in particular the superbly beautiful piece depicting a lioness attacking a negro [case 10, 127412]. We must also glance at the jar and wrapper which held Dead Sea scrolls [case 6, 131444, 131444a], and the round shield of the Greek mercenary who fought for Necho against Nebuchadnezzar at Carchemish in 605 BC [case 2, 116253], and then make our way through the Hittite Room (the sculptures exhibited here are not those of the Hittite empire but come from Carchemish in Neo-Hittite times – 10th and 9th century BC) to the Persian landing.

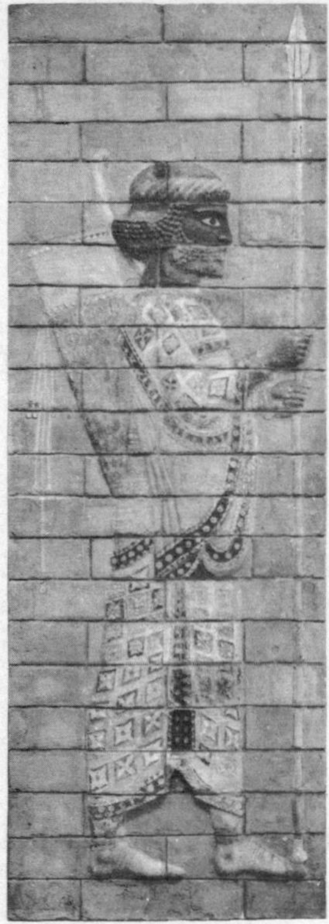

Fig. 13. A hero, possibly Gilgamesh, overcoming a lion. Cylinder seal impression, see page 104 .
Fig. 14. An archer of the Persian Royal Guard. From a frieze in the palace at Susa, c. 500 BC

The Persian Landing

The Luristan Bronzes, c. 1000–700 BC. Early Persian exhibits are the bronzes from graves in Luristan in the central Zagros region of Persia [case by entrance to Egyptian Mummy Room]. Unfortunately, not much is known about them as their excavation was not scientifically controlled. But Iranians were migrating into north-west Persia about the time the first bronzes appeared, and by the date of the latest the Medes (also Iranians) were probably in the area (p. 78).

The exhibits are such as would be required by a nomadic or semi-nomadic warrior aristocracy: bridle-bits and cheek pieces [3rd shelf, L, in form of horned or winged sheep; R: in form of winged stags and horses], as well as chariot pole tops with strange monsters, reminiscent of Celtic decorative motifs, whose bodies are expanded or curtailed to suit the design [cf. pole top, extreme R]. Harness mountings and rein rings can be seen below [L], also long pins [R] with heads of fine design and workmanship. Weapons [centre], daggers [123315] and short swords [123060] are also displayed.

One of the finest pieces is the silver dagger-hilt bought with a grant from T. E. Lawrence's Seven Pillars of Wisdom Fund, in which the silver was cast on to the iron blade and hilt by the lost wax method so that the rosettes, which appear to be rivets are only ornaments. The central space in the lunate-shaped pommel was filled with wood or ivory. Another characteristic object is the vessel with a long spout in pottery and in bronze [top shelf, R]. The owners of these beautiful bronzes had nothing to do with their manufacture which was carried out by the local metalsmiths at their commands.

Reliefs

Most of the other exhibits belong to Achaemenian times (p. 78). The reliefs on the walls of this landing decorated the Achaemenid palaces, as, for instance, the glazed tile figure [132525] of an archer of the Royal Guard (the 'Immortals') from Darius' palace at Susa (Fig. 14), and from the most magnificent palace, Persepolis, which took over 50 years to build, comes the slab showing a Median servant [no. 3] ascending stairs and carrying a covered vase [see machine for views of Persepolis].

Relics of the Persian kings are displayed on the right of the bronzes: an ointment jar [top shelf, 132114] inscribed with the name of Xerxes in Old Persian, Elamite, Babylonian and Egyptian; a portion of a baked clay cylinder [bottom shelf, 90920] of Cyrus the Great (c. 538–529 BC) inscribed in Babylonian characters with an account of the conquest of Babylonia and the chief events of his reign; and the royal seal of Darius [2nd shelf, 99132], but whether Darius I, the Great (521–485 BC), or Darius II (c. 424–404 BC) is not known. (Note here the winged god, Ahuramazda, the design derived, as will be seen, from the Assyrian god, Ashur.)

The Oxus Treasure, 5th–4th century BC. The Oxus treasure [centre] is part of the Treasury of an ancient Persian temple of the 5th–4th century BC. It is believed to have been found at the city of Khandian or Kabadian in Bactria (mod. Uzbekistan) on the right bank of the Oxus (mod. Amu-Darya river). It consists of votive offerings, that is objects offered to a god by a petitioner who hopes that his request will thereby be granted.

The Achaemenid empire stretched from the Aegean to the Indus, and from the Taurus to Egypt, and the hoard contains objects from its constituent parts, as well as those which show the influence of neighbouring civilizations. For instance, the penannular gold armlet [facing stairs, 1st side, 116] of Achaemenian design with ends in the form of winged griffins, was inlaid with precious stones by the cloisonné technique, which probably originated in the Euphrates valley. Furthermore, the scaraboid seal [113] shows Greek influence and indeed may have been engraved by one of the many Greek craftsmen working for the Persian king.

On the second side [to R] is a gold model of a four-horse two-wheel chariot with two men such as was used by the king and nobles for hunting and fighting and which, in battle, had scythes attached to the axles. It was derived from the later Assyrian chariot. The two gold statuettes [2, 2a] wear the dress of a king or Persian satrap (provincial governor), a girdled knee-length tunic over which is a long-sleeved coat with fur border, possibly of the fashionable beaver, worn as a mantle with the sleeves hanging loose. The high cap is stiffened so that it remains erect, and has lappets over the ears to give protection against extremes of heat and cold, as is the case with most Persian head-dress. The silver statuette [1] represents a king, in Median dress, holding a ritual bundle of rods, while the gold horseman, whose mount is missing, rides without stirrups (which were not used till Roman times) or saddle, a cloth taking the place of the latter.

Both men and women wore jewellery. The magnificent Scythian hair ornament [3rd side, 23] and the Scythian bird's head joined to a serpent's body [39], probably for attaching to clothing, would both have been the property of a great Persian landowner.

But the gold covering of the sword scabbard showing a Median king hunting lions [22] may have been made in the 6th century before the unification of the Median and Persian kingdoms.

Some idea of the luxurious household appointments of the nobility can be gained from the Scythian gold vase in the form of a fish [4th side, 16, 5th or 4th century BC], the fine gold jug with horizontal flutings and lion-headed handle [17] and the gold and silver dishes [19, 21, 20, 25, 18].

The thin votive gold plaques, although without artistic merit, are interesting as illustrating Persian dress and other aspects of life. No. 69 [4th side] shows a man in a long coat bordered with fur, who holds a vase perhaps for a libation. On the 3rd side can be seen a clean-shaven naked man [86] holding a bird, perhaps performing a ritual act, while no. 93 [2nd side] depicts a woman whose hair hangs in a plait down the back, and who wears a long dress over which is a wide-sleeved garment hanging down in front.

* * *

Descending the staircase from this gallery, we must turn right on the ground floor and walk through the Egyptian Sculpture Gallery to the end where we shall find ourselves in the Assyrian Transept.

Assyrian Transept

The exhibits now to be seen date from the 9th–7th century BC. They come mainly from the palaces and temples built by the Assyrian kings at a time when, having consolidated the state, they were sufficiently powerful to conquer an empire. At its greatest extent the Assyrian empire comprised Mesopotamia to the Persian Gulf, Cilicia, Syria, Palestine and Egypt, a remarkable achievement considering the small area of the homeland.

The Black Obelisk

In the centre of the Transept is a monument known as the Black Obelisk [118885] of Shalmaneser III, king of Assyria (858–824 BC) who undertook campaigns in the west when he either overcame the potentates of the local small states or they prudently paid him tribute and became Assyrian vassals.

In the latter category was Jehu, 'son of Omri' (used generically: he was a usurper), king of Israel who, in the second row from the top, can be seen, in western Semitic dress, bowing to the ground before Shalmaneser (Fig. 15), while his attendants carry the tribute. Some items mentioned in the inscription can be recognized: 'a golden bowl, a golden vase with a pointed bottom, golden tumblers, golden buckets, tin, a staff for a king . . .'. This is the earliest representation of an Israelite which has survived, and the events recorded appear to have taken place about 841 BC.

On the right side of the Transept are exhibits from temples in the city of Nimrud (Biblical Calah) built by King Ashurnasirpal II (883–859 BC), whose statue [118871] is one of the very few representations in the round of an Assyrian monarch to come down to us [further notes on exhibits here can be seen behind 118894 and beside 118895].

On the left of the Obelisk are two colossal winged human-headed lions [118801–2] flanked on either side by reliefs of winged deities and eagle-headed figures of magical significance. Sculptured stone lions and bulls of this type stood at the entrances to palaces of the late empire and outside principal rooms, probably supporting arched door lintels as shown here. These two lions guarded the throne room at

Fig. 15. Detail showing Jehu, king of Israel, paying homage to Shalmaneeser III of Assyria. From the Black Obelisk

Ashurnasirpal's palace at Nimrud, his capital.

Bronze gates from Balâwât

Ashurnasirpal also built a small palace and temple a few miles south of Nimrud at modern Balâwât. Both buildings had double doors of wood, one pair set up by Ashurnasirpal and the other by his son, Shalmaneser III (858–824 BC) (the wooden reconstruction represents Shalmaneser's gates), and each pair decorated by two sets of embossed and engraved horizontal bronze bands. Those from Ashurnasirpal's gate are much damaged [see glass case, R], but Shalmaneser's are in perfect condition [left of wooden gate] and are marvels of the bronze-worker's art. Each band represents one of Shalmaneser's military victories or diplomatic successes.

For instance, Jehu's example of paying tribute rather than fighting was followed by the Phoenician trading ports, Tyre and Sidon, a transaction, so far as Tyre is concerned, which is recorded on the bands [right case, 3rd band from bottom, top reg., 124661].

Tyre was situated on a rocky island off the coast of Lebanon and [starting from the gate post and moving L to R] tribute is loaded by porters into boats which ferry it across to the mainland. Here other porters wade into the sea to unload, after which the procession of men with bales and trays on their heads and shoulders goes to Shalmaneser, preceded by two turbaned individuals, probably officials from Tyre, who crack their fingers in salute, and an escort of Assyrian officers. The king, attended by his staff and an escort of chariots, calmly awaits the arrival of the tribute which will be carried to Assyria to fill the royal treasury.

Nimrud Gallery

The Palaces

Love of architecture seems to have been an hereditary characteristic of the Assyrian monarchs (indeed of most oriental autocrats), and it appears to have been incumbent upon them, perhaps for religious purposes as well as to signify their wealth and power, to build and beautify a palace. But Ashurnasirpal II built on an ancient site, Nimrud, and surrounded it with walls some 5 miles in extent, over 50 ft in height and 120 ft wide, provided it with gardens and orchards, a canal connecting the city with the river Zab, a zoological garden and probably erected the stone quays which gave access to the Tigris.

Ashurnasirpal's palace (the north-west palace) with the ziggurat, temples and other buildings formed part of the citadel complex. It had two principal courts, both square, around which were grouped eight wings of long narrow rooms. The doors were decorated as at Balâwât with bronze bands.

Religious sculptures

The walls of the principal rooms were decorated with sculptured reliefs, and many in the gallery come from the Throne Room. The magnificent relief [124531, centre, long wall] showing two representations of Ashurnasirpal on either side of a sacred tree being anointed by two winged deities, stood behind the throne, and undoubtedly had ritual significance.

Other large slabs [124564–6] depict the king enthroned with his cup-bearer, the keeper of his bow and his eunuchs: once again there are two superhuman figures who anoint him with a magical substance from a vessel by means of a fir cone. The Assyrian artist has managed to convey here that subtle difference, the dignity and air of command, between the sovereign and his courtiers. These reliefs were coloured, probably only in certain parts such as the intricate patterns on the robes and on the sandals, which were black with red soles and the colour can still be seen [cf. 124564].

On another wall in the Throne Room was a totally different type of relief [see opposite long wall], the sculptured narrative. The slabs were divided into two registers and an attempt was made to show a sequence of events. Thus we see the king hunting wild bulls [top: 124532] and [below: 124533] pouring a libation over a dead bull to the accompaniment of two harpists, probably a ritual gesture to the gods of hunting.

The Military sculptures

The majority of these reliefs illustrate scenes of war, and their purpose was to impress the visitor, vassal king, diplomatic envoy, high dignitary, with the power and invincibility of the king and his armies, an aim which must have succeeded for the Assyrian army is invariably represented as winning every battle by its ruthlessly efficient methods of warfare.

For example, Ashurnasirpal leads his archers in an attack on a walled city [124536], covering the operation by a siege machine with a ram which dislodges stones from the city's walls, while the defenders man the ramparts and counter-attack the archers [see also 124552, 124554, 124556, for another siege]. Next we see a walled city [top: 124538] by a river towards which fugitives, attacked by Assyrian archers, are swimming. When Ashurnasirpal crosses a river, probably the Habur, he steps from the bank into a boat with curved ends (as seen in the Babylonian Room) into which his chariot has already been loaded [below: 124541, 124543, 124545]. His soldiers either swim or are supported by inflated skins. Military equipment is ferried in the round coracle, still in use in Iraq today, while the king's horses swim to the farther bank guided by a soldier in the boat holding leading reins. The passage safely accomplished, Ashurnasirpal is seen standing in his chariot about to land.

The detail given in these reliefs is astonishing. In the king's tent and royal stables [above: 124548] we can see food being prepared, and cooks cutting joints of meat [below] and placing a cauldron on the hearth, while outside, horses are watered and groomed.

The ancients had no knowledge of, and probably would have had no use for, perspective. Their object was to show what had happened. The Assyrian artist placed his figures on the base line, and if they were numerous and the action vigorous, there was no space for dead enemy soldiers. But if they were not displayed the viewer might imagine that no enemies had been killed, which would defeat the object of the reliefs. Corpses, therefore, were shown in any available space, usually in what to us would be the sky [cf. 124553–5].

* * *

Leaving the Nimrud Gallery by the opening near the Transept entrance, one arrives in the Assyrian Saloon.

The Assyrian Saloon

Ashurbanipal, 668–627 BC. The Hunting sculptures

Two centuries after the reign of Ashurnasirpal, the Assyrian sculptors reached the pinnacle of their artistic achievement: the hunting reliefs for King Ashurbanipal's North Palace at Nineveh.

On the right in the staircase recess can be seen the going out of the hunt servants with ropes, stakes, hunting nets, balls of twine, mules, and leading the savage, baying hounds [124893–99]; and their return after the day's sport with the quarry, great lions whose deadweight was such that it required 4–6 men to carry the carcases. There is also small game, hares and young live birds [124888–92].

Next comes the chase [wall by the entrance], where a series of small reliefs shows the hunting of different species: deer trapped in a net positioned by hunt servants [124871], and Ashurbanipal shooting from a pit at gazelle [124872–74], of which only the buck at the rear of the herd has wind of the danger. The king also kills lions on foot by the sword and by shooting [top], and here we learn that the animals were trapped elsewhere and brought in cages to be released in the area of the hunt [above]. Again, the king spears lions on horseback [2nd reg.]: one of his attendants seems to have come to grief, judging by the riderless horse being attacked by a lion. Another royal quarry was the onager [below R]; and the anxious gesture of the mare obliged to abandon her foal to a fierce hound is superbly rendered [124875–82].

Turning right, we can now examine the principal hunting sculptures displayed on the two long walls. On the left, the horses are being harnessed to the royal chariot by grooms [124858]. Other horses are led forward through two lines of soldiers [124859–60]. Now spectators, protected by guards, crowd on a hillock to obtain a good view of the sport [124867]. Meanwhile lions have been released from cages [124869] and Ashurbanipal slays them on both walls by bow and arrow [L: 124860], by spear [R: 124854], and dagger [R: 124850].

Although these scenes seem to represent a holocaust, we are probably seeing the same animal in a sequence as he progresses to his death. The Assyrian artist has delineated these victims with such a naturalness and delicacy of feeling that one's sympathy for the stricken beasts, the lioness whose hind legs are paralysed but who still roars defiance [R: 124856] and the lion bleeding to death [L: 124865], is immediately aroused rather than, as intended, one's admiration for the king's expertise. However the peasants whose children, womenfolk, slaves and farm animals were in daily danger of their lives from the lions which infested Mesopotamia would undoubtedly have thought otherwise. The end of the hunt is signalized by Ashurbanipal's pouring a libation over dead lions [124886–87].

The Lachish Room

Sennacherib, 704–681 BC. The Siege of Lachish

During the reign of Sennacherib, the method of presenting a subject changed, and instead of two or three registers the whole slab was employed. The result was a continuous narrative over several slabs instead of a sequence of scenes, thus achieving greater verisimilitude. In the siege of Lachish (Tell ed-Duweir), south of Jerusalem, in 700 BC when a revolt of Assyria's Palestinian vassals, supported by Egypt, took place, we can follow every stage of the operation on these enlarged reliefs, which come from the South-West Palace at Nineveh built by Sennacherib.

First [L: 2nd slab] the regiments of slingers, archers and spearmen [124904–5] mass for the attack on the double-walled city, which stands on high ground (represented by scales), so that the Assyrians have built numerous long ramps to enable their siege machines to mount to the walls for an assault [124906–7]. The defenders maintain a constant fire, and hurl stones and burning brands on to the machines. But the brands are extinguished by Assyrian soldiers who pour water on the flames with long-handled ladles [L]. They have already captured an outlying bastion, and through its gate men and women emerge carrying bundles only to pass by three fellow citizens being impaled by Assyrian soldiers.

On the other side of the city are two processions, comprising soldiers and civilian prisoners who make their way to the king. The soldiers are loaded with booty [above: 124908] while the women, one with a child clinging to her dress, carry their sparse possessions in sacks on their backs [top: 124909], or ride in carts with those too young to walk [124908]. An infant on its mother's lap holds up its head for a reassuring embrace [top procession, right] for while the adults in the sculptures are repetitive types, the Assyrian artists depicted children with truth and naturalness. The scribes check the booty [top: 124910] and naked prisoners prostrate themselves before Sennacherib (Fig. 16). Not all come before the king: some are flayed alive [below: 124909] or scalped, these victims being Jews, subjects of King Hezekiah of Judah [below: 124910]. The conqueror is seated

Fig. 16. Sennacherib receives the officers of his victorious army. Below is his chariot complete with sunshade, and to the left is the grim sight of the decapitation of the vanquished

on his throne [124911] receiving his officers. Behind the throne is the king's tent and the Assyrian fortified camp [124913–15]. The entire episode has taken place in hilly country in which grow profusely the fig and vine.

It adds to the interest of the reliefs that some of the weapons depicted on the sculptures were recovered during the excavations at Lachish [wall case]: metal and bone arrow heads, the latter used when metal became scarce, a spear head, sling balls, bronze cheek piece and also olive stones.

* * *

Retracing our steps we must now descend to the basement by the staircase near the entrance to the Nimrud Gallery.

The Assyrian Basement

Ashurbanipal, 668–627 BC. The Battle of the River Ulai

In addition to the hunting sculptures, Ashurbanipal had some splendid war sculptures, as for instance the great battle against the Elamites in 653 BC on the River Ulai [left wall] in Susiana [124801–10], which the king set up in the palace of Sennacherib, his grandfather [South-West Palace) at Nineveh. He had been brought up there and loved the place, and so redecorated it for his own use.

Elam had been a constant thorn in Assyria's side owing to its alliance with the Chaldean tribes of southern Babylonia and with Babylon. Ashurbanipal determined to remove this menace and, fortunately for posterity, he recorded it in stone [124802, 124801]. Although the slabs are broken, the main scene of the Elamite army in retreat to the river gives a singularly vivid idea of the confusion of an ancient battle when fighting was hand to hand. Here we can see the Elamites driven down a steep hill, surrounded by dead and dying [L], trying to reach the river [R] only to be speared at the last moment.

Some of the Assyrians' least engaging customs are depicted on the large slab by the staircase [top] where two men are being decapitated. To the right can be seen a collection of heads brought in by the soldiers [2nd row], while on the left an Assyrian soldier holds the head of Teumman, King of Elam, which will go to Assyria. The Assyrians are renowned for their cruelty, but all ancient nations were cruel. Nevertheless, there is no instance of cruelty to children on the reliefs. On the contrary they act with a freedom which no adult prisoner would dare to emulate, witness the child astride its captive father's shoulders who turns and waves gaily to the Assyrian guard [Siege of Hamanu, last slab, bottom reg.: 124937].

At the far end of the long wall is an idyllic scene of Ashurbanipal and his queen in an arbour of vines [124920, 124922]. He lies on a couch and she sits beside him on a chair, her feet on a footstool (Fig. 17). Both are quaffing cups. Behind them are attendants with fly whisks and servants carrying refreshments, while among the trees [L] a harpist and [R] an orchestra play softly. But this sylvan scene is marred by the sight of Teumman's head hanging from a tree, and his hand and sceptre.

* * *

Not many objects of daily use have come down to us, probably because of the looting of Assyrian cities in the last campaign. Nevertheless, there are some charming examples of Assyrian minor arts in the centre cases, and of furniture in the corner case.

Assyrian furniture. A couch, chair, footstool and tables have just been seen on the sculpture depicting Ashurbanipal and his queen in the arbour. This palace furniture would have been made of wood and decorated with ivory inlays as seen in the Syrian Room, and bronze brackets and finials. The palace would also have had bathrooms with perhaps terracotta or bronze baths [no. 1, late 7th century] such as that found at Ur. The bronze cauldron, probably from Nimrud [no. 2, 8th century BC] is of a type frequently represented on the reliefs among the tribute or spoils of war of the Assyrian kings, while the ornamental painted clay plaques were widely used as wall decoration and are in the tradition of the flowers seen in the 'Ubaid temple. Bronze lion weights

Fig. 17. Ashurbanipal and his queen celebrating in a garden after the victory of the River Ulai, 653 BC

[no. 5] found in the North-West Palace at Nimrud are nearly all inscribed with the name of the king for whom they were made with their weight in terms of heavy or light *mina* (1010 or 505g). The insignia of authority, the mace-head, is also represented [no. 6] in bronze and in stone. The bronze and iron tripod is for holding a jar or cauldron.

Arms and armour in Assyria and Urartu. One can recognize among the weapons and armour exhibited the types shown on the reliefs, which were generally similar to those of Urartu (Ararat) (p. 88), Assyria's neighbour in eastern Turkey with whom, during the 9th–7th century, she was constantly at war. For instance, the majority of soldiers, of whatever arm, wore pointed helmets [4, Urartian, 8th century BC], although there are scenes where a crested helmet is also shown [5, Urartian, 9th century BC]. Spearmen generally carried round shields [1, Urartian, mid-7th century BC], and bronze scale armour [8, Assyrian, 8th–7th century BC] and iron [10, Assyrian,8th–7th century BC] was only worn by archers under Ashurnasirpal although both were more widely used later. Most soldiers wore a belt [12, from Nimrud, 8th century BC] into which was fixed a dagger [14, from Nimrud, c. 8th century BC]. A horse's head was also protected by armour [26, Urartian, 8th–7th century BC]. In the Assyrian armies there were contingents from various parts of the empire who wore their native dress.

* * *

Leaving the Assyrian basement by the foyer, where there is an exhibition devoted to the discoverers of these magnificent sculptures for the British Museum, we mount the stairs at the side of which is a slab showing Sargon II (721–705 BC) with an officer [118822] and arrive [R] at the two human-headed bulls and their divine attendants [118808, 118809], which originally guarded the east gate of the citadel at Dûr-sharrûkin (mod. Khorsabad, Fig. 18).

Proceeding to the right we enter the Nimrud Central Saloon where the sculptures of Tiglath-Pileser III (744–727 BC) are displayed. On the left of the entrance to the Nineveh Gallery [ahead] is one which is unique. It depicts [top] an

Fig. 18. Winged human-headed bull and winged attendant with bucket and cone. East gate, citadel, Khorsabad

attack on what is probably a triple-walled Phoenician city [118931] and [below] Assyrian soldiers removing the statues of the gods of the conquered city [118934].

The Nineveh Gallery

The Nineveh Gallery is full of good things, in particular sculpture showing the building of Sennacherib's new palace at Nineveh (mod. Kuyunjik) which he had chosen as his capital city. The palace is known today as the South-West Palace, but he named it 'The Palace without a Rival' for it was a magnificent building with over seventy halls, chambers and passages, nearly all with sculptured reliefs on the walls.

Building the Palace

Five large slabs on the right wall of the Gallery [124824–124820] from one of the courts show the arrival and positioning of human-headed bulls, such as those which can now be seen through the doorway [R] outside the Nimrud Gallery. Owing to the deterioration of the stone, the operations can be followed more easily in conjunction with the drawings displayed on the desk, which were made during the excavations.

First Sennacherib is shown standing in a hand-drawn chariot, attended by courtiers, and overlooking the work [124824]. Above are marshy reed thickets probably on the banks of a stream where deer and a wild sow and piglets are concealed. The colossal bulls have been made at Balatai a few miles up the Tigris and floated to the site on a raft. The bull, lying on a sledge, is then moved forward by means of a lever beneath the back of the sledge [124823] while slaves haul it by ropes in front. Near by are handcarts containing ropes and logs, the latter for placing under the sledge runners during a hiatus. Above on the river are coracles loaded with bricks and bronze or wooden loops for the gate-posts, and men astride inflated skins in the river.

Operations are a little more advanced in the next slab [124822] on which slaves, prisoners probably from the siege of Lachish (p. 115) can be seen hauling the bull from the river to the palace which seems to be sited near woods. Next we see gangs of Phoenician prisoners [124821], guarded by soldiers, carrying earth in baskets which they empty to build up the platform on which will stand the palace, while other slaves prepare a base for the bull. Finally, a second bull is landed from the Tigris [124820], and hauled by slaves to be erected at one of the palace gates. At the top of the mound [L] stands the king in a hand-drawn vehicle overlooking the work, while soldiers guard the site. On the river bank men raise water to cool the ropes in a bucket hanging from a counter-poised arm which revolves on a brick column, a method still in use in Iraq today. Indeed what machinery is to the modern world, slavery was to the ancient world, a source of motive power.

* * *

The Siege of —alammu

At the end of this gallery [left and right walls] are sculptured slabs from the South-West Palace at Nineveh showing the siege by Sennacherib's army of a city, the name of which ends in '—alammu' [L: 124784–85; R: 124786–87] which has not yet been identified. However, these sculptures command attention for they may bear the scars of the destruction of Nineveh, and may have been blackened by the flames which consumed the Assyrian capital in its death agony in 612 BC. Alternatively they could have been damaged in the revolt when Sennacherib was murdered. But in that case it is strange that Ashurbanipal, his grandson, who, we know, redecorated part of the South-West Palace and lived in it, made no attempt to clean them, but perhaps primitive cleansing materials were inadequate for the job.

* * *

When the remnant of the Assyrian army and its Egyptian ally, Necho II, were finally defeated at Carchemish by Nebuchadnezzar in 605 BC, the kingdom of Assyria was heard of no more.

It was rescued from oblivion some 2,500 years later by Austen Henry Layard who in two short periods, 1845–7 and 1849–51, discovered Nimrud (which he at first believed to be Nineveh), and excavated the North-West Palace of Ashurnasirpal, the sculptured slabs from the Central Palace of Tiglath-pileser III and the temples of the citadel; and Nineveh where he found the South-West Palace of Sennacherib.

He was followed by a number of very able men among whom were Henry Creswicke Rawlinson, the decipherer of the cuneiform script whose notebooks can be seen in the Room of Writing, and Hormuzd Rassam, Layard's assistant, who discovered the North Palace of Ashurbanipal at Nineveh, and the king's cuneiform library. Exhibits concerning these men and others who contributed to the Museum's collections can be seen in the basement Foyer, as well as the small Ishtar temple.

4 The department of Egyptian Antiquities

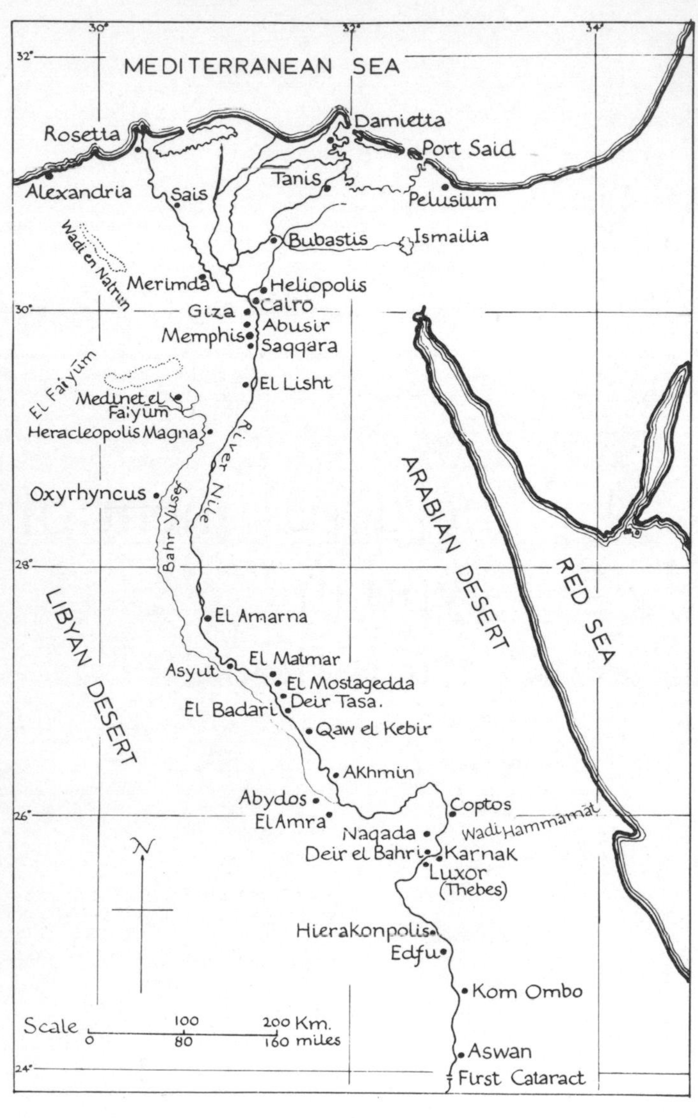
MEDITERRANEAN SEA
Rosetta
Alexandria
Sais
Damietta
Port Said
Tanis
Pelusium
Bubastis
Ismailia
Wadi en Natrun
Merimda
Heliopolis
Cairo
Giza
Abusir
Memphis
Saqqara
El Lisht
El Faiyum
Medinet el Faiyum
Heracleopolis Magna
River Nile
Oxyrhyncus
Bahr Yusef
ARABIAN DESERT
RED SEA
LIBYAN DESERT
El Amarna
El Matmar
Asyut
El Mostagedda
Deir Tasa.
El Badari
Qaw el Kebir
Akhmin
Abydos
El Amra
Coptos
Wadi Hammamat
Naqada
Deir el Bahri
Karnak
Luxor
(Thebes)
Hierakonpolis
Edfu
Kom Ombo
Aswan
First Cataract
N
Scale
0
100
80
200 Km.
160 miles
30°
32°
34°
32°
30°
28°
26°
24°

Map 3. Egypt

The department of Egyptian Antiquities

Historical Summary

Egypt

Introduction

The development of Egypt and Western Asia provides a remarkable contrast. In Western Asia all was turbulence and movement; kingdom succeeded kingdom and empire followed empire. It was the highway for migrations of peoples from central Asia, south Russia and Europe, and in it an amalgam of races struggled for survival. Many things were created and many destroyed, but it was the birthplace of nations and religions that still have a profound influence on the world today.

Egypt, on the other hand, was from historic times the land of the Egyptians, the immutable Nile valley (Map 3). Protected on either side by the desert and fertilized by the river's annual inundation, this fruitful strip provided a comparatively safe base in which a gifted people could evolve its unique civilization undisturbed by predatory interlopers.

These conditions facilitated the accumulation of great wealth (the riches of Egypt were a by-word in the ancient world) and the creation of superb works of art in sculpture and architecture as well as fine craftsmanship, which are Egypt's legacy to the modern world.

Note. The interpretation of the archaeological discoveries here follows that of the revised *Cambridge Ancient History*, volumes 1 and 2. We must point out, however, that opinion, so far as prehistory is concerned, is by no means unanimous on the interpretation of the data.

Paleolithic Age

From early Paleolithic times, man supported himself by hunting and food gathering in what is now the desert and on the hills and terraces bordering the Nile in Upper Egypt. Although there is no proof, it is probable that the tools found there were made by *Homo erectus* (p. 33).

In late Paleolithic times the climate became increasingly arid, the desert vegetation began to dry up and man was forced into the Nile valley, which abounded in game and fish, where he camped on the edge of the high flood plain in Upper Egypt.

Predynastic Period, c. 4500–c. 3100 BC

Neolithic-Cuprolithic cultures. A number of early farming settlements have been located in Middle Egypt at Deir Tasa, Matmar, Mostagedda and also at El-Badāri, after which their culture (Badārian) was named.

Sheep, cattle, goats and probably dogs were domesticated, and the villagers cultivated emmer wheat and barley. Their dwellings have not survived, but the settlements were on the spurs of the desert. From these and from the cemeteries, objects recovered show the early development of Egyptian craftsmanship in carving, modelling, drawing and painting. Later, in Upper Egypt at Naqāda, there was a fortified town, and in the Faiyūm, on the shores of a prehistoric lake, a settlement showed flint-work with analogies to that of the early Naqāda culture (Naqāda I).

But a vigorous people bringing new technical skills, probably from Western Asia, subsequently entered Upper Egypt perhaps by the Wadi Hammāmāt, and settling there, merged with the indigenous population to develop the later Naqāda civilization (Naqāda II), which spread northwards into Lower Egypt. That is one view: but some scholars consider that these foreigners migrated to Egypt from Palestine and settled in the Delta, later spreading to Upper Egypt and becoming merged with the indigenous population.

But from about 3300 BC, it would seem that the country was divided into two kingdoms or confederations of tribes: Upper (southern) Egypt and Lower (northern) Egypt. Tradition has it that Menes, King of Upper Egypt, conquered Lower Egypt. Certain it is that when, with the appearance of a developed hieroglyphic script, Egypt entered into history, the country had been unified under one king.

The Early Dynastic Period. c. 3100–c. 2686 BC. Dynasties 1 and 2

Historians have equated the legendary Menes with Narmer, the first king of the 1st dynasty. Menes is also credited with founding a capital at Memphis (Map 3) south of Cairo, on the borders of Upper and Lower Egypt, a tradition which has substance in fact.

But not much is known of the political organization of Egypt following the unification, except that the basic concept of the Egyptian state that the king was divine already existed; and that this absolute ruler had many courtiers and officials to carry out his commands both at Memphis and in the provinces.

The period was mainly one of political consolidation and technical innovation, most notably mastery over stoneworking. In art, forms and conventions were evolved and stabilized, some of which were to last as long as ancient Egyptian art was practised, that is, to Roman times.

The Old Kingdom, c. 2686–c. 2181 BC. Dynasties 3–6

The Old Kingdom was one of the most glorious periods of Egyptian history. By the 4th dynasty the state was on a secure foundation with the king as the unchallenged controller of its destiny, and the high offices of state held by members of his family. Material prosperity increased, due to technical developments and expanding trade with foreign countries. The central position of the king in the state, the efficiency of its organization, and his control over material and human resources is best demonstrated by the erection of the pyramids.

These huge stone constructions, standing on the edge of

the western desert, were the tombs of the monarchs. Erected in the lifetime of the king, the pyramid formed part of a complex of buildings which consisted of a valley temple, situated on the border of the cultivable land from which a causeway led up to a mortuary temple before the east face of the pyramid. The Great Pyramid of Cheops of the 4th dynasty at Giza, was one of the Seven Wonders of the ancient world; and standing high on the desert plateau, it still arouses awe and wonder today.

It is ironic that the pyramids, the glory of the Old Kingdom, may also have been one of the causes of its downfall, for the combined effects of supplying and provisioning a vast skilled labour force, of providing raw materials and of rewarding officials with land and office, may have both exhausted central reserves and affected adversely the agricultural economy upon which their replenishment depended. The decreased power of the king was matched by the increased power of the provincial nobility, the governors of the districts (nomes), whose appointments formerly were in the gift of the king but which now became hereditary, thus making their holders independent of the royal authority and contributing to the monarchy's collapse.

First Intermediate Period, c. 2181–c. 2040 BC. Dynasties 7–10

The Old Kingdom virtually ended with the reign of Phiops II of the 6th dynasty, for little is known of the dynasty's last three rulers. Few records remain, too, of the 7th and 8th dynasties. It was a time of chaos. Egypt, lacking strong central control, fell apart territorially and there was a struggle for supremacy between the provincial governors (nomarchs) who had established hereditary local states.

Thus about 2160 BC, Achthoes, the governor of the twentieth nome of Upper Egypt with its capital at Heracleopolis, became sufficiently powerful to seize the throne and establish his sovereignty as far south as Aswan, and his successors of the 9th and 10th dynasties also controlled the Delta. At Thebes, however, their authority was not recognized and a rival dynasty, the 11th, was set up whose fifth ruler, Mentuhotpe II, defeated the Heracleopolitan king about 2040 BC.

The Middle Kingdom, c. 2133–c. 1786 BC. Dynasties 11 and 12

Under the forceful rule of the kings of the 11th and 12th dynasties, Egypt regained her prosperity.

Trade was vigorously prosecuted with Western Asia, the Sudan, and the Horn of Africa; mineral resources were exploited; building was resumed; the capital was moved to Itj-towy, south of Memphis, to facilitate administration, and a great project of land reclamation was initiated in the Faiyūm by Sesostris II (c. 1897–1878 BC) which was continued by his successors. Territorial boundaries were also considerably extended in the south by Sesostris III (1878–1843 BC) who penetrated deep into Nubia (Sudan) and fixed the frontier above the second cataract. Egypt also wielded considerable political influence in some of the cities of the eastern Mediterranean litoral and of Syria, amounting perhaps to suzerainty in certain cases.

Second Intermediate Period, c. 1786–c. 1567 BC. Dynasties 13–17

Then for reasons as yet unknown but perhaps dynastic, the powerful 12th dynasty ended and was succeeded by a line of many kings with short reigns (dynasty 13). As always when the crown was weak, fragmentation occurred, manifesting itself by subsidiary and overlapping local dynasties.

Furthermore, Semites from Western Asia (known as the Hyksos) infiltrated into the Delta, and later became sufficiently powerful to establish their rule at Avaris, 12 miles south of Tanis, and either directly or through vassals, over the greater part of Egypt (dynasty 15). These Hyksos kings, who ruled as Egyptian pharaohs through Egyptian institutions were later execrated; but they nevertheless introduced military innovations which enabled the Egyptians to drive out those whom they designated as the 'wretched Asiatics'.

The New Kingdom, c. 1567–c. 1085 BC. Dynasties 18–20

But expulsion of the Asiatics was not enough. They must not return, and this determination transformed the easy-going Egyptians into a martial people with imperial ambitions. The times were ripe for expansion in Asia. Babylonia was in eclipse; Palestine and Syria consisted of a number of petty states no match for a powerful foe, and Egypt's only rival was the kingdom of Mitanni (p. 76), which extended from Assyria in the east to the Orontes valley in the west.

It was Tuthmosis III (c. 1504–1450 BC), the greatest of the warrior pharaohs of thc 18th dynasty, who in many campaigns conquered the independent princelings of the eastern Mediterranean seaboard, reached the Euphrates in Mitannian territory and installed Egyptian garrisons in the conquered areas to keep order.

But in less than a century, by the time of Amenophis IV (1379–1362 BC), much of this splendid Asiatic empire had been lost. The Hittites of Asia Minor (p. 76) had defeated Mitanni and secured northern Syria, which encouraged Egypt's remaining vassals in Palestine to revolt. Amenophis IV, immersed in religion and constrained by political circumstances, ignored the appeals of his governors and loyal vassal princes who, receiving no support, eventually succumbed.

Attempts were made, only partially successful, by the pharaohs of the 19th dynasty to regain the lucrative Asiatic provinces. The Hittite power could not be broken and finally a peace treaty (1269 BC) between Ramesses II and the Hittite king brought peace to the troubled area for a number of years.

The Hittites were finally overwhelmed by an invasion of immigrants, possibly of east central European descent, into Asia Minor from Thrace and the eastern Mediterranean, and the survivors fled into Syria. The invaders were joined by further overseas immigrants, known as the Sea Peoples, among whom were probably Greek contingents. The combined force attacked Egypt by land and by sea about 1191 BC, but was defeated in great battles by Ramesses III (1198–1166 BC) of the 20th dynasty, Egypt's last great warrior pharaoh.

The Late Dynastic Period and Persian Occupation, c. 1085–332 BC. Dynasties 21–30

The five centuries of the Late Dynastic period saw Egypt's decline and extinction as an independent power. In her weakness, the kingdom fell apart, the 21st–23rd dynasties ruling in the Delta and the High Priests of Amun at Thebes. About 730 BC Egypt was conquered by the kings of Napata (25th (Ethiopian) dynasty, c. 750–656 BC), rulers of Nubia

(Sudan). During this dynasty the Assyrian invasions took place (p. 77), after which the Delta was administered by local princes, one of whom, Psammetichus, founded the 26th dynasty (664–525 BC), ruled from Sais in the Delta and reunited the country with the aid of Greek mercenaries, when a political and artistic revival, already begun under the 25th dynasty, followed. But in just over a century Egypt was invaded by Cambyses (525 BC) and became a Persian satrapy, except for an interval of about 60 years, until the arrival of Alexander the Great in 332 BC.

The Macedonian and Ptolemaic Periods, 332–30 BC

Alexander was recognized as a deity by the priests, proclaimed king and welcomed as a liberator. But after founding the city of Alexandria and organizing the government, he departed to conquer the East. He died at Babylon in 323 BC shortly after his return.

His generals were then appointed governors of the imperial provinces, and Ptolemy, son of Lagus, was sent to Egypt. After the empire's dissolution and its division among the generals, Ptolemy took the title of king (304 BC). He reorganized the army, enlisting Greek mercenary soldiers, and by encouraging Greek merchants and bankers to settle in Egypt, restored trade and commerce, bringing prosperity to an impoverished country. Alexandria was his capital, and he and his son, Ptolemy II Philadelphus, made the city a renowned seat of learning by the establishment of the museum, which with its library attracted scholars from all over the ancient world.

The earlier Ptolemies were enlightened monarchs and created a strong state, militarily and economically, but from the end of the 2nd century BC the rot set in among their descendants, and Egypt was in no condition to withstand the might of Rome. When in 31 BC Antony, defeated by Octavius (later the emperor Augustus) in the naval battle of Actium (Ambracian Gulf, Greece), fled with Cleopatra VII to Egypt and was followed by Octavius, there was no serious resistance to the Roman army. Antony committed suicide and Cleopatra, failing to captivate Octavius as she had beguiled Caesar and Antony, also died by her own hand. Thus Egypt lost her independence for ever.

Rome, 30 BC–AD 640

At first she was a prosperous province, for the Romans restored order and re-established trade. But Egypt became the granary of Rome and her revenues, which in Ptolemaic times had remained in the country, were paid to the central treasury for the benefit of the empire. Her wealth, therefore, was gradually drained away. The peasant, faced with ever increasing taxation, abandoned the land which went out of cultivation. The irrigation system was neglected; once prosperous villages and towns, by the middle of the 4th century, were abandoned to the desert. The records of their inhabitants (family letters, legal, municipal and literary documents, accounts, official orders, etc.) were preserved by the dry sand. Excavated at the end of the 19th and during the present century, a number of them, including classical and biblical MSS., the texts of which were hitherto unknown, are now in the Museum [Department of MSS., Bible Room].

Egypt remained a province of the East Roman empire (usually known as the Byzantine empire, for after the separation from the West in 395 BC, its culture became that of the Hellenized East) until the rise of Islam, when the country was invaded by the Caliph Omar's Arab armies (AD 640). The Byzantine emperor, beset on all sides by barbarians, was unable to come to the rescue and Egypt became part of the Islamic empire.

Egyptian Antiquities

First Floor:
Sixth Egyptian Room; Fifth Egyptian Room; Fourth Egyptian Room; Third Egyptian Room, Second Egyptian Room, First Egyptian Room

Ground Floor:
Egyptian Sculpture Gallery

Introduction

In antiquity, Egypt consisted of the Valley of the Nile from the First Cataract in the south, to the Mediterranean in the north, some 750 miles by river. It was (and is) a narrow, winding country confined on each side by the cliffs of the desert plateau until, just before Cairo, the Nile emerged into the broad plain of the Delta, where its three branches – there are only two today – flowed to the Mediterranean. In the Libyan desert to the west are several oases and the Faiyūm depression with its lake which in ancient times was much larger, while on the east is the mountainous Arabian desert (Map 3).

Without the Nile, Egypt would never have become a populous and prosperous country, for rainfall is negligible and the scorching sun parches the land. But at the end of the first week in June the Nile begins to rise between Aswan in southern Egypt and Cairo, due to the annual flood waters (resulting from melting snow in the Abyssinian highlands and rains in central Africa) which flow down the White Nile, the Blue Nile and other rivers, and unite at Khartum.

The inundation reached its greatest height in September and October when it spread over the Nile Valley and deposited on the land the fertilizing silt brought down by the flood waters, which afterwards slowly subsided until the following May. Only the villages and towns on their artificial mounds and the dykes were above water level.

The height of the flood, which varied from year to year, was a matter of life or death in ancient times. A series of low Niles, when the water was insufficient to fertilize all the cultivable land, resulted in famine. Too high a flood did immense damage; but an average flood covered the valley to the rising ground on the edge of the desert and ensured that the population would be adequately fed.

Sixth Egyptian Room

The centre cases in this room are marked A to F. When subdivided, the divisions are marked at the top.

Prehistory

Paleolithic Age, before 12000 BC

Entering from the Hittite Room we can see in case A, A1 rough flint tools from various stages of the Paleolithic period which were found in Upper Egypt in the Theban region, some types of which will already be familiar to visitors to the Early Man Gallery, for example, hand-axes and scrapers.

Neolithic–Cuprolithic Period, c. 4500–c. 3100 BC

c. 4500–c. 3500 BC. There are numerous exhibits from the Badārian cultural group of settlements in Middle Egypt (p. 128) and from those of Upper Egypt at Naqāda, which demonstrate the inherent skills of the Egyptians in the applied arts, in particular the production of small objects.

For example, the exquisite Egyptian jewellery of historic times [wall cases 18, 20, 22] has never been surpassed, and in the child's ivory bangle with carved animal's head, the string of nerita and ancillaria shells [A, B1, 62062, 62070] from Mostagedda, and the ivory bracelets [A, C1, 62224], horn bangles [59708], shell necklaces and studs from Badāri and Qau [62215, 59702], we see its beginnings. Indeed such was the ingenuity of the prehistoric craftsman that a vitreous glaze was invented which, when applied to steatite (soapstone), produced a passable imitation of turquoise, although semi-precious stones, including turquoise, were also frequently employed [A, C1, 59687, glazed steatite and carnelian bead necklace. See also case D, A1 for Badārian jewellery].

Cosmetics were used by both sexes, green malachite being ground on rectangular palettes with notched ends in slate or stone [A, B1, 62036, alabaster palette; B2, 59635, slate palette], mixed with some fatty substance for application to face or body, and stored in carved ivory containers [above A, C2, 63057, toilet box in form of hippopotamus]. Other carved ivory objects were combs and spoons which can be seen in the Fifth Egyptian Room [centre case G, 63067, 62171].

In addition to ivory, copper was also known, but although some copper beads have been found, the metal was not in general use. Objects of everyday life were often made of bone, for example, fish-hooks [A, B1, 62015–6], awls [A, B2, 62078] and needles [A, B2, 59709, 62072]. The Badārians made flint tools [A, B2, 59713, saw-edged knife; 59717, sickle blade], but few weapons have been found, and these mainly arrow heads, leaf, tanged and winged shape [A, B3] used for hunting. Another Badārian achievement was the modelling of the human figure for the first time [above B2, 59679, Fig. 19].

Owing to lack of dwellings made from durable materials, habitation in the villages was attested by hearths and cooking pots and by the granaries which were lined with basketwork [A, C2, 62254].

Badārian pottery [case 17] can be divided into two classes: fine and coarse ware. The most popular types of the fine ware were the black topped red or brown vessels [62126 from Mostagedda; 59664 from Badāri], the polished red, and the polished black [59721 from Badāri]. A characteristic of this class was the rippling of the exterior surface [62126] while the interior was also occasionally decorated [59721]. Black topped pottery was made in Nubia and the Sudan, so the Badārian culture may have emanated from those regions. The coarse ware was brown [62156 from Mostagedda] and

Fig. 19. Pottery figure of a woman. Badārian culture, see page 137
Fig. 20. Queen Tetisheri as a young woman, see page 142

the shapes were principally bowls and deep cooking pots.

The cultures of Upper Egypt, both early and late, were represented in the cemeteries and settlements found at the modern village of Naqāda. The early phase (Naqāda I) was a development of the Badārian, as can be seen from its pottery [case 16], among which are many black topped red vessels. The fabric, however, was of much better quality, and an innovation was a red ware decorated with white cross lines, probably imitating basket-work [case 14, 30987, 58199]. Stone vessels, perhaps first made by the Badārians, were also produced.

Slate palettes were often in rhombic form, some large [A, D2, base, 66070], others very small [C, A3, 63072]; and the latter must have been amulets which were of great magical significance to the Egyptians. Palettes were also made in the form of animals, hippopotamus [case B, 29416], turtle [B, 37913] and other animals. Ivory and pottery figures continued to be popular, witness the carved figures of men and women [A, D1] and the ivory combs [D2, 63406, from Matmar].

As befitted a people who inhabited a walled (and perhaps fortified) town, tools and weapons were of excellent quality, for by now flint was specially mined. The disc-shaped mace head [A, D3, 63092, from Mostagedda] is characteristic of Naqāda I culture and also of a settlement in the Faiyūm (A). Indeed many weapons and tools are common to both sites, so they must have been almost contemporaneous. Weapons from graves were large and excellently made. Their flint work is indeed most accomplished as can be seen from the rhomboidal double-edged knives [C, D1, 30750, 30749, 49723, 34297], and flint lances with concave tops [C, D2, 30128].

Very little copper was found in graves although gold, which was available in the neighbourhood, may have been known. But in spite of the technological advances, the community was still dependant on farming, supplemented by hunting and fishing, for its livelihood.

c. 3500–c. 3100 BC. The foreigners who had entered Upper Egypt and mixed with the native population (p. 128) had transformed it into a strong homogeneous people with a desire to develop and expand. It is thought they came from

Western Asia for they introduced the Mesopotamian cylinder seal [wall case 23, cylinder seals, Early Dynastic, 2800 BC; Old Kingdom, c. 2700–2350 BC].

Asiatic influence is also obvious in the pottery. The black topped ware almost disappeared although the red and black polished vessels continued in production. A new clay was now employed which, after firing, became pink or buff [case 13] and this light background was painted with designs inspired by those of the Mesopotamian Jamdat Nasr period. These were mainly scenes from contemporary life which emphasized the vigorous and manifold activities of the Naqāda II people.

We can see that they were accustomed to travelling in large boats with many oars, two cabins and an emblem flying from a pole [case 14, base, 36326]. Animals and birds were also depicted, as well as men and women (perhaps deities) taking part in religious ceremonies [case 14, base, 49570, 36326]. Among innovations was the wavy handled pot [case 13, 30908]. Stone vases were also made during this period [see Fourth Room].

In one of the Naqāda settlements (the South town), roughly rectangular houses were excavated which were probably similar to the terracotta model house found at El-Amra [case B, 35505], which consisted of one room roofed over and a walled forecourt in which was a door on the short side. But in a rural settlement at Merimda of this time on the western edge of the Delta the huts at the top level were partially sunk below ground.

Tools and weapons were now made of copper, but flint continued to be worked and some of the finest implements hitherto made in Egypt were turned out by Naqāda II craftsmen [C, D2, 30232, flint lance with fishtail top; D3, 30097, curved knife; 59235, curved knife; 30225–7, chisels or scrapers].

Prehistoric craftsmen found it easier to model or carve representations of animals than the human form, and the porphyritic frog [B, 66837] is a masterpiece.

According to tradition Egypt, at the end of the Naqāda II period, was divided into two kingdoms, Lower (northern) and Upper (southern) Egypt, each with its ruler and capital. Incidents in the fight for supremacy between the two kingdoms are recorded on the great carved slate palettes of the period. The Hunter's palette [B, 20790] shows armed men hunting lions and other wild animals, symbolizing the enemy; and on the Battlefield palette [C, top, 20791] we see a lion, probably representing the conqueror, attacking his prey (opponents).

Again, according to tradition, Menes, King of Upper Egypt, conquered the north and unified the country. Historians equate Menes with Narmer, the first king of the 1st dynasty, whose name is inscribed on a wooden label and on a fragment of alabaster [C, C1, 35519; B1, 32640] both from Abydos. One wonders whether the exceptionally fine statuette of a king wearing a woven robe and the crown of Upper Egypt could possibly represent Narmer (Menes)? [B, 37996, from Abydos, 1st dynasty, c. 3000 BC].

Writing

The sudden emergence of the hieroglyphic script at the beginning of the Early Dynastic period (c. 3100 BC) without, so far as is known at present, the evidence of development such as occurred in Mesopotamia (p. 98), is due, it is believed, to Sumerian immigrants transmitting the basic principles of their system.

This accomplishment abolished the anonymity of individuals who now acquired personalities. We know their names, their religious beliefs, their customs, and much else besides; and in the Fifth Egyptian Room [through the entrance into the Fourth Room and turn right] we can also study their appearances and some of their attributes.

Fifth Egyptian Room

The Historic Egyptian

The Egyptian was broad-headed and the length and breadth of his face were about equal [A, 47568. Head and part of torso of a high official, 6th dynasty, c. 2300 BC]. With eyes set wide apart, a large mouth and a prominent and slightly broad nose, he was of medium height and sturdily built, with powerful shoulders and thick wrists and ankles, as, for example, Meryre-Hashetef [55722, 6th dynasty, c. 2350 BC].

His womenfolk were small and slender [case 192, 24619, 5th dynasty, c. 2450 BC].

Marriage

He was a family man, fond of his womenfolk and children. He had one legitimate wife, the mistress of his house, and married couples are frequently portrayed together, affectionately holding hands or with arms around each other's waists [case 193, 1181. Ka-tep and Hetepheres, 4th dynasty, c. 2550 BC]. In addition a wealthy man's household would include concubines, the women of his harem. The king, on the other hand, had more than one wife, but these marriages were usually for political purposes. It is also probable that the governors of the nomes and other high officials followed the king's example, because Egyptian women were able to inherit property, were customarily daughters of rich men, and so brought wealth to their husbands.

Indeed, they appear to have enjoyed a good deal of liberty. They moved around freely, attended entertainments, and a wife often accompanied her husband on rural outings, at any rate in the 18th dynasty, as will be seen later [Third Egyptian Room].

So far as the royal ladies were concerned, the queen consort was a person of importance and received honours in her own right: indeed it is conjectured that inheritance descended through the female line. But the king's other ladies in the household lived in seclusion in the harem.

During the 18th dynasty (1567–1320 BC), royal women stepped into the limelight. Queen Tetisheri, wife, mother and grandmother of the last three kings of the 17th dynasty, and grandmother of Amosis, founder of the 18th dynasty, played a significant role in the expulsion of the Hyksos by her grandson. Although her statue represents her as a charming girl (Fig. 20), she became a woman of strong character [C, 22558, 17th dynasty, c. 1600 BC].

The next queen to take the stage was the dowager Hatshepsut, regent for her stepson, Tuthmosis III (1504–1450 BC) [case 197, 487, c. 1450 BC] (p. 132), then a child. Within two years she had herself crowned 'King of Upper and Lower Egypt' with full pharaonic powers, and with the youthful Tuthmosis as nominal co-regent. It was over 20 years (1482 BC) before he was sufficiently powerful to claim his birthright as the sole occupant of the throne. Hatshepsut's subsequent fate is unknown.

Another prominent royal lady was Queen Tiy, wife of the easy-going and luxury-loving Amenophis III (1417–1379 BC) [case 199, 30448. Head of a king, probably Amenophis III, c. 1400 BC] great grandson of Tuthmosis III . The Queen was the daughter of non-royal, untitled parents, but Amenophis held her in great esteem and affection. They are frequently represented together on the monuments; and can be seen here [recess 198, 57399, 1370 BC] in a pose which is far removed from the traditional calm dignity of royal sculptures, for the portly Amenophis is relaxing in a chair in front of a table loaded with food, and has flung his arm round his wife's shoulder. Not only were the royal manners less conventional, but Amenophis inaugurated a trend to naturalism in art in the delightful scenes from nature in his vast palace at Thebes.

The Amarna period

These trends were accelerated by his son, Amenophis IV [case 199, 13366; recess 198, 26810, 1370 BC]. But while the father fulfilled his duty to the state god, Amun (see below), by building temples to his glory, the son attempted to destroy this deity and other Egyptian gods, and to supersede them by the monotheistic worship of the solar deity, Aten (Disk), under whose life-giving rays he was often depicted [recess 198, 24431, Fig. 21]. His animosity to Amun naturally aroused the enmity of the god's adherents.

Amenophis changed his name to Akhenaten, and built a new Residence city (capital) at El-Amarna (mod.) in Middle Egypt named Akhetaten (Horizon of the Aten) in which were workmen's villages, houses for the nobles, temples for the Aten, and palaces for the king, his beautiful wife Nefertiti [case 199, 935, c. 1370 BC], and his offspring. Two of the youthful princesses, Meritaten and Meketaten [recess 198, 55616, c. 1370 BC] can be seen riding in a chariot (extreme right), while a plaster death mask possibly again represents Meketaten, who died and was buried at El-Amarna [case 199, 65517, c. 1370 BC].

The trend to natural plant and animal forms in art continued, for example, the relief of deer feeding from a manger

Fig. 21. Amenophis IV (Akhenaten), the heretic pharaoh, see page 143

Fig. 22. Ploughing, with a man to drive the animals and another to control the plough, see page 150 [recess 198, 57395], and the painted scenes of birds in the marshes from the Northern Palace, El-Amarna [Sixth Room, end by Room of Writing, 58830]. The Amarna fine pottery [Sixth Room, case 9] is also very distinctive.

Akhenaten reigned for 17 years, and towards the end of this period there must have been grave unrest. The Asiatic empire, consolidated by Tuthmosis III, had been lost: Akhenaten had been so engrossed in Aten worship that he neglected to send help to his Syrian and Palestinian vassals and allies who were overcome by the Hittites and the desert tribes. In Egypt foremost among the disaffected was the priesthood of Amun, and the pharaoh's youthful co-regent, son-in-law and half-brother Smenkhkare was sent to Thebes apparently to effect a reconciliation. But Akhenaten and Smenkhkare died within a few months of one another and the throne descended to the latter's brother Tutankhaten [case 199, 37639, c. 1350 BC], a boy of 9 or 10. The court returned to Thebes, Egypt reverted to her old gods and the youthful pharaoh changed his name to Tutankhamun.

The Gods

Who were Egypt's old gods? A glance at the collections in cases 207–221 makes one realize that, owing to their number and diversity, that question cannot be answered in detail here.

Generally speaking, however, the Egyptian gods originated in prehistoric times as the protecting deities of the community. These units, in due course, amalgamated with others probably on a tribal, and later territorial (nome) basis, and the god of the dominant unit became the god of the enlarged community. By means of this progression Horus, the god of Nekhen, capital of the rulers of Upper Egypt before the unification, became after it the patron deity of the conquerors of Lower Egypt.

The Egyptians emerged into history with a profusion of deities, often with overlapping functions. To preserve their local deities, they overcame these difficulties by believing that one god was merely an alternative form of another, or a part, aspect, or associate of it: alternatively they grouped gods and goddesses in families, and to a male divinity they added a wife and son. Some gods, though anthropomorphized in myth and legend, retained also animal incarnations, and were often therefore represented in human form with animal heads. Furthermore there were the cosmic deities representing natural forces: the sun and moon gods, those of the stars, and the goddess of the sky; the gods of the earth, air and of the primeval waters.

The Egyptian religion was, in effect, the worship of many gods; of which it is only possible to mention those which were pre-eminent: Horus, the falcon god [case 218, base, 11593. After 600 BC], Re, the sun god of Heliopolis [case 218, 2nd shelf, 16037], and Amun elevated to be state god by the powerful pharaohs of the New Kingdom and associated with the sun god to become Amun-Re [case 207]. To these must be added Osiris [case 219] whose restoration to life after death through the devotion of Isis, his wife, and Horus, his child [case 221] (one of the latter god's manifestations) was the pledge of immortality to even the humblest citizen, and was consequently worshipped throughout Egypt.

Before leaving this room, note should be taken of two statuettes [case I, 38442, 38443, c. 250 BC] of Ptolemy II Philadelphus and Arsinoe II represented in Hellenistic style. We shall see later (p. 191) how the Macedonian sovereigns were formally represented to their Egyptian subjects.

Fourth Egyptian Room

The way of life of the Egyptian is admirably illustrated in the Fourth Egyptian Room. At the time of writing, however, the room was in the process of rearrangement and a number of cases without exhibits: therefore although the type of exhibit to be shown can be indicated and where it is likely to be found, it is not always possible to give specific examples.

Building materials

The principal building material was brick made from Nile mud. It was not a stable material and mud-brick buildings disintegrated comparatively rapidly, and the decayed material was used as a fertilizer. In course of time the sites of ancient cities were ploughed up for corn growing, which accounts for the almost total disappearance of Egyptian dwellings [see case I for architectural and other measuring equipment].

Houses

During the Early Dynastic period when the superstructures of tombs were built of brick, it is a reasonable assumption that the palaces of kings and the houses of the nobles were similarly constructed.

Middle Kingdom houses of the well-to-do in the crowded towns had narrow frontages on the street, but were sometimes of several storeys. The narrow width was compensated for by the depth, in which were reception halls and living quarters for the family: suites of bedrooms for the males and quarters for the harem, as well as for the domestic offices.

Rural dwellings in their simplest form, judging by models [case 150, 32609, 12th dynasty, c. 1900 BC] found in tombs (see *The Eternal Life*, p.154f) had a courtyard in front used for storage (note beer jars) in which was a water tank. Only the façade of the dwelling was shown, and the number of rooms behind it probably depended on the owner's prosperity. From this humble beginning there developed the nobleman's elegant establishment with its columned and painted portico, large wooden doors behind which were the porter's lodge and the reception rooms.

In the New Kingdom (c. 1567–1085 BC) a rich man's country house comprised spacious rooms for entertaining, sleeping quarters for the owner and his family, bathrooms and lavatories. There were also separate quarters for the harem, and the servants, and kitchen and storage rooms. The buildings, which were extensive, were situated in a charming garden, surrounded by a wall, within which were shady trees, flowers and a lily pond, such as will be seen later [Third Egyptian Room].

Music [case B]. Music had been enjoyed in Egypt from time immemorial. There were musicians in the palaces of the king and in the households of men of rank, at royal ceremonies and religious festivals, and at banquets and entertainments. There must also have been street singers and players. In case B, musical instruments in use throughout the ages are exhibited.

Furniture [cases 184–91], *Domestic equipment* [case H]. We know from the tomb of Tutankhamun that the palaces of the 18th dynasty pharaohs contained superb works of art, and that their furniture was elegant and luxurious. The wooden bed [case 188, 21574, 18th dynasty, c. 1400 BC] decorated with silver and gold exemplifies the innate good taste of the Egyptian, and may have belonged to a member of the royal family. Even the more simple bed, possibly a child's [case 190, 18196, c. 1250 BC], with the carved bull's feet, has a certain grace. Although the Egyptians made feather cushions [case 184, 15710. Date uncertain], experience since prehistoric times had taught them that a wooden head rest [cases 189–91] was more suitable for use in a hot climate.

Some pieces had a surprisingly modern appearance. The wooden chair with the high back and woven seat [case 184, 2479, c. 1250 BC] would not be out of place today in a children's playroom; and the handsome acacia wood chair with the high back inlaid with ebony and ivory lotus flowers [case 185, 2480, 1250 BC] would arouse no comment in a modern sitting room, unless on its unusual elegance. Instead of cupboards, the Egyptians kept their clothes and other property in wooden chests, such as that of ship's captain Demeg-ro [case 187, 5907, c. 1250 BC] only probably larger.

That the carpenter was able to undertake such high quality work was due to his comprehensive range of tools [case L], but above all to the Egyptian genius for the applied arts.

Some domestic equipment is as familiar to cooks of recent times as it was to cooks of ancient Egypt, although now superseded by electrical gadgets, for example the mortar and pestle [case H, 173, 29301, after 30 BC] and sieve [55130, c. 1370 BC]. Other types of equipment, buckets [23558, c. 50 BC] and jugs [38229, c. 1300 BC] are still in use today. But unfortunately our tables are not graced by the exquisite faience bowls [4790, c. 1450 BC] and cups in the form of an open lotus flower [26226–7, 22731, c. 1000 BC. See also Sixth Room, cases 24 and 26]. The locks and bolts exhibited are mainly of late date (after 650 BC) although in use much earlier for the Egyptian workman was always a most accomplished thief, witness the fact that Tutankhamun's tomb was the only king's tomb found with its contents comparatively intact.

Toilet and cosmetics [case 139]. *Toilet objects* [case A]. The toilet chest of Tutu, wife of the scribe Ani, contains many of the items required for the toilet of a well-bred woman [case 139, 24708, c. 1300 BC]. In addition, she would require, *inter alia*, a mirror [case A, B1–3], perfume flask [A, A2, 64041, 1300 BC], tweezers [A, D3, 37213–37217, c. 1500 BC–AD 100], and hair curlers for the dressing of wigs [case 139, 2560–61, c. 1400 BC] worn by both sexes at all periods. The composite bronze implement, razor, hair curler and trimmer [case A, D, base, 67448, 18th dynasty, c. 1450 BC] was probably the property of a barber, either one who served his customers in the open air, or a more superior tradesman who attended the houses of the great, or better still, a humble member of the staff of a great temple or palace where his livelihood was assured.

Servants at work [cases 148–9]. The objects described above were principally the appurtenances of the upper class who maintained large establishments with numerous servants, who can be seen carrying out their duties in the lively wooden models in this room, mainly of Old and Middle Kingdom date, c. 2686–1786 BC.

For instance, two female servants carry ducks in their right hands, and a basket of bread or fruit on their heads [case 148, 45074–5, 12th dynasty, c. 1900 BC], presumably to the kitchen. In a bread-making scene [55730, 6th dynasty, c. 2250 BC] a woman grinds the corn on a quern [R], while a man kneads the dough [L], and another woman in front [R] tends the oven of circular stones, and raises a hand to protect her face from the heat.

Food and drink [cases 150–1; case D]. The end products which would result from such activities provide a cross section of Egyptian diet: a triangular loaf of barley bread [case D, 40942, c. 2050 BC], cooked ducks on the upper shelf of a wicker offering table to the dead [5340, c. 1450 BC], and several fruits – dates [5369, c. 1250 BC], fruit of the dom-palm [35939, 35952, c. 1240 BC] and dried figs [5368, c. 1450 BC]. Large estates would also have their own butchery and slaughter house [case 151, 58083, 12th dynasty, c. 1900 BC]; and since beer was the national drink, in large establishments it would be brewed in considerable quantities, often in conjunction with bread-making, as barley was the common raw material [case 151, 40915, 11th dynasty, c. 2050 BC].

Agriculture [cases 156–9]. Full-scale farming equipment is displayed in conjunction with models which show how some of it was used, for instance, the bronze shod plough [case 156, 50705, c. 1400 BC] was usually drawn by a pair of oxen harnessed to the pole [case 157, 51090] (Fig. 22). If the ground were hard, however, it was broken up by a hoe [22863, 41193, c. 1300 BC]. The sower usually followed the plough and the seed was trodden into the earth by flocks of sheep and goats.

When the corn was ripe, it was cut by hand with wooden sickles in which were set flint teeth [case 157, 52861, c. 1400 BC]. It was then threshed by cattle trampling upon it on the threshing floor, winnowed [case 158, back, 18206, winnowing fan, c. 1300 BC], carried in sacks [158, 63195, c. 1300 BC] and stored in a granary [158, 2463, c. 1800 BC], whose owner, in the model, sits on a platform above the storage chamber, while a woman in the court below grinds grain. A granary containing ancient corn is also exhibited [case 159, 41573, c. 1800 BC].

Spinning and weaving [cases 144–5]. *Clothing and footwear* [cases 140–3]. One of the oldest crafts was spinning and weaving which, in the Old Kingdom was carried out by household slaves but later by the wives of the peasants, who as serfs were tied to the land of their masters, either an individual, a department of state or the estate of a god.

From the Old Kingdom, the principal male dress was the kilt in all its variations [cases 141–3, 55261; 1818, kilt with stiff front]. High ranking New Kingdom officials favoured a long pleated garment [1820]. Women's dress throughout the pharaonic period was a robe wrapped tightly round the body and held up by shoulder straps [29595].

Navigation [cases 152–5; E]. The Nile, from time immemorial, has been Egypt's main internal highway: the ancient Egyptians were as much at home on the water as they were on land and many could swim. But Egypt lacked timber for boat building, which had to be imported from the Lebanon and shipped through the Phoenician port of Byblos (Jbail).

From prehistoric times the Egyptians used a boat made from papyrus stems lashed together [case 155, 21805, c. 2250 BC]. Propelled by a pole or oars its shallow draught made it admirably suited for use in the marshes where noble and commoner went fishing and fowling.

Manufactured products and raw materials went by water, and so also did the dead, the mummy of those of high rank making a pilgrimage before burial to Abydos, the cult centre of Osiris [case 152, 23560, 12th dynasty, c. 1800 BC]. A great Officer of State would travel in an ornate cabin fitted on to the deck of his ceremonial barge [case E, 37160, c. 1350 BC. See painting of Viceregal barge in Third Room corridor]. The Egyptians also built warships and sea-going ships, rowing boats, sailing boats, and cargo barges designed for towing. Transport by land, however, was by litter, donkey and sledge until the horse and wheeled vehicle were introduced from Asia, but the latter conveyance was always the prerogative of royalty and the governing classes. The ordinary Egyptian travelled on his feet.

Scribes and artists [case J]. *Script development* [case K]. Nothing was undertaken in Egypt under government (free enterprise was minimal) without the production of documents. This 'mania for writing' necessitated a large body of scribes, from the high officials of the Treasury (House of Silver) to the lowly clerk in the nome, although the letter writer who sat at the gate of the city or other public place was probably a freelance.

The scribal pupil had a rigorous training at school, where boys of high and humble birth were educated together for the profession. Papyrus was too valuable to waste on students, so they wrote their exercises on potsherds (ostraca) and limestone chips [case K, 50724, c. 1250–1150 BC].

The scribe had to be familiar with the forms of writing in current use which, for the greater part of the pharaonic period were the hieroglyphic script [case K, 10793, caption to illustration, c. 1000 BC], and hieratic in its many varieties. However writing, like language, changes over periods of time, and whereas hieroglyphs were only used for royal and religious inscriptions, hieratic [10735.12, from Abu Sir, Old Kingdom], which was a cursive form of abbreviated hieroglyphs employed for literary and business documents, continually evolved [10819.1, 18th dynasty]. Indeed, the late cursive script, used from mid-7th century BC to mid-5th century AD and known as demotic, eventually had no resemblance to hieroglyphs [23040, receipt for delivery of wine at Thebes in year 2 of Emperor Hadrian, AD 127].

From the 1st century AD, attempts were made to write the Egyptian language in the Greek alphabet, Greek being the *lingua franca* of the Near East and the most frequently written language. These early texts were mostly of magical import [case K, 10808, from Oxyrhynchus, 2nd century AD]. In the 3rd century, with the rapid spread of Christianity among the native population, translations of Christian literature appeared written in Greek uncials [14030, pottery ostracon containing opening lines of Psalms in coptic, 6th–7th century AD], supplemented by seven characters taken from demotic to indicate sounds for which there was no equivalent Greek letter. This script is known as coptic, the word 'copt' being the westernized version of the Arabic *qubt*, from the Greek *Aiguptios*, indicating the people and language of Egypt. Coptic is the ultimate stage of the Egyptian language before it was supplanted by Arabic. Scholars can read ancient Egyptian in all its forms but their knowledge of its pronunciation is limited to what can be deduced from coptic.

The scribe was conventionally represented sitting cross-legged with his papyrus roll stretched across his knees, as shown on the pottery flask [case J, 24653, c. 1400–1300 BC], and in the statuette of the sage Imhotep [64495], who lived about 2650 BC and was chancellor and architect of King Djoser of the 3rd dynasty. Here, too, are items of a scribe's equipment [see photograph and exhibits], including the wax tablets of the Graeco-Roman period [29527, after 30 BC].

In addition, there will be an exhibition dealing with scribes and artists in case 178 and the following cases; and in cases 167–77, examples from the Department's collections of stone vessels.

Third Egyptian Room

First Section: Tomb paintings

A Scribe's Estate

A scribe could rise to high position and affluence, for example, Nebamun, an assessor of grain in the New Kingdom about 1400 BC, whom we see here [37977] fowling with a throwstick in the marshes in a papyrus stem boat, accompanied by his wife and daughter. He lived in an elegant country house, and in his garden was an ornamental stretch of water stocked with fish [37983] with a pair of geese and their young swimming among the waterlilies. Heavily laden fruit trees surrounded the water which was edged with plants and flowers.

He was also a cattle breeder, and his large herds can be seen rounded up for inspection [37976], probably at the biennial census held for taxation purposes. The animals are shown in two scenes, and in the lower [L] are two scribes, one listening to a servant bowing low before him. The herdsman, holding a coil of rope, urges the servant to stop talking, as the scribe abominates chatter [caption]. Nebamun's geese also came under the scribe's scrutiny [37978].

Banquets

The Egyptian upper classes relished good food and wine, and were much addicted to parties [37984, 37986, 37981]. Nebamun was no exception; furthermore these paintings from his tomb had a magical potency, and ensured that he could offer entertainments to friends in the afterlife.

The guests were waited upon by male and female slaves (the latter naked except for a necklace and narrow girdle) who offered a lotus flower, a scented cone to place on the head, necklaces and a bowl of wine to each guest. Female musicians [37981, below] played the lute, double pipe and perhaps a tambourine. Another group consisted of a pipe player and three singers [37984] who clapped their hands to mark the rhythm, while two female dancers performed what appears to be a belly dance near to wicker baskets containing wine bottles (Fig. 23). But partaking of wine in quantity before eating is apt to have disastrous results, and it was by no means rare – in fact almost *de rigueur* – for both male and female guests to end up in an advanced state of inebriation.

Fig. 23. Guests at a banquet with musicians, dancers and a goodly supply of wine in jars

Other interesting paintings are *Jewellers at work* [920], and the *Presentation of tribute by Semitic envoys from Syria*, probably to Tuthmosis IV or Amenophis III [37991, c. 1420 BC].

The remaining sections of the Third Room (opposite side of corridor) are mainly concerned with aspects of religion which can be better understood after a visit to the First and Second Egyptian Rooms.

Second Egyptian Room

It is well known that the Egyptians preserved the bodies of their dead by the process of mummification; but what is not so familiar is their reason for doing so.

The Eternal Life

The Egyptians, of all the peoples of the ancient Near East, were the most determined believers in a future life. Man, they believed, consisted of several elements, physical and immaterial; but as the functions of these elements varied through the centuries and were complex and confused, it is best here to mention only two, the Ka and the Ba which together represent what we understand as the spirit. After death the spirit was released from the body and was free to go where it pleased; but its dwelling was the body to which it returned. Therefore the body must be preserved in perpetuity: hence the process of mummification.

The future life was envisaged as an extension of earthly existence so that all those things required in this world were placed in the tomb for use in the next. As it is mainly the contents of upper class tombs that have come down to us, it can be seen that a man of rank cherished his family and home, and among other things held in high regard his herds and flocks, sport, services rendered by servants, entertainments, and food and drink, which were all represented in his tomb in one form or another. By magical potency they would be transformed into actuality in the other world.

Mummification

In prehistoric times the dead were buried in a contracted position in rectangular or oval pits in the desert, and the hot sand dried the body, conserving its appearance [centre, case A, 32571, c. 3300 BC]. But shallow graves provided no security, and burials took place in wooden coffins [centre, case B, 52888, 1st dynasty, c. 3000 BC] which, however, must have hastened the body's decomposition. In the 2nd dynasty (2890–2686 BC) attempts were made to preserve the body by binding it to keep its shape. By the 4th dynasty, it was realized that the first essential for preservation was the removal of the internal organs, but it was not until the New Kingdom that a satisfactory process of mummification was evolved.

Coffins

Mummification necessitated large rectangular wooden coffins because the body was buried in an extended position. This type appeared in the Old Kingdom and continued in use until the later Middle Kingdom [cases 80 and 81, 44631, c. 2000 BC]. Magic Udjat eyes of the falcon god, Horus, which enabled the mummy to look out, were painted on the outside [centre case C, 55315, c. 2000 BC], as was a representation of a palace façade, with its doors and panelling, the then customary habitation of an Egyptian nobleman [12270, c. 2000 BC]. Inner and outer coffins decorated with texts on the insides were in use during the First Intermediate period and the 11th and 12th dynasties [centre case E, 30839, outer coffin, c. 2000 BC].

During the 12th dynasty, the head of the mummy was covered with a mask moulded to the features of the face [case 76, 29770, c. 2000–1700 BC], and from this development evolved painted wooden coffins in the shape of a heavily bandaged mummy [case 77, 52951, c. 1600 BC]. The feathered decoration of these mummiform coffins is thought to represent the wings of the goddess Isis, protecting the body of Osiris: in the case of a king (Inyotef, possibly Nubkheperre, 17th dynasty, Fig. 24), the decoration was in gold [case 79, 6652, c. 1600 BC].

In the New Kingdom coffins were made of wood [case 71, 29580, c. 1400 BC] or cartonnage (moulded linen or plaster), and were simply decorated, but became more elaborate towards the end of the 18th and during the 19th dynasty [case 67, 48001, inner coffin with modelled face and wig; case 68, 48001, openwork cover of mummy; case 69, 48001A, outer coffin, all of the Lady Henutmehyt, 18th–19th dynasty, c. 1300 BC]. In the 20th and 21st dynasties, inner and outer mummiform coffins were heavily decorated inside and out with various religious scenes and magical symbols, some of which were modelled in gesso (plaster of Paris) before being painted [case 84, 24789, 21st dynasty, c. 1050 BC].

First Egyptian Room

Animal worship

Animal worship in Egypt went back to the remote past when a primitive people regarded the strength and virility of animals with awe, and the cult never entirely died out. But in the Late period it was resuscitated by the priests in an en-

Fig. 24. Mummiform coffin of King Inyotef. Note the feathered decoration (L) by the lappet of the head-dress

deavour to counteract the effect of foreign religions, and it flourished especially during the Ptolemaic and Roman periods, as can be seen from the animal mummies and exhibits in cases 2–4.

Later coffin styles

After the 21st dynasty the mummy was placed in a close-fitting cartonnage case [case opp. 8, 6686, 20th–22nd dynasty, c. 1200–700 BC]. It was then enclosed in at least an inner and an outer wooden coffin of inferior decoration and large and clumsy shape [case 6, 6676, 26th dynasty, c. 600 BC]. High officials had stone mummiform coffins, as will be seen later in the Sculpture Gallery. In the Late period, too, a new outer coffin, a rectangular chest with a vaulted roof and a post at each corner, again of uninspired decoration, became fashionable [case opp. 36, 15655, c. 25th dynasty, 650 BC].

The Ptolemaic sovereigns, whose culture was Greek, nevertheless adopted Egyptian burial customs, even to the vast mummiform wooden coffins [cases 24 and 25, 6677, 6677a, c. 200 BC]. They also favoured the vaulted rectangular coffin [centre, opp. 45, 6710, Ptolemaic period, c. 200 BC].

In the Roman period a most striking innovation took place: a painted portrait of the deceased, remarkably modern in style and execution, was placed over the face of the mummy, for example, in the case of Artemidorus, aged 19–21 [case 44, 21810, early 2nd century AD]. These portraits, apart from their value as a visual record of the Graeco-Roman upper class, are also important because they are practically the only body of painted portraits to have come down to us from classical times. An alternative to the painted portrait was a rendering of the deceased's features in plaster. In the Coptic Gallery (off Fourth Room) there is a splendid collection of these portraits and plaster heads [cf. 29772, portrait of a woman. Early 2nd century BC] (Fig. 25).

In the cartonnage case of the mummy of a Greek woman [opp. 50, below, 29585, 2nd century AD], the features are moulded to represent the deceased's, and she is depicted in the gaily coloured garments and jewellery of everyday life [see case 51, 29586]. At this time mummies were kept in the

Fig. 25. Mummy portrait of a woman in the Roman naturalistic tradition except for the eyes which seem to stare into infinity, later a characteristic of Roman Christian portraits

house for considerable periods before burial in coffins with movable sides, so that relatives and friends might view the corpse.

Such changes in age-long customs show the influence of the many foreigners (Greeks, Jews, Libyans, Persians and Romans) who had entered the country during the last centuries of the 1st millennium BC and early in our era. The time was ripe for widespread changes in religious beliefs, and Christianity, brought to Egypt in the 1st century AD, made great headway in the 2nd and 3rd centuries (see the Coptic Gallery, the Department of Medieval and Later Antiquities, and the Department of Manuscripts).

In cases 9 and 10 can be seen the Canopic jars in which the viscera were placed after removal from the body during mummification. In the adjacent recess is a limestone relief [326, 19th dynasty, c. 1250 BC] which shows the Canopic chest being carried by priests in a funeral procession.

On returning to the Third Egyptian Room (2nd section), we must take note in the First Egyptian Room of the mummy [case opp. 44, 6714 top. Roman after 30 BC] with the amulets strung across the chest, the significance of which will shortly be explained.

Third Egyptian Room

Second Section: Magic

We can now investigate a very potent factor in Egyptian religion – magic – which bridged the gap between reality and the Egyptian's desires and fears, and which could be invoked by speech and action but was at its most powerful when called forth by the written word.

For instance, it was early realized that priests and families whose duty it was to bring food offerings for the deceased to his tomb, did not always fulfil their obligations. But a magical spell inscribed in the tomb, such as a list of food for the owner's funerary feast (p. 163) was sufficient to ensure that he never lacked sustenance, should human assistance fail.

Originally, magical spells were the prerogative of the king, and during the 5th and 6th dynasties were inscribed in his pyramid (*Pyramid Texts*). During the First Intermediate period they were appropriated by the local rulers and later, in the Middle Kingdom, by the nobles who had them painted, suitably adapted, on their coffins (*Coffin Texts*). By the New Kingdom, a substantial body of material had accumulated (known now as *The Book of the Dead*) from which selections were copied by the priests on to papyri and placed on mummies. These compilations were in use up to the 30th dynasty, and were often beautifully illustrated in ink and colour [wall frames 10470, Papyrus of Ani, 19th dynasty, c. 1250 BC; 10472, Papyrus of Anhai, 20th dynasty, c. 1150 BC; 9901, Papyrus of Hunefer, early 19th dynasty, c. 1300 BC; 10558, Papyrus of Ankhwahibra, Ptolemaic period, c. 200 BC].

Magical powers also assisted the living: there were spells to dispel headaches [case 111, 10685, c. 1200 BC] and to give protection against scorpions [case 112, 10687, c. 1250 BC]; nor were they confined to the written word. They could be evoked by certain objects designed to give protection against specific dangers, such as funerary amulets placed on the body [cases 96, 97] as we have just seen in the First Egyptian Room, and ivory wands [case 96] which protected both living and dead against snakes. They were also inherent in the image of things, such as the *shabti* figure which would act as a substitute for the tomb owner when he was called upon to undertake burdensome toil in the next world, for instance, the communal duty of repairing the dykes and cleaning irrigation canals which he avoided in this world by providing a deputy [cases 98, 99, 100 and 101]; and the miniature ritual vessels of the priest Idy [case 93], which would by magic prove adequate for use in the hereafter.

The king, nobles and high officials with their costly and well equipped tombs and magical spells were assured of a comfortable after-life. But the peasants, who toiled in the fields during their lifetime and had few possessions, magical or material, to take with them, probably did not expect any better conditions in the next world. Nevertheless, they were as equally determined as their betters to get there, for the preoccupation of all classes with death and burial really arose from their love of life and their fixed resolve to prolong it indefinitely.

Egyptian Sculpture Gallery

We must now descend by the north-west staircase to the great Egyptian Sculpture Gallery. Here can be seen sculptures and architectural features which give some idea of the magnitude of the Egyptian achievement. For although the Egyptian was the skilled craftsman of the Ancient Near East, he was also a great builder, monumental mason and sculptor.

Tombs

Having just examined many of the objects placed in tombs, we can now learn something about the construction of these 'eternal dwellings'.

In the Early Dynastic period, the tombs (called mastabas) of kings and high officials consisted of rectangular excavated substructures with compartments for the burial and storage of food and drink, and objects required by the owner in the next world, which were covered by brick superstructures, also containing storage chambers. The exterior walls of the superstructures were decorated with recessed panelling in series, reproducing the façade of a dwelling house or palace. Later the recesses were reduced to two, both containing false doors, one being used as a chapel. In the early Old Kingdom, the chapel was either a separate small building or constructed partly inside and partly outside the superstructure, with a false door through which the spirit could enter and leave the tomb.

The funerary panel of Rahotep [bay 8, 1242, 4th dynasty, 2600 BC] comes from the false door of an early Old Kingdom chapel (Fig. 26). It is especially notable for the beauty of the carving, in particular the hieroglyphs which list [R] the standard food offerings, while individual items, which the owner hopes to enjoy in the next world, are inscribed above and below the table.

The Museum possesses many false doors, but we will examine that of Urirenptah [bay 6, 718, 5th–6th dynasty, c. 2400 BC], a priestly official attached to the Sun Temple, built by King Neferirkare of the 5th dynasty. He was buried at Saqqara, the necropolis of Memphis, and in 1904 the

Fig. 26. Funerary panel of Rahotep, 2,600 BC. Note the beauty of the hieroglyphs

Museum bought the entire superstructure of his mastaba from the Egyptian government and re-erected it in London. Unfortunately climatic conditions caused some deterioration of the stone, but the false door, architrave, and many of the reliefs which decorated the original chapel can still be seen.

At the back of the bay are two false doors, the principal one on the left. Here Urirenptah is seated on a chair while his wife sits on the ground. In front and above them are food offerings, and the five registers below are devoted to their preparation and provision. On the right of the door, Urirenptah and his wife are seated on chairs with offerings on low tables again before and above them. Below [reg. 1], two sons and a daughter take part in the funerary feast. Another son [reg. 2] sits at a table, listening to a small band, while below four women dance to the rhythm of hand-clapping.

In the centre of the doorway is a list of offerings, the hieroglyphs being coloured blue. An offering table (see p 169) would have stood in front of this false door on which would be food provided by the family and the priest, who had received an endowment from Urirenptah to perform the funerary ritual.

But victuals were not Urirenptah's only consideration. He was a landowner, and any existence which did not include a country estate and its activities would have been intolerable to him. He made sure, therefore, of these amenities by placing reliefs depicting rural life in his tomb.

Unfortunately Urirenptah's sculptures [left wall of bay] are damaged and only his head [reg. 1, L], and part of the kilt, his staff and legs [reg. 3] can be seen, but this is sufficient to show that the figure of the deceased in these funerary monuments is represented in outsize.

Here Urirenptah reads 'the accounts of the work in the fields' presented by a scribe [reg. 1] while two scribes stand on either side of a small chest, one making up his accounts, the other dragging forward a cringing servant. Simultaneously the master surveys his herdsman who is parading cattle, now mainly lost except for the feet [reg. 1], and the asses and sheep driven by his stockmen [reg. 2], while yet another reluctant servant is dragged before him. Below [reg. 3, by hieroglyphic panel], a scribe, pen behind ear and scroll under arm, records the activities of the farm labourers, who will scatter seed to be trodden into the earth by sheep driven by farm hands with whips.

The scene now changes to the marshes by the Nile [reg. 3, right], where naked fishermen and their overseer (the 'chief bird-catcher') snare wild birds in a clap-net on a stretch of water near a reed thicket. The net is crammed with wildfowl, and the foreman unfurls a piece of linen as a sign to the men to close it by hauling on the ropes. The next stage is the removal of the trapped birds in cages to the house, but evidently one scene from the sequence is sufficient to invoke magically the entire operation in the hereafter.

Urirenptah's harvest, however, is shown in more detail. Barley is cut [reg. 4, R] with sickles, while flax is pulled up by the roots, made into bundles and placed on the ground to dry [reg. 4, L]. The sheaves of dried barley are loaded on to donkeys [reg. 5] and carried to the threshing floor. Beneath Urirenptah [L], servants make up a bed (note the head rest) and take linen from a chest [reg. 4]; another [reg. 3, extreme left] prepares a chair for the master, who is also provided [narrow register below] with a table, chests, ointment jars and a ewer. In the lowest register there was originally a flotilla of ships on the Nile but nothing now remains save the tops of the masts and the rigging. All these reliefs were originally coloured.

These lively scenes give a vivid idea of the tastes and habits of an Old Kingdom nobleman, but not his appearance. But the tomb could furnish an idealized likeness, for a portrait statue of the owner was placed there as a substitute dwelling place for the spirit should the body be destroyed. This was a very necessary precaution in a country where the dead attempted to take their worldly goods with them, which ensured that tomb robbery and mummy despoliation were endemic. Urirenptah's tomb statue is not available but that of Nenkheftka [bay 2, 1239, 5th dynasty, c. 2350 BC] is a fine representation (though idealized) of an Egyptian aristocrat who lived nearly 5,000 years ago, a man accustomed to command, conscious of the achievements of his age, and well endowed with this world's goods [the entrance to the type of house he lived in can be seen on 157b, top, L and R].

The Divine King

The Gallery also contains portraits of many of Egypt's kings (the term 'pharaoh' used in the Bible, is a Hebrew transliteration of the Egyptian word *per-o*, the great house, a synonym for the king which came into use during the 18th dynasty. The aim of the Egyptian sculptor was to depict the king-god with an air of dignity, majesty and power, and to stress his isolation from his subjects, an aim frequently achieved, but often at the expense of the delineation of character.

But in the Middle Kingdom, a more realistic style came into fashion, which produced the superb portrait of Sesostris III (c. 1878–1843 BC) (Fig. 27) [bay 3, 686, 12th dynasty]. This statue was found in the ruins of the mortuary temple of King Mentuhotpe II (c. 2060–2010 BC) [bay 3, 729 and 1397, 11th dynasty] at Deir el-Bahri, Thebes, whose walls and columns were decorated [see back of bay] with painted reliefs of gods and the divine king, and adulatory inscriptions to both, as were all Egyptian temples. The statue of Sesostris was one of six he set up there, each representing

Fig. 27. Sesostris III, c. 1878–1843 BC

him at a different age.

Here we see a man with protruding eyes and penetrating glance, high cheek bones and sunken cheeks, with a firm yet disdainful mouth and an expression of weary disillusionment; in short, a middle-aged man, accustomed to the burdens of kingship but not overcome by them. Sesostris III was, indeed, one of Egypt's most illustrious kings and a man of both imagination and action, as is shown by the unusual inscription he composed to mark his conquests in the Sudan.

> I have made my boundary, my going up-stream, farther than my fathers; I have added to what was decreed to me; I, the King, I say it and I have done it. What my heart conceived, my hand brought to pass . . . And if any one of my sons shall have maintained this boundary made by my Majesty, he is verily my son, begotten by my Majesty myself . . . but if he shall have slackened it and not fought for it, no son of mine is he, and none begotten by me. And bchold! my Majesty hath caused to be made a statue of my Majesty upon this boundary made by my Majesty, not desiring that ye should venerate it, but that ye should fight for it.

A contrast to power and majesty in this bay [L] is the touching stela of Sobkaa, an Overseer of Transport [1372, 11th dynasty, c. 2050 BC], which illustrates delightfully the Egyptian as a family man. Lying on his couch [reg. 3] he caresses an infant in his arms, while another child watches at the end of the couch. At the presentation of offerings Sobkaa [base, R] inhales the scent of a lotus flower and holds the hands of his wife and small child, while an older daughter clings to her mother's arm.

There were other splendid royal sculptures in the Middle Kingdom besides that of Sesostris III, for example, the head from a colossal statue which probably represents Ammenemes III [between bays 1 and 3, 1063, 1842–1797 BC], Sesostris' son, found near the entrance to the great temple at Bubastis in the Delta. If we compare these portraits with the seated statues of Amenophis III (1417–1379 BC) on either side of the north-west entrance [4 and 5], the difference between the two styles – the realistic and the blandly dignified – is immediately apparent.

On the other hand the facial characteristics of the seated

statues are totally different from the two mottled brown quartzite heads which also represent Amenophis III [between bays 6 and 8 and 7 and 5, nos. 7 and 6, 18th dynasty] and are scarcely recognizable as the same person. But these heads have been influenced by the new art style introduced during this monarch's reign (p. 143).

The Temple

Many royal statues stood in temples, either in a mortuary temple where the daily ritual of offerings for the dead king took place, or in the temple where the god was worshipped, the house of the god. From very early times the column, in wood and stone, was employed in these temples to form colonnades in courts and on terraces, and in the interior as supports for the roof.

There are four temple columns in the Central Saloon of the Sculpture Gallery, one at each corner. The most ancient [1385] comes from the pyramid temple (i.e., funerary temple in the pyramid complex) of King Unas of the 5th dynasty (Old Kingdom) at Saqqara, is of red granite and has a plain shaft, with palm leaves at the top which fan out to form the capital. Plant forms were much favoured, and in addition to the palm-leaf capital, there was the papyrus and the lotus bud. The latter can be seen on the column opposite [64, c. 2000 BC] which also has the square block (abacus) on which rested the roof or architrave. Of the two other columns, one [1123, 19th dynasty, c. 1250 BC] from the temple built by Ramesses II at Heracleopolis, is made from a single block of stone and is 17 ft 2 in. in height, while the other [1065, c. 850 BC], which came from the great temple at Bubastis, is 20 ft 9 in. in height and weighs 11¼ tons.

As we already know, the interior walls of temples were decorated with painted reliefs and inscriptions [bay 23]. Temple doorways also carried inscriptions (see p. 171). But little could be seen of the interior of these huge buildings unless illuminated by torchlight processions, for windows in Egypt were small and placed near the roof (see p. 170). In front of the temple pylons (monumental gateways) might be a pair of obelisks similar in shape to but of greater height than those which can be seen at the Gallery's south end near bay 30 [523, 524, 30th dynasty, 350 BC] as, for example, that of Tuthmosis III from the temple of Heliopolis which now stands on the Embankment, London (Cleopatra's Needle).

Statues of the kings were also placed in temples, as was that of Ramesses II in the Central Saloon of the gallery [19, 19th dynasty, c. 1250 BC] which came from the Ramesseum, this king's mortuary temple at Thebes.

Here also is a display of offering tables which, though mainly of late date, are of a type which would have stood before Urirenptah's false door (see p. 163).

Stelae

The Museum has a most comprehensive collection of stelae, commemorative stone slabs or tablets which carry a sculptured, painted design and/or an inscription. They were used to record notable achievements, mark boundaries and as memorial stones, when they were placed near, or in, the tomb.

The Museum's funerary collection is large and representative of people in many walks of life at different periods: it is, therefore, a notable contribution to ancient Egyptian social history.

For instance, Penamun [bay 16, 916, 19th–20th dynasty] was one of the labourers and craftsmen in the service of the pharaoh at the Theban necropolis who lived in the necropolis workmen's village of Deir el-Medina about 1200 BC. His stela is pathetically small (8 in. deep by 6 in. wide) as befits his humble station.

On the other hand that of the master craftsman Qaha [bay 18, 191, 19th–20th dynasty, c. 1200 BC] is more spectacular because he was higher in the hierarchy. On the top section is the Syrian goddess Qadesh standing on a lion with [R] the Egyptian fertility god Min, and [L] the Syrian god Reshef, both of whom are on a shrine. Below, Qaha, his wife and son are worshipping another Asiatic goddess Antet. These foreign gods were introduced into Egypt along with less ethereal objects during the great conquests of the pharaohs of the 18th dynasty in Syria and Palestine.

In theory the land of Egypt and everything therein was the property of the king; although circumstances inevitably modified this state of affairs, a high proportion of the population was nevertheless in his service. Whatever their position, it was proudly stated on the stelae, for apart from a desire for renown, there was magic in the written word and a name once inscribed ensured survival for its owner. In a sense this is true for our attention brings these people to life, if only for a fleeting moment.

Thus we meet Naia, keeper of the royal stables [between bays 15 and 17, L, 795, New Kingdom, c. 1200 BC]; Neb-nefer, a royal bodyguard [between bays 15 and 17, 1184, New Kingdom, c. 1200 BC]; Hori, diplomatic representative of Ramesses IV [bay 19, 588, 20th dynasty]; Rauben, a judge [bay 19, 320, Late New Kingdom]; Userheriatef, royal scribe and general [wall between bays 17 and 19, 357, New Kingdom, c. 1250 BC]; Ptahser, a chief mason [bay 17 (rear), 165, 19th dynasty, 1250 BC]; Baenāa, a royal scribe, and [below] the launderer Huy, which seems a very strange combination [bay 17, 149, New Kingdom, c. 1250 BC].

These are just a few examples, but there are many more funerary stelae in the Gallery which would well repay study.

Sarcophagi

It was customary for Egypt's kings, from the Old Kingdom onwards, to be buried in stone sarcophagi which were either rectangular or mummiform in shape and the high officials sometimes copied their masters, for example, Setau, royal scribe and governor of Nubia [bay 19, 78, 20th dynasty, c. 1200 BC].

When we examine the sarcophagus of King Nectanebo II [between bays 27 and 25, 10, c. 350 BC], the last native king of the last three native dynasties (28th–30th) which ruled during the interregnum (404–343 BC) between the two Persian periods, we can understand why the use of this type of coffin was restricted to royalty and the upper classes, for it was a most costly item of equipment. Constructed from granite, the exhibit is large enough to hold several inner coffins, each fitting over the other, and weighs nearly 7 tons. The exterior is carved with scenes and texts from the *Book of what is in the Underworld* to assist the occupant in the hereafter, who was not Nectanebo II; he was driven from Egypt by the Persians and died in Ethiopia. It may, however, have had a far more illustrious occupant – Alexander the Great.

It was mentioned (p. 168) that temples must have been dark. In bay 25, a temple window grating [1153, Ptolemaic period, c. 200 BC] emphasizes the point.

A fine stone sarcophagus was made for the Princess Ankhesneferibre [between bays 24 and 26, 32, c. 590 BC], daughter of Psammetichus II of the 26th dynasty, and wife of Amasis II. She held the high position of Divine Adoratrice in the hierarchy of the god Amun at Thebes. On the cover (wall) she is depicted with the insignia of royalty, the uraeus (cobra) on the brow, and holding the crook and the flail, while the sides of the sarcophagus are inscribed with texts from *The Book of the Dead* (Fig. 28).

On page 168 it was stated that temple doorways carried inscriptions, and an example can be seen in bay 26 [1519, c. 525 BC. The inscription refers to Psammetichus III, the last king of the 26th dynasty].

Ptolemaic and Roman periods

The majority of exhibits so far examined have come from the pharaonic period, but Egypt was a Hellenistic kingdom for 300 years (332–30 BC) and formed part of the Roman empire (if one includes the East Roman, later Byzantine, empire) until the Arab conquest in 640 AD, that is, for nearly a thousand years, of which the last 200 or so are generally considered as the beginning of the Middle Ages. There are, however, comparatively few exhibits from these times in the Sculpture Gallery.

But from a bust of one of the Ptolemies [bay 28, 1641, c. 200 BC] wearing the *nemset* head-dress, we can see that members of this dynasty were represented in the traditional style of the pharaohs, with a restrained and dignified appearance rather than with the naturalism of a Hellenistic monarch (for example, the statuette of Ptolemy II Philadelphus, to which attention has already been drawn (p. 146). A Roman emperor, too, lord of the civilized world, was represented as the king of Egypt (and without much technical skill) wearing the crown of Upper and Lower Egypt [bay 27, back, 2nd row, 1696, c. 300 AD].

But Egypt, although under alien rule, still had one inestimable – if involuntary – contribution to make to civilization. When archaeological excavations were undertaken at the end of the 19th and in the present century in towns and villages in Middle Egypt which had been enveloped by the desert in Byzantine and Arab times when the irrigation

Fig. 28. Lid of the stone sarcophagus of the Princess Ankhesneferibre

system broke down (p. 134), vast numbers of papyri from the Greek and Roman periods were discovered preserved by the dry sand. These consisted of literary texts, new and already known, official decrees and correspondence, legal documents, private letters and early biblical MSS., which have proved of the utmost importance for the history of the period and also for the verification of classical and biblical texts. Large numbers of these papyri are in the Museum, and examples can be seen in the Bible Room, Department of Manuscripts.

The Rosetta Stone

It is due to the use of the Greek language and alphabet in Egypt that the hieroglyphic script came to be deciphered. In 1802 the Rosetta Stone [centre of gallery, no. 25] was brought to England with other antiquities collected by the French in Egypt (p. 17). The text (a decree passed by the General Council of Egyptian priests at Memphis to celebrate the first anniversary of the coronation of Ptolemy V Epiphanes,27 March, 196 BC) is in two languages, Egyptian and Greek, and three scripts, hieroglyphic [top], demotic [centre], and Greek uncials (capitals) [below.] It aroused great interest among European scholars.

Foremost among them were J. D. Akerblad (1760–1819), a Swedish diplomat, and Thomas Young, the physicist and physician (1773–1829). By 1802 Akerblad was able to identify the proper names in the Greek text and some of its words (a total of 19) with their equivalents in the demotic inscription, and furthermore to show that demotic signs used for writing these words were mostly alphabetic. Young, availing himself of Akerblad's discoveries, found 86 words in the demotic text the meaning of which he inferred from the Greek version, and also that demotic characters and hieroglyphs were closely related. Thus the alphabetic (phonetic) values discovered by Akerblad in demotic were probably present in hieroglyphs. In addition he drew up a list of 200 words as they were written in demotic and hieroglyphs, and postulated their coptic equivalents but not always accurately.

But it was the great French scholar, Jean François Champollion, who was the decipherer of the hieroglyphic script. Through his knowledge of coptic (see p. 152), he was able to translate Greek words on the Rosetta Stone into coptic and, when he had mastered the basic principles of the hieroglyphic script, i.e., the different signs and the significance of each class, to find the spelling equivalent to the coptic word in the hieroglyphic version. Indeed before his death at the early age of 42 in 1832, he had drawn up a classified list of Egyptian hieroglyphs and formulated a system of grammar and decipherment which is the basis on which Egyptologists have worked ever since.

5 The department of Greek and Roman Antiquities

Map 4. Greece and the Aegean

Byzantium
Samothrace
Aegospotami
Ilium
Scamander R.
Lemnos
Myrina
Hellespontus
TROAS
PHRYGIA
MYSIA
Mytilene
Pergamum
Caicus R.
Lesbos
Hermus R.
Magnesia
Sardes
Smyrna
LYDIA
Chios
Smyrna Nova
IONIA
Cayster R.
Ephesus
Magnesia
Samos
Maeander R.
Priene
Miletus
CARIA
Delos
Patmos
Halicarnassus
Naxos
Paros
Cos
LYCIA
Cnidus
Ios
Anaphe
Thera
Rhodes
Mallia
Palaiokastro
Karpathos
Knossos
40°
39°
38°
37°
36°
26°
27°
28°
29°

The department of Greek and Roman Antiquities

Greece and Rome

Historical Summary

Introduction

The civilization of Greece and Rome is the source of our Western civilization.

The contributions of the Greeks to civilization were their superlative artistic achievements and the expansion of the range of human thought; for while the peoples of the Ancient Middle East were of necessity engaged in the solution of practical problems, when it came to those of a speculative nature, their vision was limited.

But the Greek mind soared into the spheres, and the results of its questing were the rational and inductive processes of thought applied to the investigation of natural phenomena and other subjects, many of which now form part of our intellectual disciplines, the sciences and medicine, philosophy and politics, literature and the arts.

The Roman genius, on the other hand, was political, not with the narrow patriotism which caused Greece to waste her substance in internecine warfare, but on a large and generous scale. Imperial Rome conferred immense benefits on humanity, bringing order into areas distracted for years by anarchy and civil war; by the humanization of society through the development of law; by making the roads safe for travellers and merchants thereby fostering trade, and above all by bringing peace, the Roman peace, to the greater part of her peoples for nearly three centuries.

Furthermore, although the population of the Empire consisted of many races, Roman civilization achieved, perhaps more than any other civilization has so far achieved, a homogeneity on the plane of intellect and politics, so that a man of talent of any colour or creed – even a slave – could and did take his place among the élite. Imperial Rome, the mistress of the civilized world, was never exclusive.

Prehistory

Paleolithic and Neolithic Ages of the Aegean

Hunting and food-gathering Neanderthal man was roving in Greece from about 100,000 years ago.

The first farmers, as far as is known at present, settled on the Greek mainland in Thessaly during, perhaps, the 8th and certainly the 7th millennium BC. Stock was raised and crops grown, but there was no pottery until about 6000 BC. The date of settlement in Crete is more problematic, but it may have occurred during the late 7th millennium BC. The Cycladic Islands were not settled until the latter half of the 4th millennium.

The Bronze Age, c. 3000–1100 BC

Early in the 3rd millennium, copper and later bronze, an alloy of copper and tin, gradually superseded stone for weapons and implements which resulted in the brilliant civilization of the Aegean Bronze Age, comparable with those of the Near East and Egypt.

This civilization was not uniform over the area, for there were differences between the three principal regions – the Cycladic Islands, Crete and Greece – each of which reached its apex at a different time (Map 4).

Cycladic Civilization

The Cycladic Islands were the first region to reach maturity. Strung out across the Aegean, the islands earned a prosperous living by trading, supplying Greece and Asia Minor with obsidian, a volcanic glass for blades, copper, marble and emery.

But even at the height of their prosperity life on these rocky islands must have been austere. However, agriculture was practised, barley, chick peas, aniseed and coriander being grown, and the olive and vine cultivated. The inhabitants raised sheep, goats, cattle, pigs, donkeys for transport and dogs to guard the flocks. There were numerous settlements throughout the archipelago, the majority sited on bays. Owing to the sparsity of clay for bricks, the houses often had stone walls, and their inmates were buried near their settlements. It is probable that fishing and trade were always more important to the islanders than agriculture.

Minoan (Cretan) Civilization

Bronze Age skills were brought to Crete about 3000 BC mainly by immigrants from Asia Minor where they acted as a catalyst on the Neolithic inhabitants to produce by 2000 BC a most elegant and artistic civilization.

It is known as Minoan, after the mythical king of Crete, Minos, and was based on the control of the island by powerful princes who lived in magnificent palaces at Knossos, Phaistos, Mallia, Zakro and probably elsewhere, round which, at Knossos, were smaller palaces, probably occupied by members of the royal family and high officials, and the houses, often of two storeys, of the people.

But about 1700 BC due to some catastrophe – possibly destruction by an earthquake – most of these palaces were rebuilt and it is their ruins which can be seen today. This elegant civilization lasted until about 1470 BC when, once again, the palaces were destroyed following an explosion of the volcanic island of Thera (mod. Santorin) some 90 miles to the north-east. This disaster laid waste the coastal towns and brought fire and pestilence to their populations. Afterwards only the palace at Knossos was rebuilt which was perhaps subsequently occupied by Mycenaean Greeks (see below).

Helladic (Greek) Civilization, 3000–1100 BC

Copper-working skills were brought to Greece soon after 3000 BC from north-west Asia Minor and the Cycladic islands. As a result prosperity increased: palaces were built, settlements became sizeable and overseas contacts were made. But most of the settlements were destroyed by mass burnings, mainly in the Peloponnese, by invading warriors in two waves before and after 2000 BC who are thought to have been the first Greek-speaking peoples.

Greece was reduced to poverty. However, conditions gradually improved, and by about 1600 BC contacts had been renewed with Eastern Mediterranean lands and Crete. Therefore, when Heinrich Schliemann, a wealthy German businessman, unearthed in 1876 at Mycenae a royal grave circle, it contained gold and silver vessels and jewellery of Cretan workmanship. Schliemann, who believed in the *Iliad's* historicity, was convinced he had found the graves of Agamemnon and his court, and discovered a 'new world for archaeology'. But while his grave circle was three centuries earlier than the Trojan war, his second supposition has been fully substantiated by intermittent excavations at Mycenae ever since.

Mycenae (1550–1100 BC). How Greece acquired such wealth is not known. But by the 14th century the country was controlled by warrior princes whose power was centred on the Peloponnese probably under the leadership of the Lord of Mycenae. They lived in fortified palaces, of which the 13th century ruins of Tiryns, Pylos and Mycenae are the best known examples, although others have been located at Iolcus (Thessaly), Gla and Orchomenus (Boeotia), Athens and elsewhere. Furthermore Greece had trade contacts in Sicily and south Italy, the Islands, Asia Minor, Troy, Rhodes and Cyprus, Syria, Palestine and Egypt so that her ships must have sailed the seas unmolested. She had indeed become a Mediterranean power, known to the Hittites with whom she had political contacts, possibly through Rhodes.

This brilliant civilization collapsed between 1200–1100 BC. Invaders entered Greece, probably in several waves (this was the period of the great migrations when the Hittite empire was overwhelmed, and the Sea Peoples attacked Egypt by land and sea in about 1191 BC and were repelled by Ramesses III) (see p. 132) and partially or wholly destroyed Mycenaean centres, so that refugees moved to other parts of Greece or fled overseas. It is thought that the Dorians, another branch of the Greek family, arrived about this time.

Protogeometric and Geometric Ages, c. 1100–700 BC

After the collapse of Mycenaean civilization Greece was illiterate and impoverished for about two centuries, although the use of iron became more prevalent, and Athens, whose life had escaped the interruption of the invasions, created a new style of pottery (protogeometric) which spread to other centres. Athens was, therefore, strong enough to lead a Greek revival, when interest was once again shown in countries overseas and migrations to other areas.

The migrants sailed from Attica about 1000 BC or even earlier to Asia Minor and settled on the coast between Smyrna and Miletus known later as Ionia. At the same time or earlier, Aeolians founded settlements between the gulf of Smyrna and the plain of the River Caicus, and later further north in the Troad. During the 8th century Dorians settled in Caria and the Cnidus peninsula in southern Asia Minor. These terms are derived from the Greek dialects as they were spoken in historic times.

The immigrants took with them to Asia Minor some poems enshrining the tradition of the Trojan War and its aftermath which were subsequently lengthened and elaborated. Some time, probably in the 8th century BC, this diverse material was fashioned into the epic masterpieces of the *Iliad* and the *Odyssey* by a poet of genius in Ionia (for the poems were predominantly in the Ionian dialect) whom the Greeks knew as Homer. At first they were transmitted in song by itinerant musicians at festivals and in palaces and later recited unaccompanied by the rhapsode, but when exactly the poems were committed to writing we do not know. After Homer came Hesiod, probably at the end of the 8th century, who in *Works and Days* told of the hard life of the Boeotian farmer, an exercise in realism far removed from the heroic exploits of the Trojan war.

In the 8th century, Greece renewed her overseas contacts in the Aegean and Eastern Mediterranean. At Al Mina, at the mouth of the Orontes (mod. Nahr el Assi) in North Syria, she established an important trading post. It must have been through this and other Levantine contacts that she adopted the Phoenician (North Semitic) alphabet which she adapted to Greek, and thus again became literate.

Trade, too, combined with the fact that the populations of the Greek states outstripped the capacity of the land to support them, played a great part in the founding of Greek colonial enterprises. In the west the first settlement was on Ischia in the Bay of Naples by the Euboeans who subsequently moved to Cumae near Naples in the mid-8th century and traded with the Etruscans.

The Archaic Period, 700–480 BC

Greek colonizing ventures were generally so successful that

by about 500 BC, settlements had been established on the coasts of southern Italy, Sicily (except the north-west), Marseilles, the Black Sea and its approaches, and North Africa.

In addition the period was immensely fertile intellectually with the series of great lyric poets beginning in the middle of the 7th century: Archilochos of Paros, a mercenary soldier and bitter critic of life, Alcman, the choral poet of Sparta, Alcaeus of Mytilene, an adept at political invective, his compatriot, Sappho, of the exquisite love songs, and the greatest of all, the choral odes of Pindar. This was also the period of the first scientists, Thales (fl. 585 BC), Anaximander (c. 610–540 BC), the first to consider man in evolutionary terms, Anaximenes (fl. 546 BC), Ionians from Miletus, and Heraclitus of Ephesus (fl. 500 BC), who all rejected the mythological and magical interpretations of the universe hitherto current, and gave explanations of its structure based on observed phenomena.

In politics we find that monarchy had disappeared in illiterate times, and that the government of the Greek states was aristocratic and exclusive, which caused the mercantile classes and prosperous farmers to stir up revolt. The leadership was often taken by a dissident noble who skilfully made himself dictator. Athens did not escape these troubles; but the great reforms introduced by Solon (594/574 BC) and Cleisthenes (507 BC) partially mitigated their effects, and also laid the foundations of Athenian democracy.

Sparta, a Dorian state of the Southern Peloponnese, was the greatest military power in Greece. Her educational system trained Spartan children to be soldiers under rigorous discipline from the age of seven, and the political system exempted the ruling aristocracy from any form of work except military service so that she always possessed a proficient standing army. By means of it she formed an alliance of most of the Peloponnesian states, known now as the Peloponnesian League, which in the 6th century and later exercised a preponderating influence on Greek affairs.

The Persian Invasion, 490–479 BC

The Greek states were soon to have need of military virtues. In 499 BC the cities of Ionia, which had formed part of the

Persian empire after the defeat of Croesus of Lydia by Cyrus the Great in 546 BC, revolted and help was sent to them by Athens and Eretria (Euboea).

The Persian king, Darius the Great, suppressed the revolt by c. 494 BC, and determined to punish these two cities. A Persian army landed in 490 BC on the island of Euboea, capturing Eretria, and then crossed over to the bay of Marathon in Attica, where the Athenians marched out to meet it. A fierce battle was fought in which the Persians were utterly defeated.

However, Persia, a mighty power, was not deflected from her purpose, and Xerxes, the successor to Darius, returned with a large army. He crossed the Hellespont on a bridge of boats in 480 BC, marched through Thrace and Thessaly, and reached the pass of Thermopylae defended by the Spartans and their allies, for the defence of Hellas was a combined effort of Sparta, Athens and some (but not all) other states. Xerxes, however, turned this strong position, the Spartans were annihilated, and the way to central Greece lay open. The Greek fleet, mainly Athenian ships, evacuated the population of Athens, and on the island of Salamis in the Saronic Gulf new headquarters were set up.

When Xerxes reached Athens, he disposed of the few men fighting a delaying action on the Acropolis and burned its temples; but by then it was early September, and it would soon become difficult to supply the army by sea. He decided to bring the campaign to a quick end by a naval victory, and ordered his fleet to attack the Greek navy. But the Greeks lured the Persian ships into the narrows between Attica and Salamis and there destroyed them, inflicting great loss of life. Xerxes returned overland to Asia, leaving part of his army in Greece which, in the following spring, although reinforced, was defeated by the Greeks at a great battle at Plataea in Boeotia. The threat to Greece was removed; but the war was not over.

The Classical Period, 479–336 BC

Athens

The defeat of Persia was followed by fratricidal struggles among the victors, and the next hundred years saw the attempt by the three most powerful states – Athens, Sparta and Thebes, to control the Greek mainland and the Aegean area.

Athens made the first attempt. After Salamis her navy was supreme in the eastern Mediterranean, and a maritime League was formed, with its headquarters on Delos, under her leadership to liberate the Asiatic Greek cities still in Persian hands and to continue the war against Persia. But by the mid-5th century, Athens employed the League fleet to force Greek states to become subject to her, thus transforming the League into the Athenian empire, although she continued to fight the Persians wherever they were accessible. Many were her successes, but she finally met disaster in 454 BC when about 200 of her ships supporting a revolt by the Egyptians against the Persian king were trapped on the Nile and destroyed, as was later a relieving force.

This disaster, combined with her attempt at pre-eminence on the mainland which had eventually caused revolts against her in central Greece, supported by the Spartans and their allies, had so taxed her resources that she made peace with Artaxerxes, king of Persia, in about 449 BC, and with the Spartans in 445 BC.

The process of democratization begun by Cleisthenes had been continued under the guidance of the aristocrat Pericles, and by this time any citizen of Athens was eligible for election to high office and those who served the state in whatever capacity were remunerated. With the conclusion of peace, Pericles initiated a vast building programme to replace the temples on the Acropolis destroyed by the Persians (Fig. 29), and to erect new temples and secular buildings, all of which were paid for out of the funds of the Delian League and gave relief to unemployment.

Literature, too, had a prodigious flowering. The tragedies of Aeschylus (525/4–456 BC), Sophocles (c. 496–406 BC), and Euripides (c. 485–c. 406 BC) were performed at the Dionysiac festivals in the great theatre of Dionysos at the foot of the Acropolis, as were later the comedies of Aristophanes (c. 457/445–c. 385 BC). The first extant complete history, that of Herodotus (c. 491–c. 431 BC), was written, and later the analytical history of Thucydides (460/455–c. 400 BC), which was continued more prosaically by Xenophon (428/7–c. 354 BC). It was also an age of moral philosophy taught by Socrates (469–399 BC), who never wrote a line, Plato (c. 429–347 BC), and Aristotle (384–322

Fig. 29. Model of the Acropolis, Athens, as it was about 400 BC. In the centre foreground is the Propylaea (entrance), and to the right the small temple of Athena Nike. Beyond on the north (left) side stands the Erectheum and opposite, dominating the Acropolis, is the Parthenon

BC) who was concerned, too, with the natural sciences.

Sparta

The Peloponnesian War. In 431 BC war broke out again between Athens and Sparta which, with one short respite, lasted till 404 BC. Its cause, says Thucydides, was Sparta's fear of the increase in Athenian power. This fear was fully justified by the growth of the Athenian empire.

But after the death of Pericles in 429 BC, the Athenian leaders, although obtaining some notable successes, were not of the same calibre intellectually. A vast expedition to Sicily in 415 BC to stop corn supplies to the Peloponnese was, through bad generalship, utterly destroyed; and although the Athenian fleet was rebuilt it never regained the overall command of the sea. In 405 BC the Spartan admiral, Lysander, was able to wipe out the last Athenian ships at Aegospotami on the Hellespont (Dardanelles), thus cutting the Athenian corn supplies from south Russia. In 404 BC Athens was starved into surrender.

After the fall of Athens Sparta took over the Athenian empire, except the Asiatic Greek cities which reverted to Persia. But they rebelled and called on Sparta, as the current defender of Greek liberty, for assistance. A considerable army was sent which campaigned successfully from 396–394 BC.

But the Persian king, Artaxerxes II, realized that this success could not have occurred without Spartan command of the sea, and he caused a large fleet to be built which in 394 BC destroyed the Spartan fleet. Meanwhile Persian envoys had distributed gold to Sparta's former allies, Corinth and Thebes, Boeotia (who realized that the sole result of their war effort had been to increase Sparta's power), and to Athens, who had now restored democracy and was rebuilding her fleet to regain her empire. Sparta, therefore, was faced with a formidable coalition of central Greek states. But neither side could prevail; and in 387/386 when the Persians called a conference, the weary Greeks agreed to the terms imposed by what is known as the 'King's Peace'.

Thebes

One of the stipulations of the King's Peace was the autonomy of states, interpreted by Sparta as the right to prevent any combination inimical to her interests. But Sparta was now a broken reed, deficient in military manpower. Her weakness became obvious when in an attempt to break up the Boeotian federation recently founded by Thebes, she was utterly defeated by Epaminondas, the Theban general, on the plain of Leuctra in 371 BC.

Thebes now menaced Greek liberty. She campaigned in Thessaly, intervened in Macedonia, and placed a garrison on Athenian territory. Above all she invaded the Peloponnese four times and twice unsuccessfully assaulted Sparta; but on the last expedition the Peloponnesian states and Athens were allied against her. A great battle was fought at Mantinea in Arcadia in 362 BC, which the Thebans won; but Epaminondas was slain and his victorious troops made peace.

As a result Athens became once again the leading power in Greece. Since her defeat in 404 BC she had partly re-established her Aegean empire.

Macedonia

But in the north a power had arisen, Macedonia, whose population was of Greek stock, and whose king, Philip II (359–336 BC) had been trained in the military arts at Thebes under Epaminondas. After securing Macedonia's own frontiers, Philip turned his attention to divided Greece. In 338 BC, in spite of the warnings of the orator, Demosthenes, he decisively defeated Athens, Thebes and a large coalition of states at the battle of Chaeronea. At last Greece was united by the king of a people whom she regarded as barbarians.

After his victory Philip summoned a congress of Hellenic states at Corinth, and outlined his plan for the conquest of the Persian empire. He was murdered before he could put it into effect.

Alexander the Great, 336–323 BC

However, Philip's son, Alexander, put the plan into operation. He crossed the Hellespont in 334 BC with about 40,000 men and conquered the entire Persian empire – even adding to it – in 11 years. His empire comprised most of Asia from the Aegean to the Punjab south of the Caucasus and the Caspian, and Egypt, but excluding northern Asia Minor, eastern Turkey and Arabia.

But he was never able to organize this vast area. After his return from India in 323 BC, he caught a fever and died in the palace of Nebuchadnezzar in Babylon in his thirty-third year.

The Hellenistic Period, 323–30 BC

After Alexander's death his generals at first supported the empire; but before long the members of his family were summarily disposed of, and the generals fought among themselves for supremacy.

Finally three were left: Lysimachus who controlled Macedonia, Thrace, Thessaly and part of Asia Minor; Seleucus, who ruled over most of the Asiatic provinces, and Ptolemy, king of Egypt and Libya who also controlled the sea. Lysimachus and Seleucus fought at Corupedium in Lydia, Asia Minor, in 281 BC when Lysimachus was killed. But when Seleucus stepped ashore in Thrace to claim his European spoils of victory, he was assassinated, and the last chance of uniting the greater part of Alexander's empire was lost.

From about 270 BC there were three principal Hellenistic kingdoms. Macedonia, which held a fluctuating control of Greece, and the Seleucid and Ptolemaic kingdoms, which fought one another for possession of part of Syria and southern Asia Minor. In addition a small kingdom, Pergamum, had been created in Asia Minor (c. 241 BC) during a period of Seleucid weakness which subsequently became an ally of Rome.

The three principal states were the most powerful in the eastern Mediterranean until Rome turned her attention to Greece, which occurred in 215 BC when Philip V of Macedonia made an alliance with Hannibal, then invading Italy in the second Punic (Carthaginian) war. The Roman Senate did not forget this hostile act, and in the second of its Macedonian wars, Philip was defeated in 197 BC by the army of T. Quinctius Flamininus at Cynoscephalae in Thessaly. He was forced to abandon Thrace and Thessaly, and the fortresses in Greece which had enabled him to control the country. In 196 BC Flamininus declared the Greek cities to be free and withdrew his troops to Italy.

Rome had never intended to make conquests in Greece and the East but events combined to force her to do so. In

196 BC, Antiochus the Great (223–187 BC), the Seleucid king, landed in Thrace which, abandoned by Philip, he considered as part of the Seleucid empire. He was later invited by the Aetolian League (one of the federations formed in Greece after the death of Alexander – belated attempts at unity) to liberate Greece and was promised a general uprising. The Romans, thoroughly alarmed, once again crossed the Adriatic, and as Antiochus had only brought with him a small army and as no Greek revolt took place, they inflicted a severe defeat on him at Thermopylae in 191 BC. The following year they followed him to Asia Minor and annihilated his army at Magnesia ad-Sipylum.

Antiochus was obliged to surrender territory in Asia Minor mainly to the benefit of Rome's ally, Pergamum, and the Roman armies withdrew in 188 BC. But his loss of prestige was such that the Asiatic provinces of his empire seceded. Indeed Seleucid power was so impaired that in spite of transient recoveries it had, by 150 BC, sunk to the level of a local dynasty.

Meanwhile the Romans had decided that the only way to prevent a recrudescence of Macedonian power and influence over Greece was to annexe the country, and this was achieved in 148 BC, after the fourth Macedonian war, when Alexander's homeland became a Roman province. The Senate had also discovered that the freedom accorded to the Greek states included the freedom to quarrel among themselves, which necessitated Roman interference in Greek affairs, a procedure much resented by the Greeks. As a result in 146 BC, the Achaean League (Peloponnese) voted for war. But its armies were heavily defeated in central Greece by the Romans, and also later at Corinth which was razed to the ground. Thus the Romans brought peace to the Greeks, a peace they had never been able to attain themselves.

In 133 BC the last king of Pergamum died, leaving his kingdom to the Roman people which the Romans transformed into the province of Asia. In the 1st century BC, the Hellenistic world became involved in Rome's Asiatic wars and its terrible civil wars.

Ptolemaic Egypt suffered least. It did not experience a serious Roman invasion until the end of the civil wars when in 31 BC the fleet of Octavius, Caesar's great-nephew and heir, defeated that of Antony at Actium, off the west coast of Greece. Antony and Cleopatra (she had provided some of the ships), fled by sea to Egypt, and were followed in the winter of 31–30 BC by Octavius. Rather than fall into his hands they both committed suicide. Egypt became a Roman province and Octavius the first Roman emperor, Augustus (27 BC–AD 14).

The Roman Empire, 27 BC–AD 476

Augustus, the victor of the civil wars, was the founder of the Roman empire. The greatest of Roman statesmen, his legislative, administrative and military reforms formed the basis of Roman government for the next 300 years. He also understood and sympathized with the ordinary man.

His most important task was to make the frontiers secure; and immediately after the battle of Actium the first steps were taken which resulted in the frontier being moved to the line of the Danube. He carried out territorial rectifications round the Mediterranean basin so that by the end of his reign he laid down the principle that the empire had reached the limits of profitable territorial expansion. The majority of his successors agreed with him, although Claudius (AD 41–54) invaded Britain (p. 57), and Trajan (AD 98–117) crossed the Danube to conquer Dacia, and to extend Roman territory beyond the Euphrates, the latter conquest being abandoned by his successor.

But the Romans, for all their statecraft, were never able to settle satisfactorily the problem of the Imperial succession. At the end of Augustus' dynasty (the Julio-Claudian) there was no recognized heir, which provided the opportunity to the Praetorian Guard and the armies to nominate a successor and resulted in civil war and four emperors in one year. From the reign of Nerva (AD 96–98) to that of Antoninus Pius (AD 138–161) the emperors, who were childless, adopted as heirs during their own lifetime men of proven ability so that there were no dynastic crises. Unfortunately, the adopted heir of Antoninus Pius, the philosopher Marcus Aurelius, reverted to the hereditary principle and was succeeded by Commodus, his unworthy son, who was subsequently murdered at the instigation of the Praetorian prefect.

In the 3rd century, from about AD 235, the empire sank into military anarchy, when emperor after emperor was proclaimed by the troops or occasionally by the Senate and then murdered. The barbarians seized the opportunity to invade along the Rhine-Danube frontier; but thanks to the military genius and determination of some of the emperors, in particular the Illyrian emperors, Claudius Gothicus (AD 268–270) and Aurelian (AD 270–275), the empire survived to become under Diocletian (AD 284–305) and Constantine the Great (AD 306–337) a complete autocracy. In AD 313 by the Edict of Milan, Constantine accorded freedom to each individual to worship as he pleased, thus legalizing the practice of Christianity.

According to tradition, which contains some elements of history, Rome was founded about the middle of the 8th century BC, and in the 2nd century AD ruled over the civilized world. In AD 330 the capital was transferred to Constantinople, and at the end of that century the empire was divided into the Western and Eastern empires under separate emperors. In the 5th century the Western empire (including Britain) was overwhelmed by the Germanic invasions, and the last Western emperor was deposed in AD 476. But the East Roman empire protected the European nations from the Asiatic nomads until they were securely established. Constantinople finally fell to the Ottoman Turks in 1453.

Greek and Roman Antiquities

Ground Floor:
1. Cycladic Room; 2. Bronze Age Room;
3. Early Greek Room; 4. Room of the Kouroi;
5. Room of the Harpy Tomb; 6. Bassae Room;
7. Nereid Room; 8. Duveen Gallery; 9. Room of the Caryatid;
10. Payava Room; 11. Architectural Room;
12. Mausoleum Room; 13. Hellenistic Room;
14. First Roman Room; 15. Second Roman Room

First Floor:
Terracotta Room; Greek and Roman Life Room;
Greek Corridor; First and Second Vase Rooms;
Cyprus Room

The Geographical Area

The Mediterranean basin, where the summers are hot and dry and the winters mild with occasional short-lived cold spells, is the area where the Greeks and the Romans created Western civilization.

The Greek mainland is divided by mountain ranges running mainly north and south, and the coast is deeply indented. The cultivable land, of which there is comparatively little, is mostly situated in the east. The centre of the Greek world was the Aegean, and the majority of ancient Greek cities of Europe and Asia were sited within sight and sound of it (Map 4). The sea was the lifeblood of the population for Greece was dependant, particularly in classical times, on imported grain from Sicily, southern Italy, South Russia and Egypt. Egypt, too, was imperial Rome's granary. After Alexander's conquests, the Greek world included both European and Asiatic geographical and climatic features.

The Roman empire, on the other hand, included all the lands of the Mediterranean seaboard as well as Britain and those areas of Asia to the Euphrates, and of Europe south of the Rhine and the Danube, the latter with its greater rainfall and more severe winters. But it was unified by the Mediterranean and a fine system of roads which facilitated the movement of troops. Such mobility was vital for the

Roman army was always too small for the tasks allotted to it, probably never at any time more than 500,000 men.

Prehistory

The Department's prehistoric exhibits date from the Greek Bronze Age (3000–1100 BC) (p. 179), and are displayed in the order in which the three principal regions reached the apex of their prosperity.

The Cycladic Room

Cycladic Civilization

Sculpture

The inhabitants of the Cycladic islands lived sufficiently above the subsistence level to be able to export their surplus goods to many parts of the Mediterranean, such as marble idols (Fig. 30), at first fiddle-shaped and then the more lifelike female figure [case 2, A5, A6, 2800–2500 BC; 1932 10–18 1, c. 2500–2000 BC; case 3, A17, 2500–2000 BC]. These idols are thought to represent the Mediterranean fertility goddess, and they were found in both houses and graves on the islands.

Stone vessels and pottery

A stone vessel of characteristic Cycladic shape is the large marble vase [case 2, 43 5–7, 76, 2800–2500 BC], but the circular marble box [TB614, 2500–2000 BC] is Egyptian inspired. Pottery was hand-made, and among characteristic shapes and designs are the incised, burnished jar [case 1, A301, 2800–2500 BC] and the 'sauceboat' covered with a lustrous black paint [A263, c. 2500–2200 BC]. Later, linear decoration in black paint was employed, as on the multiple cluster vase, probably for offerings [A343] and the jug [A341], both dated c. 2000 BC, followed by spiral and curvilinear designs and representations of animal life.

After 2000 BC no more marble idols and vases were made and Cretan influence began to permeate the region. Finally, Cycladic art, after 1550 BC, could not be distinguished from that of Crete and mainland Greece.

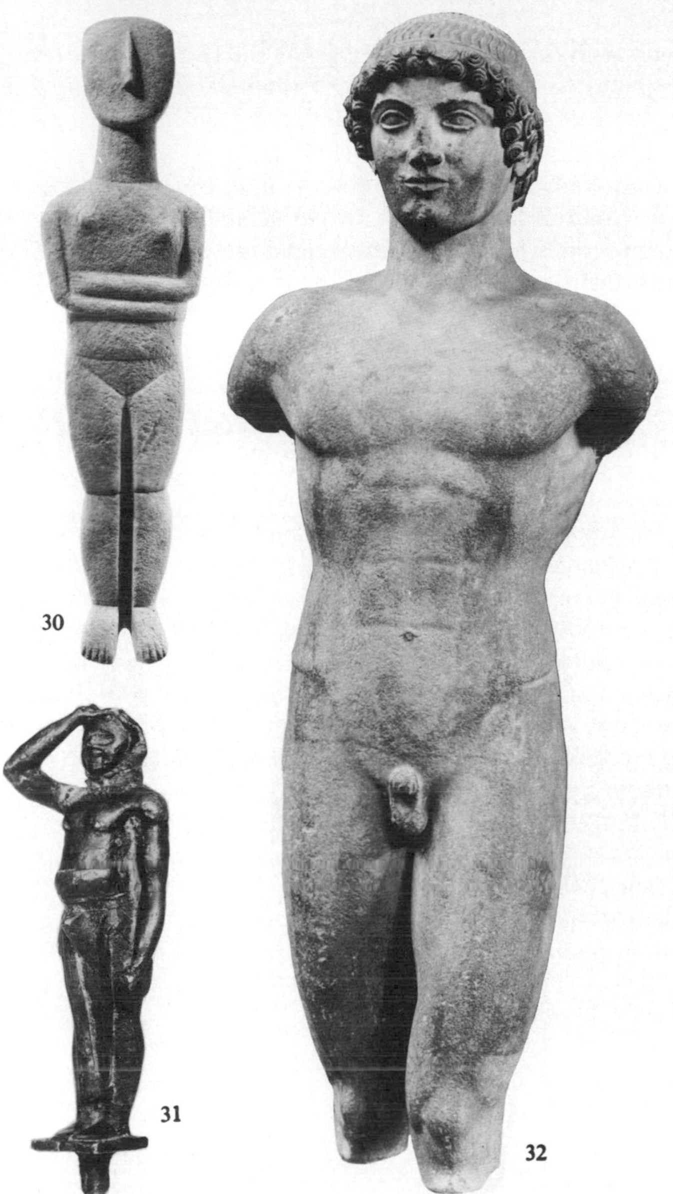

Fig. 30. Cycladic marble idol, c. 2500–2000 BC
Fig. 31. Bronze figure of a worshipper, arm raised to forehead in a gesture of adoration, see page 196
Fig. 32. The Strangford 'Apollo', still with a faint trace of the archaic smile, but with the body anatomically correct, c. 490 BC

Bronze Age Room

Minoan (Cretan) Civilization

The Palaces

Little is known about the first great palaces (built c. 2000 BC). However, their successors of c. 1700 BC (p. 180) were probably similar but on a more imposing scale. The various sections of the palaces were grouped round a central rectangular courtyard, and were often several storeys high.

The palaces were without fortifications and consequently grew outwards, but the important buildings, such as the state apartments, faced inwards on to the court. The interior walls were painted, the majority of the surviving frescoes dating from 1550 BC. They consisted of two classes: court ceremonial, religious festivals, the national sport of bull acrobatics [case 1, 1966 3–28 1, c. 1600 BC], and scenes from nature.

The palace populations were large and necessitated vast stocks of food. Oil and grain were stored in huge jars [A739, 1450–1400 BC] in the palace basement. Although little plate has been found, the king almost certainly ate and drank from gold and silver vessels [case 1, no. 4. Aegina cup, 1700–1500 BC]. The palaces were surrounded by houses and narrow, cobbled streets, and there were small villages and isolated farms in the countryside.

Religion

The chief deity of Cretan religion was a Nature Goddess under various aspects. Other deities were immanent in natural objects such as streams, and tree and pillar worship were also practised. Kings and queens were evidently priests, and large areas in the palace, probably the court, were used for religious ceremonies, ritual dances and perhaps even the sport of bull leaping in which girls took part.

There were no temples: worshippers brought their offerings to shrines and sanctuaries in caves and on mountain peaks sacred to particular gods, such as the votive clay jar found in the Kamares cave [case 1, 1938 11–19 1, 1700–1550 BC], where pottery offerings predominated; and the bronze male worshipper (Fig. 31) in the act of adoration [1918 1–1 114, c. 1600 BC]. Terracotta animals, too, were offered as a substitute for sacrifice [1907 1–19 33, 34, 31, 2000–1700 BC]. There were also domestic shrines in palaces and large houses.

Burial practices varied. Clay coffins were first used from about 2200 BC but only became popular after 1400 BC. Two shapes were made, the bath tub [A744, 1400–1300 BC] and the rectangular chest of four legs with a pitched roof [A746, 1400–1300 BC], a copy of a wooden clothes chest.

Dress, jewellery and seals

Male dress was a tight belt, sheath and loin cloth [1918 1–1 114], while women wore a long bell-shaped skirt with a girdle at the waist, and a bodice with a high collar open at the breast.

Both sexes wore jewellery of which the Department has a fine collection [case 1, nos. 1–8]. The gold pendant depicting the 'Master of Animals', a deity, who clasps a water bird in each hand and stands in a field of lotuses, is a superb piece (see also Greek and Roman Life Room).

Cretan seals were made in the form of beads and pendants and were worn from the wrist.

Pottery

Only a few examples are exhibited of the many beautiful Minoan pottery styles. An interesting early piece is the Vasiliki ware 'teapot' [case 1, A425, c. 2500 BC] with the mottled surface in imitation of stone vases. Its shape is based on a metal vessel which originated in Asia Minor.

Subsequently, white designs were drawn on the mottled background and then on black paint. The drinking cup, decorated with pink and white lines and sometimes spirals, was a characteristic shape of this time, and also of the first palace period [case 1, A477, 2000–1900 BC, from Knossos; A579, 1700–1550 BC, from Zakro] when the most beautiful wheel-made Kamares pottery, made mainly for palace use, was decorated with natural forms and curvilinear patterns incorporated in numerous imaginative and colourful designs.

Pattern and floral styles, with sometimes the two combined, were characteristic of the late second palace period (1550–1450 BC), with the addition of marine life, all depicted in dark paint on a light background [case 1, A650,

1500–1450 BC. Ritual vessel from Palaikastro]. After 1450 BC natural forms became stylized, as they were on the Greek mainland.

Stone vessels

Beautiful stone vessels were made at all periods for the Cretan carver knew how to take full advantage of his materials, as can be seen from the stone dish [case 1, 1921 5–15 23, 2500–2000 BC], and the stone bowl [1914 3–21 1, c. 1600 BC].

Writing

A civilized society cannot exist without writing, and from the time of the first palaces (2000 BC) the Cretans used a hieroglyphic script. Between 1900 and 1700 BC they evolved a linear script known as Linear A, not yet deciphered but which almost certainly recorded a non-Greek language, as on the bronze axe head [case 1, 1954 10–20 1, 1700–1550 BC]. After 1470 BC, Linear A was supplanted by Linear B, deciphered as an early form of Greek in 1952 by the late Michael Ventris. Tablets inscribed in this script have been found at Knossos [1910 4–23 1, c. 1400 BC], which may indicate that it was occupied by mainland Greeks and that the hegemony of the Aegean had passed to Mycenae.

Mycenaean (Late Helladic) Civilization

The palace at Mycenae stands on a spur of the mountains overlooking the Argive plain. Its principal feature, common to Mycenaean palaces, was a *megaron*, a unit consisting of an entrance porch on a court, a vestibule and a large hall with a central hearth and a throne. The ceilings and walls of the hall were decorated with frescoes, Cretan in technique but Mycenaean in subject – a battle scene.

The palace and its dependant building were surrounded by a massive wall about 50 ft high and 15 ft wide. Inside this fortification was an open space, perhaps as a refuge from invaders for those living near the fortress. The majority would be in the service of the king and would include farmers who would bring animals for food during a siege.

Today the ruins of Mycenae stand gaunt and sombre, but in the 14th and 13th centuries BC Mycenaean palaces must have been swarming with people, judging from administrative records written in Linear B script on tablets found in the citadel at Mycenae and in the palace at Pylos.

Arms

For instance, military equipment for the garrison was kept in the stores, such as the bronze sword with the central spine and wooden hilt probably ornamented in metal [case 2, 2753, 1400–1100 BC], and the socketed bronze spearhead [23, 1400–1100 BC]. There would also be chariots, represented in the Department by the stylized terracotta two-horse chariot from Rhodes [case 2, B2, c. 1300 BC], and the amusing painting of a chariot procession on a mixing bowl [case 3, 1925 11–1 3, from Maroni, Cyprus, 1400–1300 BC. See also Greek and Roman Life Room].

Dress

Upper-class women in Minoan Crete and Mycenaean Greece appear to have had a good deal of liberty in contradistinction to women in classical times, and a boar-hunting fresco from Tiryns shows two aristocratic young women driving a chariot, presumably to watch the sport. They are wearing long belted robes, the customary outdoor dress and most likely indoor garb too; but the ceremonial dress of court ladies was a short-sleeved jacket with a blouse, and a long skirt with flounces.

Men wore a tunic of wool or linen with short sleeves, and a short flaring kilt over the thigh. The cloth for these garments was made by spinners, weavers and fullers who, so Linear B tablets record, were on the establishment of Mycenaean palaces.

The young women mentioned above have elaborately curled hair which would have been dressed by personal servants or slaves, and they may have looked at their reflections in a bronze mirror with ivory handles [case 3, 97 4–1 872, 12th century from Cyprus]. Perfume was also available, and was probably used to scent the ointment kept in painted pottery containers (alabastron) [case 2, A651, probably from Egypt, 1500–1450 BC].

Metalwork

Jewellery [case 2, 1–9] adorned both sexes and was influenced by Crete. The rock crystal and carnelian beads made handsome necklaces, while the relief glass beads were worn as bracelets and round the neck. A finger ring much in vogue in Minoan and Mycenaean times was that with a plain convex bezel [873, see Greek and Roman Life Room for Mycenaean jewellery from Cyprus].

In addition the palace goldsmiths made plate for the king's table, for example, the gold cup [case 2, 820, c. 1500 BC], the silver cup [case 3, 821] with the spool handle of Cretan origin, and the silver bowl [97 4–1 300], the latter two from Cyprus and dated 1400–1300 BC.

Pottery

At the beginning of the Mycenaean period the pottery of mainland Greece was a poor reproduction of Cretan pottery, but the fabric was of excellent quality. From 1500 BC natural forms were employed for decoration, but unlike Cretan pottery, they were stylized and formal. The only piece exhibited here from the Early Mycenaean period is a cup from Knossos which is not particularly representative [case 2, A634, 1500–1400 BC].

But there is a most comprehensive collection for the period 1400–1200 BC which demonstrates the uniformity of the Mycenaean style over a wide area. The shapes include tankards [case 2, A848, 1300–1200 BC]; stemmed cups [case 3, C608, 1300–1200 BC]; deep bowls [case 3, C416, 1300–1200 BC]; cut-away neck jugs [case 4, C579, 1400–1300 BC]; stirrup jars for the storage and export of wine and oil [case 4, C501, c. 1300 BC]; ointment jars [case 4, C488, 1300–1200 BC]; and jars [case 4, C372, c. 1400–1300 BC].

There were two styles of decoration: the pattern style with motifs which included scales, spirals, chevrons, octopuses and flowers, although often the greater part of the vessel was painted with horizontal bands, leaving little space for decoration; and the pictorial style which concentrated on chariot scenes on large jars in the 14th century, and animals, sphinxes and birds on deep bowls in the 13th century.

The later styles, when Mycenaean power was breaking up (1200–1100 BC) are regional and are represented by the Rhodian bowl with statuettes on the rim [case 2, A950].

Religion

The religion of the Mycenaeans is thought to have been similar to that of the Minoans, a nature religion (p. 196), yet it is known that some of the deities were those familiar in later times, Zeus, Demeter, Dionysos, Hera, Poseidon, Athena, Artemis and Ares being mentioned on Linear B tablets. Probably the stylized terracotta figures of the 14th and 13th centuries represent goddesses [case 2, B12, B5].

Mycenaean princes were buried in vast, domed tombs excavated in the hillside and lined with stone. They were entered by passages cut through the slope of the hill. The best preserved, the 13th century 'Treasury of Atreus' named erroneously after the father of Agamemnon, is about 50 ft high and about 50 ft wide. Its doors, probably of bronze, were flanked by green marble engaged columns which, restored from original pieces, can be seen on the wall outside the entrance to the Cycladic Room [A51 and A52], with indications above of the structure of the upper façade, giving an idea of the immensity of the tomb. A suggested reconstruction of the entrance and its decoration can be seen also in Room 2 where there are fragments of its carved marble façade [A54, A53, A55, c. 1250 BC].

Early Greek Room

Protogeometric and Geometric Ages 1100–700 BC

Pottery

The unbroken sequence of Athenian pottery from the debased sub-Mycenaean style through the Protogeometric [case 2, A1123, Attic, c. 950 BC] to the vigorous and highly original Geometric style, such as the circular toilet box with four horses standing in a row on the lid [1910, 11–21 1, Attic, 760–740 BC] indicates continuity at Athens when other centres were partially or wholly destroyed by the invaders of Mycenaean centres.

Metalwork

The large brooches (fibulae) from Macedonia and Boeotia

[case 1; case 3], and the rare gold brooches to be seen later [case 9], denote the change at this time to Greek dress; while the bronze ornaments and the figures of men and animals [case 4] are characteristic of the period. But we can see the results of contact with the East in the 9th and 8th centuries (Geometric period) in the gold jewellery in case 9 where the eastern techniques of filigree, granulation and inlay are freely employed.

The Archaic Period, 700–480 BC

The Archaic period was not only creative in literature and science (p. 183), but due to the Near Eastern contacts was equally so in art. The Greeks, as we shall see, appropriated oriental motifs, modifying and beautifying them far beyond anything accomplished in the East.

Sculpture

The earliest Greek statues in stone and bronze now in existence were made between 675–650 BC. The Department's exhibits come from the Ionic cities of Asia Minor and from the native states in the south which were greatly under Greek influence.

Map 4 shows that Ionia's neighbours were Mysia, Lydia, Phrygia (the latter succeeding the Hittites on the Anatolian plateau) in the east, and Caria and Lycia in the south; and from Xanthos, capital of Lycia, comes the Lion tomb [B286, 600–575 BC], probably carved by a Greek artist working for the Lycian nobleman who proposed to occupy it. The tomb stood on the top of a 10 ft pillar, both being cut from a single block of marble. On one side, in low relief, are a horseman and attendant and a heavily armed warrior; on the other, in which was the entrance, a combat between a man and a lion. The front depicts a lion in high relief holding a bull's head between its paws.

Adjacent to the Lion tomb are four seated statues [B280, c. 510 BC; B276, c. 560 BC; B278, c. 560 BC; B271, c. 580 BC], which, with other statues, recumbent lions [B281, c. 575 BC; B282, c. 520 BC] and stone coffins lined the Sacred Way from the pilgrim port of Panormus to the Temple of Apollo at Didyma, 11 miles south of the Ionic city of Miletus. In the 6th century the oracle at Didyma attracted pilgrims from all over the Greek world who, with their offerings, brought much wealth to the temple.

The first statue [B280] represents a woman, while the third [B278] is identified by an alphabetic inscription on the right side of the chair: 'I am Chares, son of Kleisis, ruler of Teichioussa. The statue belongs to (i.e., is dedicated to) Apollo'. Chares was a petty potentate of the modern Karakevi. The temple at Didyma was eventually sacked and burned by the Persians in c. 494 BC.

Another famous temple was that of Artemis at Ephesus, a prosperous Ionic city situated near the mouth of the river Cayster. Three temples had already stood on its site when Ephesus and other Ionic cities were conquered by King Croesus of Lydia, whose riches were, and still are, proverbial [see the reliefs B269, B270, from Sardis, Croesus' capital]. But the conqueror, a Philhellene, made substantial contributions to the new fourth temple, dedicating, Herodotus says, 'several pillars'; and on the inscribed marble fragments from a column base on the wall [B16], one bears the letters 'BA', probably representing 'basileus' (king), and the other 'KR', perhaps the beginning of the king's name, Kroisos (for the development of the Greek alphabet see Greek and Roman Life Room; Western Asiatic Antiquities, Room of Writing).

Architecture

In architecture the Greeks were undoubtedly influenced by Egypt, with which they became familiar as mercenaries and traders from about the mid-7th century; and those huge Egyptian stone temples with their carved columns certainly contributed to the evolution of the two principal orders of Greek architecture at the end of the 7th century, the Doric on the mainland and the Ionic in East Greek lands [see Room 11].

The Archaic temple of Ephesus was a vast building of the Ionic order, with its central chamber surrounded by a double row of columns to which a third row was added on the main front [see restoration]. An unusual but not unique feature was the sculptured figures at the base of the columns, of which only fragments now remain [B89, B121, B90, B91] and the sculpture from the parapet of the roof [B161]. But the most arresting fragment is the head of the young woman

[B91], with its enigmatic smile which is more subtle than the customary joyful expression on archaic statues.

Metalwork

By the 7th century BC gold and silver plate were being dedicated in Greek sanctuaries. The vessels were either imported from the eastern Mediterranean or, when metals became available, made in Greece. Little plate has survived, but the Department possesses a gold bowl [case 6, 1574, 7th century BC], found in Sicily which may be of East Greek manufacture.

Jewellery is represented by a votive deposit from the archiac Temple of Ephesus [case 9, 8th–7th century BC] which has a strong oriental element. The Rhodian pectoral ornaments [case 11] consisting of embossed plaques, often with granulations, show both Asiatic (the winged deity with lions) and Egyptian influence.

Bronze-work too was influenced by the Near East. Cauldron attachments (and undoubtedly cauldrons) were imported from the metal-working country of Urartu (eastern Turkey), which for a time in the 8th century controlled North Syria. These attachments were copied and modified to suit Greek taste as, for example, the handle in the form of a siren which, in position, peered into the cauldron [case 6, 1914 4–11 1, Greek, c. 725 BC], and the head of a griffin [case 6, 70 3–15 16, Greek, c. 650 BC]. In addition, lions, palmettes, floral designs and other oriental motifs were taken over and embellished.

The period is also notable for the development of the bronze statuette and an early example from Rhodes, the man on a camel [case 6, 222, c. 700–600 BC] shows the influence of the Orient. From about 575–450 BC bronze figures had reached a state of perfection rarely equalled, witness the mounted warrior from Grumentum, south Italy [case 7, 1904, 7–3 1, c. 550 BC], and the bibulous, smiling banqueteer [case 8, 1954 10–18 1, c. 520 BC].

Pottery

In the 7th century the maritime city of Corinth which was well placed to trade with both Asia and the West, developed a new pottery style suggested by the stylized human, animal and plant forms which had long been a feature of Asiatic art.

Corinthian potters adapted these motifs by painting human and animal figures in silhouette, and incising their inner structures with a sharp point through the black paint – the beginning of the Greek black figure technique.

This pottery is known as Protocorinthian and is seen at its best in small vessels such as the tiny perfume bottle from Thebes [case 6, 89 4–18 1, c. 640 BC], where three friezes featuring a battle, a horse race and a hare hunt are fitted into three registers totalling less than 2 in. in height. Furthermore, Corinthian pottery became exceedingly gay with the introduction of colours, as on the wine jug showing the oriental motif of a beast with one head and two bodies [case 6, 60 2–1 18, c. 600 BC]. Large quantities of Corinthian wares were exported, but in order to meet the demand, potters were obliged to lower their standards of painting.

But in the first half of the 6th century the Athenians entered the export market, as can be seen from the Attic wine jug from Nola, southern Italy, depicting Hermes between two sphinxes [case 7, B32, c. 600–580 BC]. Their superior technical skill and superb figure drawing as, for example, on the drinking cup from Vulci, Italy [B421, c. 550 BC], enabled them to displace Corinth. Indeed from about 565–535 BC, they produced some of the finest Greek vases ever made, many of which are proudly signed by the painter, such as the storage jar [B210, c. 540 BC] portraying Achilles slaying the Amazon queen, Penthesilea, with the signature of the painter Exekias.

Moreover between 530 and 520 BC, they invented the red figure technique, i.e., the background was painted black while the figures were reserved in the red clay, and the details indicated by black lines within the silhouette, for example the plate from Vulci [case 8, E135, c. 520 BC], painted by Epiktetos.

Terracottas

After a lapse of five centuries terracottas were made again in the 7th century. They were used as votive (dedicatory) offerings to a god in temples and shrines; toys for children; scent bottles; decoration of houses and furniture, and as personal possessions or special funerary offerings buried with the dead.

The new technique of the mould enabled large quantities

to be made at a number of centres, each with its local style. In the 7th century the head of a statuette was moulded and the body hand- or wheel-made, as, for instance, the two goddesses made in Corinth [case 6, 897, c. 620 BC].

But in general the terracotta statuettes followed the trend to naturalism of stone sculpture (see below p. 208), and after passing through several phases, finally achieved the representation of the human form in the round [case 8, 49, c. 550 BC, from Rhodes].

Seals

Harder stones from the Near East were used for seal-engraving – carnelian, chalcedony and jasper – during this period. The Egyptian scarab was much in vogue. Greek engravers adapted and transformed Asiatic themes to produce some of the most remarkable seals ever made, while also employing Greek subjects, witness the reclining satyr with an empty wine cup in his hand [case 10, 7, 2nd half of 6th century BC].

The Room of the Kouroi

The development of Greek stone statues was at first much influenced by Egyptian sculpture, those great frontal figures with broad shoulders, narrow waists, hands generally clenched and one leg before the other which nevertheless give the impression of monolithic immobility. These features are reproduced in the representation of what was, during the 7th and 6th centuries, the standard form of nude standing youth (*kouros*) [B474, c. 560 BC], in this instance from Boeotia.

Splendid figures of this type, some more than life-size, have been found in many parts of the Greek world; but as anatomical and technical skill accumulated and was transmitted from sculptor to sculptor, the body was more accurately represented [B325, 520 BC].

Room of the Harpy Tomb

Early Classical Period, 480–450 BC

Sculpture

A later stage of development of the human figure can be seen in Room 5 in the Strangford 'Apollo' probably from the Aegean island of Anaphé [B475, c. 490 BC] where the body is now anatomically correct but the figure is still symmetrical and frontally posed Fig. 32, p.195.

In reliefs the archaic sculptors often found it difficult to differentiate between the near and less near. But in the Harpy tomb [B287, c. 480–470 BC] the problem has been tackled and partially resolved, although in some of the figures the farther limb is larger or longer than the nearer, such as the left arm of the seated figure holding a pomegranate on the south side of the chamber.

The Harpy tomb stood on the acropolis at Xanthos in Lycia. It was a pillar tomb, and the reliefs on the marble slabs of the sepulchral chamber on top of the pillar are Greek in style and were probably sculptured by Greek artists from an East Greek city. They show offerings made to seated male and female figures, perhaps deified ancestors of the tomb's occupant(s). At the ends of the north and south sides are the harpies or sirens carrying away small human figures. Greek reliefs were painted, and traces of blue on the background and painted patterns on the throne and costumes on the west side are visible.

The three sculptured friezes on the walls, the Cocks and Hens [B299–306, c. 480 BC], Animals and Satyrs [B292–298, c. 470 BC] and Chariots and Horsemen [B311–313, c. 470 BC] also came from Xanthos. The last named is historically the most interesting because it depicts a procession, and familiarizes us with equestrian practices (no stirrups, for instance) and chariot harness and equipment in about the year 470 BC.

Pottery

It can be seen from the representation of figures on vases that Attic painters rendered the anatomy of the human form with vigour and zest. They had difficulties with perspective, but as they worked from a uniform base line, these are not much apparent.

Some lively scenes, mythological and from daily life, were depicted. A girl dances to the tune of a flute player [case 1, E38, c. 510 BC]; the hero, Heracles, struggles with Apollo over the Delphic tripod because his question to the oracle has gone unaswered [E255, c. 510 BC], or attacks the river god, Achelous [case 2, E437, c. 520 BC] whom he has to overcome before winning a wife. Homer is represented by scenes from the death of Hektor who was chased round the walls of Troy by Achilles and then slain by a spear thrust [case 3, E468, c. 490 BC].

Returning to more mundane scenes we see a man heating the contents of a vessel over a brazier [case 4, E53, c. 480 BC], while his possessions, as was customary, hung on the wall; and a youth reclining on a couch at a drinking party [case 4, E68, c. 490 BC] with a young woman dancing beside him.

Demeter, the corn goddess, her daughter, Persephone, and Triptolemus, a minor Attic god, are represented in a scene [case 5, E140, 490–480 BC] from the well-known myth of the rape of Persephone by Hades, who carried her off to the underworld. During Demeter's frenzied search for her daughter the earth became barren and nothing would grow. Here, however, the goddess (after a compromise with Hades) has recovered her daughter, and she is despatching Triptolemus with seed corn to teach the art of corn planting to lands ignorant of it, thus restoring the earth's fertility. The detail in this painting is most remarkable: embroidered on Demeter's mantle are a chariot race, foot race, dolphins, panthers and birds.

In addition to vase painting we know that the walls of sanctuaries and other buildings were decorated with paintings. The vases which are considered to give the best idea of these murals are the Attic white *lekythoi* [case 9] used for funerary purposes, being buried with the dead or placed on tombs.

Bronzes

Up to this time Greek statues in stone and in bronze (large bronze figures appeared at the end of the Archaic period) had been immobile; but during the first half of the 5th century there were startling innovations. The frontal, four-sided pose was abandoned, and the weight of the body was unevenly distributed with the result that the figure rested more on one leg than another. Thus it now acquired elasticity to move and walk. These developments were also copied in the small statuettes [case 7, 514, c. 460 BC; 212, c. 470 BC; case 9, 270, c. 450 BC].

Dress

Interest in the nude female figure was a thing of the future (4th century), and women were generally portrayed in contemporary dress. This could be the one-piece Doric woollen peplos, fastened with a pin or buttoned on the shoulders, such as on the stone statue [B318, c. 470 BC], and sometimes worn open at one side. For variety it could be girdled and pouched and covered with a short overfold introduced from the top. The alternative was the elegant Ionic linen chiton made from two rectangular pieces sewn together at each side, and either buttoned or pinned along the upper arm to form sleeves [case 5, E140, Robe of Demeter; case 10, 243, Ionic chiton and himation]. It, too, could be varied in the same way as the peplos. The outer garment for men and women was the woollen himation, a large rectangular piece of cloth which could be wrapped round the body in a variety of ways and even brought over the head [case 2, 119].

The male chiton was short when worn by young men, warriors [case 5, E458] and children, and worn long by old men and charioteers. Another masculine garment was the chlamys, a short cloak pinned on the right shoulder and worn open at the front. In the 5th century the Doric peplos superseded the Ionic chiton as the fashionable dress for women.

The Bassae Room

The Temple of Apollo Epikurios: frieze

The Doric temple of Apollo Epikurios (Fig. 33) is situated in the Arcadian mountains at Bassae near Paulizza .

Fig. 33. A fallen Amazon pleads for mercy as her Greek opponent prepares to strike. Temple at Bassae, Arcadia

The temple was begun about 450 BC but was not finished until about 425 BC, perhaps because the architect, Iktinos, was called to Athens to build the Parthenon, begun in 447 BC.

The frieze here displayed depicts two subjects immensely favoured by Greek artists: the battle of the Greeks and Amazons [slabs 12–23], those warlike but legendary women who, it was believed, emanated from Asia and invaded Attica; and the fight which broke out with the Lapiths (who lived in the mountains of Thessaly), and the centaurs (a barbarian tribe only half human) [slabs 1–10] at the wedding feast of Perithous, the Lapith king. A drunken centaur assaulted the bride while others attempted to carry off women and boys.

This frieze was placed in the temple 22½ ft above the floor. Consequently it is conceived in bold outlines and high relief, and depicts violent movements and flying drapery in order to be visible from below. Today with an eye-level view and modern lighting we can appreciate more fully than the ancients the splendid craftsmanship of the unknown sculptor.

From these tumultuous scenes we now go to the peerless sculptures of the Parthenon in the Duveen Gallery.

The Duveen Gallery

South Slip Room

Before entering the Duveen Gallery, where we shall see the noblest works of classical Athens at the peak of her artistic achievement, the sculptures of the Parthenon (Elgin Marbles), it is advisable to turn left into the South Slip Room and study first, the model of the temple at the farther end of the room, and secondly, the reproductions on the walls which illustrate the 2,500 years of its history briefly summarized below.

The Parthenon

The Parthenon (Fig. 29) was built to replace an unfinished temple sacked by Xerxes in 480 BC. As can be seen from the model, it was a rectangular building with an outer colonnade within which, at each end, were porches formed by six columns. Above the colonnade on the exterior of the temple was a series of alternating reliefs (metopes) and vertical grooves and bands (triglyphs); and at each end of the building in the triangular space below the roof were pedimental sculptures in the round.

The temple was divided into two adjoining chambers, the eastern section containing the gold and ivory statue of the patron deity of Athens, Athena Parthenos (the Virgin), by the great sculptor, Pheidias. On the exterior walls of these chambers, and above the porches, was a continuous sculptured frieze [see model].

The Parthenon Frieze

This frieze represented the principal event of the Great Panathenaea, the most magnificent of Athenian festivals, celebrated in July every fourth year by athletic and musical contests and a procession from the city's Dipylon Gate to the Acropolis. The purpose of the procession was to escort a newly-woven garment for presentation to an ancient statue of Athena, and instead of the usual mythological subject, all the various groups taking part in the procession were portrayed on the frieze, a most startling innovation.

This was a deeply religious occasion and the sculptor has heightened its effect by showing the robe being presented not to a wooden statue of Athena but to the goddess herself before the other Olympians assembled to witness the ceremony. This scene appeared on the east end of the temple, i.e. the near end of the model.

Furthermore, the procession was divided sculpturally into two similar parts in order to cover the long sides of the building (north and south), and it began on the west side with horsemen preparing to mount and join its rear.

The Parthenon was of the Doric order. Constructed of Pentelic marble, it was begun in 447 BC, but does not seem to have been finished until about 432 BC. Iktinos and Kallikrates were the architects, and the entire undertaking was under the direction of Pheidias whom Pericles [549. After a 5th century BC bronze statue] had appointed to superintend all public building.

Later History

For over 2,000 years the Parthenon stood on the Acropolis, undamaged except for comparatively minor modifications to convert it to a Christian church and a mosque during the East Roman (Byzantine) and Ottoman empires respectively. But in 1687 it was reduced to a ruin when the Venetians, besieging the Turkish garrison on the Acropolis, fired a shell into the gunpowder stored in the Parthenon. The entire interior was destroyed and the central portions of the north and south colonnades blown outwards.

By 1799, when Thomas Bruce, the seventh Earl of Elgin was appointed ambassador to the Ottoman court at Constantinople (Greece then formed part of the Ottoman empire), the building was in danger of total despoliation. Its peerless sculptures were being removed for building materials by the local Greek population, destroyed in the lime kiln or mutilated by religious fanaticism.

Lord Elgin, appalled by this vandalism, sent architects and craftsmen to make drawings and casts; and when the work was obstructed by the Turkish military governor, he obtained a firman from the Sultan for its continuance and also for the removal of the sculpture and inscriptions from the 'Temple of the Idols'.

It is, therefore, due to Lord Elgin that this sculpture, the most beautiful the world has ever known, is preserved for posterity; and to appreciate fully the magnitude of the Greek achievement, we must remember that the sculpture exhibited here constitutes less than half the frieze.

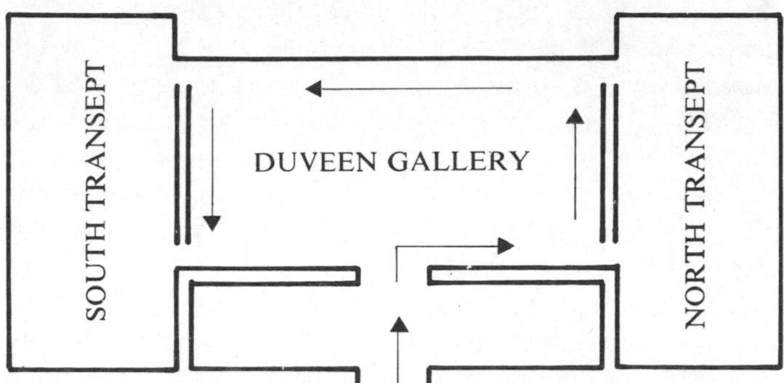

Fig. 34. Plan of the Duveen Gallery. Visitors should follow the arrows

The Main Gallery

Note. The Parthenon frieze is arranged in the gallery as far as possible in the order the slabs appeared on the temple, that is in two sections which begin on the walls on either side of the gallery's entrance and continue on the wall facing it (Fig. 34). Roman numerals identify each slab, and Arabic numerals each individual on a slab.

On entering the Main Gallery we turn right and face the last two slabs of the West frieze (Fig. 34), most of which, as already stated above, is still in place on the Parthenon.

West frieze

Here are two young horesmen [II, 3, 2] and one of the marshals [I, 1] controlling the procession.

North frieze

Next we see a boy [XLII, 134] adjusting his master's [133] dress, while beside them a young man [131] wearing a short cloak (chlamys) holds his horse's head and puts on a wreath prior to mounting and joining the troop of horsemen.

The procession then gathers speed, the horses passing from a trot to a canter and massing, sometimes seven overlapping [XXXVIII, 119–116; XXXVII, 115–113], although the height of the relief never exceeds $2\frac{1}{4}$ in. The youths wear short tunics and sometimes only a cloak (chlamys), and the majestic solemnity of the ceremony is reflected in their grave and rapt expressions. The reins and bridles of the mounts were in bronze [the rivet holes are still visible, XXXIII, 101] or were painted, as was the background at the top and bottom of the frieze. As the horsemen approach the next group, the chariots, their pace slackens [from XXXIV], and on the final slab [XXIV] can be seen the shield of the warrior in the rear chariot.

Unfortunately, the four-horse chariot sequence, continued on the wall opposite (Fig. 34), is incomplete; but we can identify a charioteer, wearing the customary long tunic [XXIII, 67], a soldier in his crested helmet [XXII, 65] and marshals who regulate the speed of the chariots. The middle-aged marshal [XVIII, 59] with the gleaming overweight flesh is a realistic masterpiece.

At this point many slabs were destroyed in the 1687 explosion; but it is known that preceding the chariots were elders, probably branch-bearers, musicians, boys carrying pots for ritual water and trays of offerings, and resident aliens in Athens bearing trays of small cakes [V, 12]. These groups were again preceded by sacrificial animals – heifers and sheep – also missing.

East frieze

The procession now turns on to the East frieze with girls carrying vessels and tall incense burners [VIII, 61–57], of which eight are missing. In front are two marshals and four elderly men conversing, probably magistrates [VI, 48–43].

Now comes the presentation of the garment before the assembled deities, of whom the first five, Eros, his mother, Aphrodite, Artemis, Apollo and Poseidon are not available here. But between the two doors in the wall of the gallery (Fig. 34) can be seen the lame deity, Hephaestos [V, 37] who turns to speak to the goddess Athena herself [36]. Behind her (left) stands a boy and a priest [35, 34] who display the sacred garment, and the priestess of Athena [33] who is about to place the stools brought by attendants [32, 31]. Then before us is the enthroned Zeus, king of the gods, sceptre in hand [30], and his consort, Hera [29], beside him (Fig. 35). As she turns to him she holds up her veil. At her

Fig. 35. Presenting the sacred garment to Athena (R) before the seated gods, represented on a larger scale than the central figures, members of the procession, who unfold the sacred garment and bring stools as symbolic invitations to the deities

side is a girl [28] Nike (Victory) or Iris (messenger of the gods).

To the left of the august couple are Ares, god of war [IV, 27], Demeter, the corn goddess [26], Dionysos [25] and Hermes, herald and messenger of the gods [24], flanked by magistrates [23–20], one of whom [20] may be Pericles, and the leading groups of the other part of the procession, marshals [III, 19, 18], and maidens whose leaders [17, 16] are empty handed, perhaps because they had carried the sacred garment. Across the gallery doorway (Fig. 34) another marshal beckons to the oncoming groups.

South frieze
Sacrificial animals and attendants constitute the first group of the South frieze on this wall. A heifer tosses her head [XL, 117], while another tries to escape and is restrained [XXXIX]. Then follows the gap caused by the explosion, and the missing groups, with the exception of the elders [XXXV, 97–88] are the same as those of the North frieze. Then once more we see the chariots (the four overlapping horses' heads – XXX – are exceptionally fine) and, finally, on the opposite wall, the horsemen of the South frieze [XXV–I, 63–4), which brings us back to the gallery's entrance.

North Transept (*right of entrance*)

The East pediment
The subject portrayed was the birth of Athena, who sprang fully armed from the head of Zeus. The central figures of the pediment, which demonstrated the method of this unusual birth, disappeared about AD 450, but some (if not all) of the figures on the 1st or 2nd century altar at Madrid (South Siip room) are thought to reproduce the scene.

Of the existing sculptures we can see [left] the arms and head of Helios, the sun god, and the heads of his chariot horses rising from the waves [A, B, C]. Next Dionysos [D] (Fig. 36) (some say Heracles and other interpretations) reposing on an animal's skin, beside whom are the goddess Demeter [E] and her daughter, Persephone [F], both seated, while a girl, probably Zeus' cup-bearer, Hebe [G] or Iris, starts forward with astonishment at the central scene but nevertheless glances back at it.

Across the gap are, probably, Hestia [K], goddess of domestic life, and Dione [L] supporting Aphrodite, her daughter [M]. Next, but now missing, was Selene, goddess of the moon, in her chariot which was sinking below the horizon. Of her horses the one here [O], nostril and mouth quivering with exhaustion after its long journey through the firmament, is superb (Fig. 37).

All these figures are in the round in spite of the fact that on the pediment their finely carved backs would never have been seen.

The Metopes

There were ninety-two metopes on the Parthenon covering several subjects, of which the Museum has fifteen from the south face depicting the legendary struggle between the Lapiths and centaurs. They are in very high relief, in some cases as much as 13 in. and their outlines are bold and striking. Of the seven in this transept, the centaur trampling triumphantly upon the dead Lapith [XXVIII] and the centaur who tries to flee while staunching the wound in his back as the Lapith prepares to strike again [XXVII] are the most impressive.

South Transept

The West pediment

The subject of the West pediment is the contest between Poseidon, the sea god, and Athena, goddess of wisdom, for the land of Attica. Both gods had arrived in chariots accompanied by Hermes and Iris, the divine messengers. Poseidon struck the Acropolis rock with his trident and brought forth a salt stream, and Athena produced an olive tree and was deemed the victor.

The figures of this pediment, with two exceptions, are so damaged that without Carrey's sketch [South Slip Room] there would be difficulty in identifying the fragments. The best preserved are Iris [N], whose body and drapery are superbly modelled and, in the acute angle of the pediment, the recumbent figure of an Athenian river god [A], Cephisus or Ilissus who, awoken by the tumult, raises himself to see what is happening.

Fig. 36. Dionysos, the Parthenon, East Pediment, see page 216
Fig. 37. The horse of Selene. East Pediment, see page 217
Fig. 38. The restored eastern end of the Nereid monument, a temple-tomb, c. 400 BC.

The Metopes

The metopes were placed on the building during its construction, and were the first sculptures to be carved which accounts for the fact that some of them have later been altered and even added to. Thc battles of Lapiths and centaurs are symbolic of the struggle between barbarism and civilization, and of the eight metopes in this transept those showing the centaur dashing a wine jar on a fallen Lapith [IV], and the violent struggle between a centaur and a Lapith [VII] are remarkable for their beautiful postures.

The Nereid Room

Outside the Duveen Gallery is the Nereid monument from Xanthos (Fig. 38), erected for a Lycian nobleman who died about 400 BC. The idea of a tomb in the form of a small Ionic temple seems first to have arisen in Asia Minor, for contemporary tombs on the Greek mainland were generally unostentatious in design and construction until after the building of the Mausoleum (see below), the splendour of which aroused emulation.

The Nereid monument stood on a platform on the top of a slope overlooking a main route into the city, its base being built against the side of the hill. The monument consisted of a central rectangular chamber surrounded by an Ionic colonnade, with four columns at each end and six at the sides, interspersed with female figures with clinging drapery, Nereids (sea nymphs) or Aurae (personified breezes) [see also central pedestal, 912, 910, 909]. There were also figures on the roof above the pediments [927, 926. Man carrying off woman], and crouching lions [929, 930] which probably guarded the approaches to the tomb. At the eastern (restored) end of the monument, the sculptures of the pediment represent the ruler and his wife receiving homage; and the remains of the western pediment sculptures [925] indicate a battle between foot soldiers and cavalry.

There are four friezes, each representing incidents in the life of the tomb owner. The first [lowest on base of monument and on wall] depicts battles involving barbarians and

Greeks, on foot and mounted. The second frieze is of great historical interest: on the front of the base [L–R] can be seen a heavily fortified city, with towers, battlements and gates, which is being stormed by an assault party with ladders supported by troops of soldiers. On the side of the base [R] is another city with its defenders, who seem to be parleying with their opponents. But the besieged, as can be seen on the adjacent wall [869, 870], sometimes make a sortie from the city, although on this occasion without much success as prisoners [884], hands bound behind back, are escorted by soldiers, and the elders of the city surrender to the enthroned oriental prince, who is shaded from the sun by an attendant with an umbrella, and surrounded by attendants and soldiers [880, 879].

The fourth frieze [on top of chamber wall and across porch] depicts a priest sacrificing at an altar, while sacrificial animals are led forward; and [on wall facing monument] a banquet at which the guests recline on couches, and drink wine drawn from a jar and served by attendants [898–903]. Their host, the prince (for these are scenes from the tomb owner's life), alone on a couch [903] under which lies his dog, holds a cup and drinking horn while an elderly official whispers in his ear.

The third frieze [above columns on architrave] shows a hunt in which the quarry, a bear, can be seen attacking a hound while horsemen approach, and [on wall] battles [892, 894] and a procession of men bearing gifts or tributes [896, 895, 897, 886, 893].

Passing behind the monument we now come to rooms containing exhibits from the later 5th and 4th centuries.

Room of the Caryatid

The Erectheum

The Erectheum (Fig. 29) stands on the north side of the Acropolis. It may have been begun about 421 BC and seems to have been finished about 406 BC. It replaced a previous temple in an adjacent position, and also protected certain venerated sanctuaries as, for instance, the spot where the salt-water fountain gushed forth when Poseidon struck the rock in his contest with Athena (p. 217).

Consequently its design was complex. Built of Pentelic marble on two levels, it had four entrances and was most richly decorated, as can be seen on the Ionic column [408, c. 415 BC] and the ornamental band [409, c. 415 BC] which ran round the exterior of the building. The caryatid opposite [407, c. 415 BC] is one of the six maidens who supported the roof of the south porch. The Erectheum suffered much damage during subsequent centuries, and was rebuilt, so far as the remaining material permitted, in 1903–1909.

Temple of Athena Nike

Another Ionic temple, the small but perfect Athena Nike (Victory) (Fig. 29) was also erected on the Acropolis during the Peloponnesian War about 427–424 BC, although designed after 449 BC by Kallikrates, probably to mark the long-delayed peace with Persia.

It stood on a Mycenaean bastion in the south-west corner, and is represented in the Museum by four slabs from its frieze [421–424] which portray battles of Greeks against Greeks, and Greeks against Persians. The swirling cloaks of the combatants which fill the background and weld the scene together are an innovation much repeated in later times. The temple was rebuilt for the second time in 1936–1941 from its original material.

Building on the Acropolis and elsewhere was continued throughout the Peloponnesian war (431–404 BC), and at the end of it Athens must have looked very fine, more like a victorious than a vanquished city.

Pottery

But although splendid buildings were erected, painting, as represented on pottery [except the white lekythoi, case 1] had degenerated. Experiments in perspective were not wholly successful, and the figures no longer have the clear outlines and vigorous movements in a balanced composition. The design is overloaded and consequently obscure, as on the clay water jar [case 1, E224, c. 410 BC] by the Meidias painter, and on the two-handled jug [case 4, E424, 350–340 BC].

Tombstones
From about 440–317 BC tombstones were in the form of shrines with the figures within the framework and the whole sculptured in relief. They evoke grief without sentimentality. For instance, the seated woman [2232, c. 400 BC] obviously died in childbirth, for the nurse who stands before her holds a swaddled baby. Such a subject could easily descend to bathos, but here it is rendered with dignity. A large tomb, however, would probably be surmounted by an animal as guardian, such as the young bull [680, 4th century BC], while a plain memorial stone (stela) with an inscription might carry the palmette [438, 400–350 BC] across its top.

The Fourth Century BC

The defeat of Athens in the disastrous Peloponnesian war, the loss of her empire, the lack of faith in the gods who had failed her and even in the city state, had repercussions on art. For Athens was ruined and state patronage almost ceased, to be replaced by private patronage. The noble austerity of 5th century art was succeeded by works with a softer and more individualistic appeal.

Sculpture
These qualities can be seen in the marble head (Fig. 39) of the young Heracles [1600, 4th century] which is in the style, and may well be the work of Praxiteles, one of the great 4th century sculptors.

Metalwork
Most 5th century gold and silver plate was made for dedication to the gods out of treasure captured from the Persians at Plataea, and it vanished in later times when the temples were despoiled. The surviving pieces have been found in the graves of Greece's rich barbarian neighbours, or in the colonial periphery of the Greek world, as for instance the silver libation dish portraying the apotheosis of Heracles [case 4, 8, 4th century BC] found at the hill town of Eze, Alpes Maritimes.

Gold jewellery was made again and the Department has a magnificent collection [case 5] which includes elaborate boat-shaped ear-rings, circular bracelets of rod or tube with

Fig. 39. Marble head of the young Heracles, 4th century BC, perhaps the work of Praxiteles

animals' heads at each end, a necklace of interlocking rosettes and other ornaments from which hang birds and human heads, and gold rings with embossed or engraved bezels, for the signet ring now came into common use.

Engraved stones became part of the goldsmith's stock in trade for he set them in pendants and wristlets and, in the latter part of the period in signet rings [case 5]. The stones were now larger and mainly of chalcedony and white jasper, and subjects much in vogue were seated women, animals and birds.

The bronzes of the period are superb, for example, the 4th century repoussé reliefs in case 2, and the Corinthian bronze mirror with the gay engraving of Aphrodite and Pan dicing together [case 4, 289, 350–300 BC].

The Payava Room

The Tomb of Payava, 375–350 BC

The gabled tomb in this room belonged to Payava, a Lycian and an important official, judging by this imposing monument which stood originally on a rectangular base on the top of a hill overlooking the city of Xanthos.

Above the base and on the reconstruction here, are sculptured reliefs depicting, presumably, scenes from the life of the tomb owner. Over the sculpture and covered by the gabled roof, is the principal sepulchral chamber which, although in the local limestone, imitates a wooden building, that is with a mortised frame, projecting beam ends and recessed panels, as was customary in Lycia.

The roof, which can be seen from the upstairs gallery, has reliefs on its ridge, gable ends and sides, the latter depicting galloping four-horse chariots, and also the foreparts in the round of the tomb's guardian lions.

But in spite of these pictorial records all we know of Payava is contained on his inscription: that he was the 'son of Ad—, secretary to A—rah, by race a Lycian' and that he built his tomb, i.e., it was erected in his lifetime. He would, however, be serving the Persian king for at that time Lycia was part of the Persian empire.

Pottery

When the Greeks first settled in Italy they imported vases from the Greek homeland. But in the last half of the 5th century BC manufacture took place in Italy, and by the end of the century all Attic imports had ceased.

Various Italian schools emerged, which are well represented in this room, whose wares have a distinctly provincial appearance. They mainly reproduce Attic shapes, but the painting never approaches that of the Attic artists, although some scenes have the merit of liveliness and humour. For example a Lucanian clay mixing bowl [case 1,F157,390–380 BC] depicts a scene from a phylax play, i.e., a local farce, which satirized scenes from life and ridiculed legendary and mythological episodes, in this case from the *Iliad*, in which Dolon, the Trojan spy, is chased and ambushed by Odysseus and Diomedes.

The mythological or dramatic scenes portrayed on the larger vases are valuable inasmuch as they record rare myths and episodes from tragedies since lost, such as Alcmene on the pyre [case 3, F149, 350–325 BC] which is from a lost play of Euripides.

Portraiture

The concentration on the individual, of which Socrates and Plato were the principal exponents, deepened interest in portraiture, and a fine example is the head of a Libyan (Berber) [268, 375–325] which comes from a bronze statue and was found in the temple of Apollo at Cyrene in the Libyan Pentapolis.

Even the humble terracotta reflects the everyday activities of ordinary individuals, in this case the two crouching young women absorbed in a game of knucklebones [case 4, D161, 340–330 BC, probably from Capua], a pastime very popular with the Greeks and later the Romans.

Bronzes

Two bronze shoulder pieces from a ceremonial cuirass with a Greek overcoming an Amazon on each [case 3, 285, 400–350 BC] found near the river Siris, Lucania, in southern Italy, are one of the finest and most famous examples of Greek bronze relief work. Another splendid piece is the woman seated in a chair, which was found in the sea off Pozzuoli, near Naples [case 1, 666, c. 400 BC].

The Mausoleum Room

On the confines of Hellenism in south-west Asia Minor Mausolus, prince of Caria [377–353 BC], a Hellenized native dynast and Persian satrap [1000, c. 350 BC] supported the revolt of the Carian off-shore islands, Rhodes, Chios and Cos, against the resuscitated Athenian empire and federation in which once again Athens was acting high-handedly towards the members. He had established his capital at the Greek colony of Halicarnassus in about 367 BC and built a great port there in order to become a naval power. He had also extended his authority to Lycia and Ionia, but before he could continue his policy of expansion he died.

The Mausoleum

Shortly before his death, however, work had been started on his tomb, and Pythios and Satyros had been employed as architects, and Bryaxis, Timotheus, Leochares and Skopas as sculptors. After his death his widow and sister, Artemisia [1001, 350 BC] carried on the work.

Unfortunately it is impossible to reconstruct the Mausoleum (a term later coined by the Romans for any magnificent tomb) because ancient descriptions are confused. Furthermore, although the monument stood till the 10th century, it was destroyed when the stone was looted in the Middle Ages by the Knights of St John of Jerusalem to build their castle of St Peter at Halicarnassus (mod. Bodrum). We know, however, that the building consisted of three parts, a high base on which stood thirty-six Ionic columns; and on these was superimposed a pyramid of twenty-four steps leading to a platform where there stood a four-horse chariot, probably containing the statues of Mausolus and Artemisia. But the position of the sepulchral chamber, the friezes, and of the statues of human and animal figures cannot be determined at present.

The Mausoleum had three friezes, chariot races [1037], battle of Lapiths and centaurs [1032], and battle of Greeks and Amazons [1006–1022]. This latter frieze is much less crowded than the Parthenon frieze, but care is nevertheless taken that the figures should interconnect. Especially notable for bold poses and violent movements are three slabs [1013, 1014, 1015]. They can only be the work of a great master, and have sometimes been attributed to Skopas.

The Temple of Artemis, Ephesus

In the other section of this room is a sculptured drum [1206] of a column from the last temple of Artemis at Ephesus (the 'Diana of the Ephesians' mentioned in *Acts*, chap. 19) (Fig. 40). The previous temple was destroyed in 356 BC (p. 203).

The new temple was begun soon after the destruction of the earlier sanctuary, which it much resembled. The outstanding feature, which caused it to be classed as one of the Seven Wonders of the ancient world was the beauty of its

Fig. 40. Sculptured drum from the last Temple of Artemis at Ephesus, c. 340 BC

sculptured columns, thirty-six in all. One was the work of Skopas, conceivably that exhibited here, which is thought to represent Alcestis [centre] between Death [L] and the god Hermes.

The noble lion [1350, 2nd century BC] is from another Asiatic tomb monument which stood on the edge of a cliff above the sea about 3 miles from Cnidus. It was undoubtedly a public monument, but it is not known whom or what it commemorated.

From the classical exhibits we now go to those of the Hellenistic period ('Hellenistic' is the term used to denote Greek civilization after Alexander) when the Mediterranean peoples shared a common language, the Koiné, an intermediate stage between classical and modern Greek, which greatly facilitated the spread of knowledge and ideas.

The Hellenistic Room

Politically the Hellenistic kingdoms lasted for three centuries. But elements of Hellenistic civilization were to endure for over a thousand years, throughout the Roman empire, when the culture was Graeco-Roman, and during the Byzantine empire, when it was Graeco-Oriental tempered by Christianity.

Sculpture

Mounting the steps into the Hellenistic room one approaches the seated statue of Demeter [1300, about 330 BC], goddess of the grain-bearing earth, which was found in the precinct of underworld deities at the south foot of the acropolis of Cnidus, Caria. The goddess looks straight at the spectator and her expression is tender, which is unusual for an Olympian. The pose is relaxed and the drapery naturalistic, in contrast with the late 5th and early 4th centuries, where it is decorative.

Compassion, too, is portrayed on the head of Asklepios [550, c. 300 BC] from a statue in a shrine of the god on Melos, which is natural in a deity concerned with healing. As has been seen these softer qualities continue the trend begun in the late Classical period.

The figure of Dionysos [432, 320 BC] comes from a monument erected below the south wall of the Acropolis at Athens immediately above the theatre of Dionysos. It was set up by the choragus, Thrasyllos, to mark the victory of his tribe in the dramatic contests held in the adjacent theatre. As choragus, Thrasyllos had paid the cost of training the chorus, a rich Athenian's duty. The statue stood on top of a three-pillared portico before the entrance to a cave.

An interesting middle Hellenistic relief is the Apotheosis of Homer [2191, 150–120 BC], found on the Appian Way near Rome. In the lowest register is the seated Homer with the Iliad and the Odyssey crouching beside him, Time and the World behind them, and a crowd who have come to honour the poet. At the top is the reclining Zeus with sceptre and eagle [and the sculptor's signature 'Archelaos of Priene' below) talking to Mnemosyne, mother of the nine Muses (his daughters), who occupy the next two registers.

On the right of the third register is a poet holding a roll, behind whom is a tripod signifying he has won a competition with a poem which, perhaps, has the theme of the relief. Next to him a muse is handing a scroll to Apollo.

Portrait sculpture

True portraiture was born in this period, and magnificent representations of kings and public figures in bronze and stone have come down to us. Nevertheless, although the features may be accurately depicted, these portraits are exalted and idealized in the manner of all Greek portraits.

Two portraits are exhibited here, a marble head from a statue of a middle-aged man with receding hair and furrowed brow [1965, c. 100–50 BC] which, being impressionistic in treatment, is best seen at a distance, and a representation of Sophocles in old age [847, 3rd century BC]. The latter is not contemporary for the poet was born *c.* 496 BC and died in his 90th year. Neither is it derived from the identified portraits of the poet which have survived in Roman copies, but is probably a realistic interpretation by some percipient Hellenistic artist.

Architecture

The Hellenistic monarchs were great builders. Antioch, the capital of the Seleucid empire, was built about 300 BC by Seleucus I who founded numerous other cities. Old towns were also recolonized and renamed, and in Ionia, Priene and Miletus were rebuilt in Hellenistic times.

Most of the new towns were built on a chessboard plan, and were provided with those buildings characteristic of a city of Greek culture and constitution. In the 2nd century, the principal buildings of Pergamum were erected on the crest and slopes of a steep hill overlooking a river valley, including the royal palace, theatre, library, temples and the great altar of Zeus with its dramatic frieze depicting the battle of gods and giants.

The houses of the Hellenistic wealthy were spacious, judging by those found at Priene and on Delos, particularly the latter, for the island was the Aegean corn market and most prosperous in Hellenistic times. In second century Delian houses the rooms opened out of a central court, or in the case of a very large house, two courts. There would be the men's dining room, a lecture room, library, possibly a picture gallery and a porter's lodge, and the women's quarters would certainly contain a weaving room where the cloth for the household's clothes was made. There would also be several guest rooms. Delos houses were two-storeyed and the upstairs rooms were off a gallery round the courtyard. There were mosaic floors in some rooms, and the walls were stuccoed and modelled and painted to resemble white and coloured marble slabs, sometimes with pictures inserted into the stucco.

Pottery and glass

While household furniture has not survived, a number of objects in domestic use can be seen [case 1] such as the painted cup [1947 7–14 19, 350–300 BC] and mug, water jar [1927 3–17 5, 250–230 BC], bowl [70 11–17 2, 4th century BC], faience jug with figure of Queen Arsinoe III of Egypt, [K76, 221–203 BC] and the bowl of the type known as 'Megarian' [case 3, G103, 300–200 BC], the forerunner of Roman relief-decorated pottery.

Hellenistic glass was a much finer product than the pottery, and the exquisite gilded bowl [case 2, 71 5–18 2, 3rd century BC] is one of the most technically perfect examples of glass-making up to that time. It was made before glass-blowing was invented and was formed from an inner and an outer casing so carefully ground that the outer fitted the inner like a glove. The bowl was found in a tomb in Canosa, southern Italy, along with the elegant wing-handled cup [71 5–18 9, 3rd or 2nd century BC] and other pieces. The small coloured bowls and dish [case 3, 1st century BC] are of Greek workmanship and may have been made in Alexandria.

Bronzes

An example of elaborate bronze work is the mirror with silver inlay [case 1, 303, 300–200 BC] said to have come from Locri, South Italy, which makes one wonder what type of woman it was who had the strength to hold it.

Hellenistic houses were more comfortable than those of the classical period, and contained objects that were ornamental, for example, the statuette of Alexander the Great [case 3, 799, 100–50 BC]. The realistic trend in sculpture allied to greater familiarity with different races resulted in the portrayal of subjects rarely represented in the classical period, such as the pathetic figure of a grotesque dancer, recovered from a shipwreck [case 3, 1926, 4–15 32, 1st century BC], the head of a negress [1955 10–8 1, c. 100 BC], and in ivory, the poor hunchback suffering from tuberculosis of the spine [1959 4–15 2, 1st century BC].

Terracottas

The same tendencies can be observed in terracottas where an ugly old woman is seen with a child on her knee [case 1, C279, c. 300 BC]. The foibles of humanity are also recorded, witness the two young women gossiping on a couch [case 2, C529, c. 100 BC], probably from Myrina, Asia Minor, where in the 2nd and 1st centuries BC some of the finest terracottas were made. But the most charming are the Tanagra figures of young women [case 1, C295, c. 250 BC; 263, 300–200 BC] who are both beautiful and elegant but lack the spontaneity and vitality of figurines in the earlier periods.

Jewellery and plate

Precious metals were in plentiful supply in Hellenistic times owing to Persian booty captured by Alexander the Great, and the output from the Macedonian and Thracian mines exploited by his father, Philip II.

Consequently there is a fine display of Hellenistic jewellery [cases 4 and 5]: necklaces of gold [case 4, nos. 7, 26] and later gold with garnets [case 5, nos. 8, 26], worn with animal-head ear-rings to match [case 5, nos. 3, 5]. Garnets were also fashionable in diadems and bracelets [case 4, nos. 17, 24; case 5, no. 7], as well as finger rings [case 5, no. 15].

The Greek silver cup from Ithaca [case 2, 1920 5–29 1, 2nd century BC] is of Persian shape but of Greek manufacture, but another type of cup, the kylix [15, 2nd century BC, from Boscoreale] has a wide shallow bowl with a central boss engraved with floral ornament.

The First Roman Room

Roman Homes and Furnishings

The majority of exhibits in the First Roman Room belong to imperial times, and are for domestic use and the adornment of person and home. They must have come from the country villas and town houses of Roman nobles and officials, rich merchants, bankers, and from provincial homes of minor officials, professional men and successful traders in towns such as Pompeii.

Metalwork

Jewellery, an expensive luxury, came under official disapproval in republican times, but no such inhibition existed during the empire. Early imperial jewellery [case 3] was gold and modelled in a continuation of Hellenistic styles. Later in the period there was increased use of the hardest stones, sapphires [12], emeralds [13], and occasionally diamonds [11].

The ball ear-ring (often gold) was popular although sometimes clusters of small emeralds were substituted for the gold surface [case 3, 2]. Necklaces with linked stones set in gold [6] were fashionable in both Hellenistic and Roman times, as were circular gold bracelets, of which a fine example is exhibited in the form of a snake [9].

Gold and silver plate [case 3] reached Rome in large quantities as the result of the conquest of Greek lands. Silver plate was an important item in the domestic, political and economic life of the empire. Even a middle-class family would probably possess a set of silver plate for dining, as well as pieces for display in the house. To have none would signify extreme poverty.

The Museum possesses several magnificent collections of Roman silver in this and other departments, some of which have been saved from destruction by barbarians by being buried, such as the Chaourse Treasure, found in a field in 1853, from which can be seen the silver dish, jug, bucket and bowl [168, 147, 148, 170]. A fine exhibit is the pair of silver cups [1960 2–1 1, 3, 1st century BC or AD]. They have lost their handles and feet, but have the most delicate repoussé decoration of scrolls of leaves and flowers, among which are birds and butterflies and other insects. Another charming piece is the small silver amphora [79, 1st century AD], decorated with scrolls of vine and ivy, partly gilded, found at Bagni di Vicarello among votive offerings from those who had taken the waters.

Bronzes in large numbers were made in imperial times, and those which can be defined as Roman are recognizable by their subject (men sacrificing wearing the toga, the deities of the home, etc., gladiators, Roman emperors) and their technique, such as the Gaulish prisoner [case 1, 1913 4–16 1, 1st century AD] which has been tooled in a typically Roman fashion.

The discerning Roman collector was naturally interested in classical works and some reproductions made for him follow the originals closely while others are varied to suit Roman taste, for example, the Mercury (Hermes) [case 2, 825, 1st century AD], which appears to be derived from a work by Polykleitos. Another popular style was the 'archaistic' which copied the Greek 6th century archaic work, of which an example is the girl with the inlaid eyes [case 2, 192, 1st century AD]. But the generality of bronze figures were Hellenistic in style, and as they increased in numbers so they lost in originality.

Bronze end rests to couches, on which rested the pillows, were much in vogue, and a traditional motif was a mule's head, sometimes in combination with other embellishments [case 2, 2562; case 3, 2561, 1st century AD].

Glass

Roman glass for domestic use was of exceptional quality. Owing to the invention of glass-blowing by the Phoenicians shortly before our era (brought to Italy in the 1st century AD) it was manufactured and used on a large scale throughout the empire.

A most celebrated piece is the Portland Vase [GEM 4036] (Fig. 41), so-called because it was bought in 1784 by the Dowager Duchess of Portland, was loaned to the Museum in 1810 by the fourth Duke, and was acquired (after being smashed into over 200 pieces by a drunken Irishman in 1845 and skilfully mended by a Museum craftsman) by the Trustees a century later.

The vase was blown in two layers, a blue inside a white

Fig. 41. The Portland Vase, probably made in Italy between 27 BC and AD 37

layer. The figures were then carved in relief in the outer (white) layer, leaving the blue as background. The subject has been much debated but it seems probable that it represents the wooing and marriage of Thetis, a sea nymph, by Peleus, a mortal. But there are other interpretations. The vase was probably made in Italy during the reign of Augustus [27 BC–AD 14] or Tiberius [AD 14–37].

A great variety of glass shapes and designs can be seen here [case 3]. In the 1st century AD, glass was coloured as the cobalt blue boat [69 6–24 20], the amber-coloured beaker [1913 5–22 18], and the amber jug with white blobs [S85] In the 2nd to 3rd century vessels were mainly colourless but of new shapes and decoration, as the flask [S257] with snake-thread spiral from Cologne where glass factories were founded early in the 1st century AD, and the gladiator's helmet [81 6–24 2], also from Cologne [see also Greek and Roman Life Room, Roman Britain Room, Department of Medieval and Later Antiquities].

Pottery

The best known Roman pottery is the red gloss ware, of which the Arretine relief ware, fabricated at Arretium (mod. Arrezzo) from about 30 BC–AD 30, is the finest. It was made in a mould in which a negative impression of the decoration had already been imposed by means of stamps. The two main types of decoration consisted of formal decorative motifs and representations of figures, such as that showing the Seasons [case 1, L54, c. 10 BC]. The forerunner of this ware was the so-called 'Megarian' bowl [Hellenistic Room, case 3] which appeared all over the Hellenistic world and in Italy from about the 3rd to the 1st century BC [case 1, 39 11–9 23, 2nd century BC. Made in Italy]. In addition there was the plain Arretine pottery with its sharp outlines, such as the dish found at Vaison (Vaucluse) [case 2, L170, late 1st century BC].

When the manufacture of Arretine ware ceased, the pottery factories moved into Gaul, first in the south, then to the centre and finally the north-east in the wake of their best customers, the Roman legions.

Gaulish potters evolved many decorative styles such as the freehand drawing of stylized plant forms with a slip, as on the clay beaker [case 1, 1920 11–18 27. Probably made at

Rheinzabern, 3rd century AD], and also combined with overlapping scales which were occasionally employed alone [K38, 1st century AD]. In the Argonne (north-east Gaul), a dark coated pottery with rouletted and incised decoration was made [case 2, M155, 4th century AD], while lead glazed ware which originated, it seems, in the eastern Mediterranean, had spread to Italy and central France by the 1st century AD, for example, the jug and cup [K25, 1931 5–14 1]. These wares, like red gloss pottery, imitated metal shapes.

Painting

The Romans decorated the walls of their rooms with paintings mainly known to us from the towns overwhelmed by the eruption of Vesuvius in AD 79 – Herculaneum, Stabiae and Pompeii.

There were many pictorial subjects, landscapes, gardens and city scenes, which were framed by a painted architectural screen, sometimes of three dimensional columns which appeared as in the foreground and the painted scene was projected as a view into the background, which must have made the occupant of the room feel he could step out into these rural or urban surroundings. Life-size figures in continuous action were also portrayed, sometimes in a setting which appeared to enlarge the existing room. Varied painted architectural features combined with pictures in panels (often mythological) and covering part or most of the wall, also provided numerous decorative combinations. All these styles were in vogue at different times, and the pictures exhibited [19, 20, 24, 27, 28] must have formed part of some of them.

The coastal scene [19] illustrates one of the outstanding features of Roman painting: the effect of luminous atmosphere diffused over the entire scene, as well as the effect of depth and space. Some paintings have a modern appearance inasmuch as the artist has treated the scene impressionistically as in the 'Landscape with villa' [20] from Boscoreale, near Pompeii. Legend (or fairy tale) is represented by Ulysses [Odysseus) homeward bound [27] and strapped to the mast, listening to the enchanting songs of some not very alluring sirens, while his crew have their ears stopped with wax to prevent their being enticed to death.

Mosaics

Mosaics are akin to painting and are associated with the Romans although they were not the first people to use this form of decoration.

Mosaics became so popular in Roman times that they are found on floors (and sometimes on walls) all over the empire up to the 4th century. In this room there are two fine examples, 'The lion bound by cupids' [1], made with small tesserae, and the very fine 2nd century floor pavement showing the head of a sea god, perhaps Oceanus [15], from Carthage in Africa, a prolific source of mosaic pavements [see also 2nd Roman Room; N-W Staircase].

The artistic output of Rome was predominantly in the hands of Greeks or Orientals from Mediterranean lands with Hellenistic culture and training. But Hellenistic art towards the end, though technically superb, had become sterile in ideas; and it was Roman imperial achievements combined with official patronage which stimulated the Greek mind and hand to new artistic forms, such as the documentary continuous narrative on stone (for example, on Trajan's column), unfortunately not represented here, and the realistic portrait of which there are fine examples in the Department.

Portrait sculpture

The Romans set great store by character, and while the classical Greeks produced idealized portraits, they insisted on a realistic likeness, not only when a man was at the height of his powers but also when his writ was nearly run and his character was mirrored in his face.

All the power and majesty of Rome are manifested in the splendid head of the emperor Augustus [1911 9-1 1, 1st century AD] (Fig. 42) whose beauty as a youth was such that when elected to the priesthood his mother arranged for him to make his temple visits after dark to avoid the attentions of susceptible Roman ladies. This bronze head stands at the beginning of the long series of imperial portraits which are a most illuminating record and one of the great achievements of Roman art, and the artist may have been a Greek from Alexandria.

As a contrast we have a representation of a Roman of minor rank, the grave relief of Antistius Sarculo and of his wife, Antistia Plutia [2275, 50–30 BC]. Antistius was a

Fig. 42. The emperor Augustus, 27 BC – AD 14
Fig. 43. The Westmacott athlete, possibly a 1st century Roman copy of a statue by Polykleitos of about 440 BC. see page 239

priest of the Alban College of the Salian priesthood, and in pagan Rome religion was not a profession, nor were its priests always of elevated character. There must, however, have been something of merit in this pair, for the relief was erected by two of their ex-slaves. These portraits were probably taken from death masks.

Second Roman Room

Sculpture

The statues in this room are mainly copies of classical Greek or Hellenistic works carried out in the workshops of Rome, old Greece and erstwhile Asiatic Greek lands. For the Romans fully appreciated and were fascinated by Greek art, and during the latter part of the Republic the plunder from their conquests was dispatched to Rome to embellish public buildings, palaces and private houses. But the supply was limited, and by the 1st century of our era copies of Greek statues were being made in the workshops, mainly by the mechanical process of pointing, which are of the greatest value today because they enable us to visualize Greek works, many of which have disappeared.

For instance, the boy binding a fillet on his head as a badge of victory in an athletic contest [501, 1st century AD] is a Roman copy of a classical bronze statue dated about 440 BC. Pheidias is known to have made such a statue, and it is possible that the exhibit might be a reproduction of his work. Again the great Polykleitos, a contemporary of Pheidias, represented the boy boxer of Mantinea, Kyniskos (Fig. 43), in a bronze work, and the marble statue of a boy [1754] placing a wreath on his head, may be a 1st century reproduction of the master's work of about 440 BC.

By the pool is the crouching Aphrodite [1963 10–21 1, 1st century AD] which is a copy of a popular Hellenistic work by Doidalses of Bithynia, c. 250 BC; and the large marble Apollo playing the lyre at the top of the steps [1380], found in the temple of Cyrene, Libya, is also a 1st century AD reproduction of a Hellenistic work.

But in addition to mechanical copies, much of the sculpture here exhibited, though carved in Roman times, is in the manner of Greek work of the 5th and 4th centuries BC, such as the relief of the boy with a horse [2206] from Hadrian's villa at Tivoli, dated AD 125, and that of Apollo and Artemis [2200, 1st century BC] killing the seven sons and seven daughters of Niobe because she had insulted their mother, Leto. The figures here seem to have been copied from an Athenian work of 440–430 BC.

Portrait sculpture
There were of course original Roman works inasmuch as they represent specifically Roman subjects and individual Romans, for example, the statue of an austere-looking Roman woman [1415, AD 130–150] found in the temple of Aphrodite at Cyrene.

An exceptionally fine character study, and a most subtle delineation of a man of the world in his physical and intellectual prime [1949] is the marble portrait bust of an unknown man. This work is of the Antonine period (AD 138–192) and was probably carved by an Athenian sculptor.

Having now examined some of the choicest works of art in the Department, it is time to study the more mundane matters of everyday life, and for this we must go to the Greek and Roman Life Room on the first floor.

The Greek and Roman Life Room

First Floor

In the Greek and Roman Life Room the exhibits are arranged under subjects and not chronologically as on the ground floor, for example, *Athletes, Gladiators and Chariot Races* [case L of corridor] and *Food and Agriculture* [R of corridor]. They will be described in conjunction with objects in the Terracotta Room and the Vase Rooms which also illustrate aspects of Greek and Roman life. These complementary exhibits are given references in the text and are listed at the end of the section, so that the rooms concerned can be visited later.

Country Life

Food and Agriculture [*wall case*]. Most freeborn Greeks at all periods lived on or from the land. In Attica in classical times (5th century BC) the peasant smallholder worked his own land; the landowner lived on his estate and supervised the work of his servants and slaves; and the rich city dweller (Pericles, for instance) either employed a bailiff to manage his estates or rode out from the city to supervise them. In Sparta, however, the helots (serfs) worked the land for the Spartiates (aristocracy) whose lives were devoted to military service (p. 183).

The land was tilled by a plough not much changed since the time of Hesiod, the late 8th century BC (p. 182), which was yoked to oxen [180. Bronze ploughman with team, 6th century BC] or mules, and behind which was the sower scattering the seed [1906 12–15 1. Attic cup, 2nd quarter 6th century BC, from Camirus, Rhodes] and a man or boy to finish the job with a mattock or hoe [99 12–29 48. Mycenaean, c. 1100 BC, from a tomb near Klavadia, Cyprus]. Crops were reaped with the various types of sickles on display, and these rudimentary methods persisted throughout antiquity because of the abundance of slave labour.

The Attic smallholder in classical times lived in a house with one or two rooms, sometimes little better than a hovel. He might have a slave or two and labourers to assist him in the fields where he grew wheat and barley. His womenfolk attended to the domestic duties: they cooked mainly in the open air [234. Woman kneading dough, mid-5th century BC; 1966 3–28 22. Woman baking, from Boeotia, early 5th century BC] for Greek houses do not seem to have had kitchens before the 4th century BC.

Land suitable for arable farming was mainly limited to the fertile plains; but sheep, goats and pigs were bred and reared in the hills. The vine and olive were cultivated extensively, and the vast olive groves, such as the thousand-year-old grove in the plain of Amphissa, near Delphi, yielded a rich harvest for the export trade. The olives were either picked by hand or beaten down by long switches [B226, amphora, Attic, c. 520 BC]. After an initial treatment, the pulp was fed into an olive press [D550, Satyr at an oil press, Roman, 1st century AD].

No place in Greece was more than about 60 miles from the sea and Rome encircled the Mediterranean so that fish, which included the species illustrated on the plate (red mullet, sea perch, sargus (bream) and cuttle fish) was prominent in the diet [F267, Campanian, 350–300 BC]. Many types of fishing equipment were available [see fish-hooks; 1909 3–5 1, model keep-net, Roman period] and men fished in the sea, in busy harbours, such as Alexandria [527. Clay lamp, Roman, 2nd century AD] and from river banks and bridges, as seen in the marine landscape in the First Roman Room.

Produce for sale was carried by pack animal into the towns [967. Donkey carrying cheese, Greek mid-4th century].

Transport [*centre case*]

Sea. Roads in Greece compared with the great Roman highways were mere tracks over the mountains, and it was therefore easier to transport people and goods by sea. A merchant vessel [B436, Attic cup, c. 540 BC] went under sail, with oars to provide supplementary power. The ship stood high in the water to provide space in the hull for cargo [A202, model of a merchant ship, from Amathus, Cyprus].

Land. Both Greeks and Romans used the four-wheel wagon with wickerwork hood [612. Hellenistic Greek, probably from Alexandria], but other types of vehicles included the chariot [2695, Roman period], mule cart [B485, jug, Attic, 2nd quarter 6th century BC; see also First Vase Room, ref. 1]. In addition to the donkey and the mule, another pack animal was the camel [C544, Hellenistic Greek], but wealthy Greeks and Romans travelled on horseback.

Town Life

After the collapse of Mycenaean civilization (c. 1100 BC) living conditions in Greece were primitive and remained so for about three centuries. But by classical times (479–336 BC) the well-to-do in Athens occupied houses with tiled roofs and sometimes of two storeys, which were built round a courtyard and had an entrance in a narrow street. The poor lived in habitations consisting of one or two rooms covered with a mud roof. The Roman lower classes, however, occupied flats in large blocks with shops at street level, but the imperial nobility resided in spacious town houses, and possessed country estates for the summer.

The life of an Athenian woman in the classical period was extremely circumscribed. Her activities were mainly of a domestic nature and confined to the home where she dwelt in the women's quarters. She never dined with her husband when he entertained his friends at home (although courtesans who sang and danced were often present) [Second Vase Room, ref. 1] nor accompanied him on a visit except occasionally to festivals. She superintended (and sometimes took part in) the household tasks of her slaves, such as the weaving of cloth [centre case: *Spinning and Weaving*; equipment and specimens of textiles], which provided her family with clothes, and she brought up her children [Second Vase Room, ref. 2] who played with simple toys (as did Roman children) beloved by the young up to our technological age, for example, dolls, rattles, soldiers, wooden animals, ships, tops [centre case: *Toys and Games*] and chariots [Terracotta Room, ref. 2]. She, herself, often tried her skill with knucklebones, the Greek equivalent of dice [1907 7–11 1, from Tanagra, Boeotia, 330–200 BC]. Elsewhere she can be seen washing (Fig. 44) [Second Vase Room, ref. 3], and the water for her ablutions and other household uses would have been drawn at one of the public fountains, probably by slaves [First Vase Room, ref. 2], or from the well in the courtyard of her home.

But a married woman of the Roman upper class had in imperial times much greater freedom than her classical sister, being able to dispose of her own property, take part in her husband's amusements, marry the man of her own choice and live in his home as his equal. The material wealth of Rome was much greater than that of Greece, and while the Roman woman undoubtedly supervised her household, she would do so vicariously through a trusted house slave.

However, clothes and their concomitants, toilet articles and jewellery, interested both Greek and Roman women, and although we have seen examples of all three in the Department's ground floor rooms, there are additional exhibits here [centre case: *Dress and Toilet Articles*; gallery: *Jewellery*]. The jewellery includes some remarkable pieces made by the Etruscans whose influence on Roman art was pervasive. There is also a small but beautiful collection of

Fig. 44. Women washing at a pedestal basin. Note clothes hanging on wall and boots on the floor

coins: Greek, Persian, Lycian, Macedonian, Ptolemaic, Hellenistic and Roman.

The Home [*wall case*]. Greek furniture was made of wood and bronze, and consisted mainly of chairs, stools [2570, bronze stool, Roman period], couches which also served as beds, small tables and chests for storage, and the Romans followed Greek models. Most of it has perished except for the occasional part which has fortuitously escaped corrosion or decay, such as the wooden chair-leg in the form of an animal's leg decorated with acanthus flowers [48 8–4 25], the wooden moulding from a piece of furniture [48 8–4 27], both Hellenistic, 4th century, from Panticapaeum in the Crimea, and the end support of a couch terminating in a horse's head and a bust of Eros [2564, Roman, 1st century AD]. Ivory also embellished furniture [1909 6–23 1, Roman,

3rd century AD] as did terracotta reliefs in earlier times [Terracotta Room, ref. 1]. Lighting was supplied by pottery and bronze lamps (see below) and also by candelabra, sometimes of silver [1924 5–14 1, Roman, 3rd century AD, from Beaurains, nr. Arras] or bronze [Terracotta Room, ref. 3], into which long candles were fixed sideways on the prongs which encircled the top.

Roman kitchen equipment is easily recognizable, frying pan, ladle, baking tin, wooden and metal spoons and knives. There was even the Roman equivalent of a hot-plate [1432] in the form of a clay shrine, the food being placed in a bowl on top and heated by lamps inside the shrine.

Greek and Roman lamps [*centre case*]. Lighting from very early times was provided by pottery lamps fuelled by olive oil, and with the side pinched in to hold the wick. In course of time other developments occurred, the bridged nozzle [196, Greek late 7th or early 6th century BC, from Ephesus], handles [360, Greek, late 2nd or early 1st century BC, from Cnidus], the enclosed body [656, Roman, 1st century AD, made in Italy] and the multi-nozzle [1904 2–4 443, Roman, made in Italy in the 1st century AD]. Pottery lamps were in use throughout the Greek and Roman world wherever illumination was required.

Mosaic floors in Greek houses appeared about 400 BC, but the great achievements in this art took place in Hellenistic and Roman times. Fine examples can be seen on the north-west staircase from villas and buildings at Halicarnassus, Pompeii, Carthage, Utica and elsewhere.

Silver [*4 wall cases*]. Comparatively few silver objects of the Greek classical period still exist (p. 222), but those which have survived are often of exquisite workmanship [1st case, 9, libation dish, style of 4th century BC, from Eze, Alpes Maritimes].

To the imperial Romans, however, silver plate in the home was a status symbol. It was used for display [2nd case, 132. Bowl in form of a lotus flower, 2nd century AD, from Chatuzanges], for toilet articles, for example cosmetic box [119] and mirror [124, from a woman's tomb at Bursa, north-west Turkey], and at banquets where food was served from large dishes [3rd case, 141, 142, from Caubiac], seasoned from silver pepperpots [4th case, 145, pepperpot in the form of a Negro slave] and wine drunk from a silver cup [176], both found in a field with other pieces at Chaourse, nr. Montcornet. One of the most beautiful silver pieces in the Museum is the Great Dish of the Mildenhall Treasure, which is classical in style but of the 4th century AD [see Roman-Britain Room].

Glass [*cases below gallery*]. Glass was first made in western Asia during the 3rd millennium BC, and by the first half of the 15th century BC in Egypt. During the hiatus caused by the Sea Peoples in these areas (p.), manufacture was maintained only in Syria, mainly of small objects. But by the 9th century, small-scale production of glass took place in Italy, and by the 7th and 6th centuries probably also in Rhodes, Cyprus and possibly Greece.

Towards the end of the 4th century BC, the great Ptolemaic glassworks at Alexandria came into production and exported superb pieces to Greece and Rome and also craftsmen who settled in southern Italy. But it was the invention of glass blowing, probably by the Phoenicians just before the Christian era, which caused large-scale production and changed glass from a luxury object to one of daily use.

In the eight cases at the base of the gallery, glass vessels can be seen made by the various techniques in use from the 6th century BC to the 4th century AD.

Sports and Amusements

The home, as we understand it today, played very little part in the life of a Greek man of classical times. In contrast with the Roman, who cherished and adorned his home, it was merely a roof over his head, and his active life was spent in the open air, on his estate, in the agora, at the gymnasium, games, theatre and other places where men congregated.

Athletes, Gladiators and Chariot races. The Greeks organized athletic contests very early in their history, and Homer writes in *The Iliad* of the funeral games arranged by Achilles for Patroclus. The Olympic games were instituted in the Geometric period in 776 BC, and subsequent Pan-hellenic festivals were the Pythian (Delphi), Nemean (Argos) and Isthmian (Corinth) games, as well as the local festivals such as the Panathenaea at Athens, at all of which it was the ambition of Greek youths to win a prize.

The events of these festivals remained the same with only slight variations throughout their existence, and included chariot races [First Vase Room, ref. 3], foot races [Second Vase Room, ref. 4], wrestling [Second Vase Room, ref. 5], boxing, throwing the discus [3207, inscribed discus of Exoidas, 6th century BC], the javelin, and jumping [B134. Panathenic amphora, from Vulci, c. 520 BC].

The Romans were not interested in athletics and the spectacle relished by the Roman mob in imperial times was the brutal gladiatorial contest, which was derived from the Etruscans [1946 5–14 1, gladiator's helmet, probably 2nd century AD; 1602, bronze figure of a gladiator]. In the provinces the magistrates were responsible for providing these spectacles and troups of trained men were hired from contractors, but in Rome the entire organization from training the combatants to the actual contests was controlled by the state [for armour and arms used in war, see wall case *Greek and Etruscan armour*; centre case *Roman Weapons and Armour*, and *Greek and Mycenaean Weapons*].

Great excitement was also aroused by the chariot races in the Circus Maximus in Rome which were less cruel but excessively dangerous to the charioteers [73 8–20 690. Charioteer holding the palm of victory, 2nd or 3rd century AD] whose careers were frequently terminated by fatal accidents.

Dancing [*1st end wall case*]. The Greeks danced at religious festivals, freeborn women danced at family festivals [D336, Terracotta, 2nd century BC], and courtesans performed for the all-male banquets, often with castanets [1925 1–20 1, Etruscan, c. 460 BC]. The Romans on the other hand regarded the art as undignified, except at religious festivals.

Music [*2nd end wall case*]. Throughout their history the Greeks were passionately fond of music. The ability to sing and play an instrument was an essential accomplishment for every educated man [Second Vase Room, ref. 6]. Musical contests were an integral part of the great festivals.

The principal instruments were the single and Pan pipes [16 6–10 502. Two pipes of sycamore wood, from Athens, c. 500 BC] and the lyre [16 6–10 501, from Athens, perhaps 5 BC] which was either plucked with the fingers or with a small stick (plectrum), and of which the kithara [C20, c. 200 BC] and the lute [1919 6–20 7, c. 300 BC] were variations. Cymbals were also popular [1906 4–12 1] and an Alexandrian Greek even invented an organ which worked by water power [1965 10–11 1. Clay lamp in form of a man playing a water organ, Roman, 2nd or 3rd century AD]. This instrument was much favoured by the Romans who were also fond of music, and whose daughters were instructed in the art [staircase, 26. Music Lesson, from Herculaneum, 1 AD].

Drama (*3rd end wall case*]. Greek tragedy, which has so powerfully influenced modern drama, seems to have evolved from the choral lyric which, in the 7th and 6th centuries BC, flourished in the Peloponnese and to whose development Alcman, the lyric poet of Sparta (p. 183) contributed so much. Subsequently Thespis, a native of Attica, added a prologue and speeches in verse in the contemporary idiom, and by about 534 BC, a tragedy was regularly performed at the Greater Dionysia, the festival of the god held at Athens each year. Satirical comedies were also performed.

The actors wore masks [1195. Clay model of a comic mask of a Negro], and also played female parts [1530. Comic actor as bride, from Corinth, c. 350 BC; 747. Comic actor as an old woman with baby, from Athens, c. 350 BC]. In the Greek cities of southern Italy at the end of the 4th century BC, burlesques were popular, and on the vase [F151, Apulian bell-krater, c. 380 BC] is illustrated a parody on the myth of the blind centaur Cheiron, cured by Apollo. In the painting the fore-part and hind-quarters of the centaur are represented by two men, a stage convention still to be seen in pantomime animal representation today.

In Hellenistic and Roman times mime, in which the actors did not wear masks, was popular [1907 5–18 8–10. Three characters from a mime of about 1st century AD]. But the relative popularity of the drama in Roman times and the gladiatorial contests can be gauged from the seating accommodation of the two theatres and the amphitheatre at

Pompeii, the former amounting to 6,500 and the latter to 20,000 seats.

Writing [*centre case*]. It has already been mentioned (p. 198) that the first script in which Greek was written was the syllabic Linear B [1910 4–23 2. Clay tablet, part of an inventory of sheep, from Knossos, c. 1400 BC]. Reference has also been made to the derivation of the Greek alphabet from the form of the North Semitic alphabet current in the 9th and early 8th centuries BC (p. 101). Here the earliest Greek alphabetic script on display in the Museum can be seen on the Corinthian vase [65 12–13 1, 640–620 BC] which tells us the name of its owner, Aineta, and those of her admirers. Also displayed are objects connected with writing, inkpots, pens, stylus, potsherds, waxed writing tablets, a statuette of a girl using a tablet [see also Terracotta Room, ref. 4] and papyrus [CCCLVI, from Alexandria, 1 AD].

Religion and magic [*centre case*]. A votive offering to a god was to ensure that the supplicant's request would be granted, or as a thank-offering that it had been granted. The floral silver plaques [227, 224, 229, c. 2nd century AD] were votive offerings from a shrine or temple, as were the 7th century figures found in the sanctuary of Artemis Orthia at Sparta. The votive wheel [Bronze 253, from near Argos, 6th century BC] may have been dedicated by Eudamos as a thank-offering for a victory in the Nemean Games, perhaps in a chariot race.

To examine the vases referred to above, we must go through the temporary exhibitions in the Greek Corridor and the Cyprus Room (the latter very splendid) to the First and Second Vase Rooms, afterwards returning to the Terracotta Room via the Greek and Roman Life Room.

The vases concerned are listed on page 250

* * *

Room	*Text page no.*	*Reference no.*	*Case and exhibit no.*
First Vase	242	1	Centre case E, B132, Panathenic amphora.* Two-wheel mule cart, 500–480 BC.
,,	243	2	Case 22, B333, hydria. Women at the fountain, c. 520 BC.
,,	247	3	Centre case E, B130, Panathenic amphora. Two-horse chariot race, c. 566 BC.
Second Vase	243	1	Case 44, 2nd shelf, E453, stamnos. Symposium [banquet], c. 440 BC.
,,	243	2	Case 43, E535, oinochoe. A child crawling towards a jug, 425–400 BC.
,,	247	3	Case 17, E201, hydria. Two women washing [note clothes hanging on wall], 480–470 BC.
,,	247	4	Case 40, E389, pelike. Two torch racers, c. 430 BC.
,,	247	5	Case 32, 1928 1–17 59, kylix. Two wrestlers and trainer, 470–460 BC.
,,	247	6	Case 18, E172, hydria. Music Lesson, 480–470 BC.
Terracotta	245	1	Centre case, Melian reliefs, 465–435 BC.
,,	243	2	Case 1, 1972 2–4 5. Toy chariot, made in Athens, c. 720 BC.
,,	245	3	Glass centre case, 593. Bronze candelabrum. Youth wrapped in his cloak leaning on his staff. Etruscan, 460–450 BC.
,,	249	4	Case 17, C718. Girl with writing tablet, from Benghazi. Made in Cyrenaica, c. 300 BC.

* Given as a prize at the Panathenic festival at Athens. These vessels were black figure.

If the Roman-Britain Room has not already been visited, it should be now, for the exhibits we have been considering are mainly representative of metropolitan Rome whereas those from Britain give a fair idea of life in an imperial province and the civilizing influence of Rome.

Appendix I

The radiocarbon method of dating is based on the fact that all living matter contains minute traces of the radioactive carbon-14 atoms, which are derived from the atmosphere. Within certain limits the proportion of carbon-14 atoms to ordinary carbon is constant for all living matter, but after death the process by which they derive carbon atoms from the atmosphere ceases. The proportion of carbon-14 to ordinary carbon is therefore no longer maintained, because the carbon-14 atoms decay at a constant rate determined by the 'half-life' of carbon-14 which is approximately 5,000 years. This means that the residual radioactivity of carbon extracted from dead organic material gives an indication of the time which has elapsed since it formed part of a living organism, i.e. its approximate age.

In the past archaeologists have often had difficulty in deciding how long any given civilization may have lasted, and this method of radiocarbon dating can provide the answer within certain limits.

Appendix II

Notes on Prehistory

Evolution

Prehistory, for those unfamiliar with the subject, is difficult to understand, but it is important to realize that this planet was inhabited for millions of years by fish, reptiles and animals many of which are now extinct, before man made his appearance. That he did so appear, after a long period of development, is due, as was the case with his predecessors on earth, to evolution.

Biological evolution is a process of gradual change. It functions through the reproductive processes which, by spasmodic mutation of the genes, cause variations in individuals of a species, such as between man and man.

If a variation assists an individual in its struggle for existence, say, in the procurement of nutriment, that individual is naturally selected for survival, and its favourable variation will be transmitted by inheritance. This process repeated over many generations will result in the formation of a new species.

Dating

Scholars divide history into periods which can be dated in order to deal rationally with their material. But before scientific methods were introduced to obtain absolute dates (methods not yet perfected) dating of remote periods of prehistory was relative, i.e. it was known that certain geological conditions preceded or succeeded others in time: consequently these epochs were differentiated by name, Pleistocine, Pliocene etc., fixed dates not being available (see Fig. 1). It was thought until recently that the development of the genus *Homo* (man) was confined to the Pleistocene epoch with its glacial and interglacial periods known as the Ice Age (p. 37), but the discoveries at Lake Rudolf have proved otherwise.

Culture

Culture in an archaeological context is the way of life of a group: its ideas, customs, tools and weapons, and other material objects. The overall culture of the Pleistocene epoch is the Old Stone Age, known as Paleolithic in Europe, the Near East and North Africa. Stone Age culture begins much earlier in Africa than elsewhere, and in its lower and middle stages the remains amount to little more than collections of stone tools known as 'industries'. But the Late (Upper) Paleolithic, Mesolithic (Middle Stone Age) and Neolithic (New Stone Age) cultures were much more diversified, particularly the latter which was a farming culture with settled domiciles and more complex possessions.

But it can never be too strongly emphasized that cultures are created by people, and when the archaeologist or prehistorian refers to, say, the Badārian culture, what he really means is the way of life (or the material remains of it) of the inhabitants of Badāri and of the peasants in the villages where a similar mode of life was practised.

Books for Further Reading

1 The British Museum

de BEER, G. R. *Sir Hans Sloane and the British Museum*, Oxford University Press. 1953.

BETJEMAN, J. *et al. Treasures of the British Museum*. Collins, London, 1971.

ESDAILE, A. J. K. *The British Museum Library*. Allen & Unwin, London. 1948.

FRANCIS, F. (ed.). *Treasures of the British Museum*. Thames & Hudson, London. 1971.

MILLER, E. J. *A Brief History of the British Museum*. Pitkin Pictorials, London. 1970.

Prince of Librarians: the life and times of Antonio Panizzi of the British Museum. Deutsch, London. 1967.

This Noble Cabinet. A History of the British Museum. Deutsch, London. 1972.

2 Prehistory and Roman Britain

de BEER, G. R. *A Handbook on Evolution*, 4th ed. British Museum (Natural History), London. 1970.

CAMBRIDGE ANCIENT HISTORY, vol. 1, (revised).

CLARK, J. D. *The Prehistory of Africa*. Thames & Hudson, London. 1970.

CLARK, J. G. D. & PIGGOTT, S. *Prehistoric Societies*. Penguin Books, Harmondsworth. *In print* 1973.

CLARK, J. G. D. *The Stone Age Hunters*. Thames & Hudson, London. 1967.

World Prehistory. Cambridge University Press. 1969.

CLARKE, R. Rainbird. *East Anglia*. Thames & Hudson, London. 1960.

FOX, Aileen M. *South-West England*. Thames & Hudson, London. 1964.

HOWELLS, W. W. *Mankind in the Making*. Penguin Books, Harmondsworth. 1967.

JESSUP, R. F. *South-East England*. Thames & Hudson, London. 1970.

LEAKEY, L. S. B. & VANNE MORRIS, G. *Unveiling Man's Origins*. Methuen, London. 1970.

LE GROS CLARK, W. E. *Man-apes or Ape-men*. Holt Rinehart & Winston, New York. 1967.

OAKLEY, K. P. *Man the Tool-Maker*. British Museum (Natural History), London. 1970.

QUENNELL, C. H. B. & M. *Everyday Life in Prehistoric Times*, revised G. de G. Sieveking, Batsford, London. 1968.

ROE, D. *Prehistory: an introduction*. Macmillan, London. 1970.

ROSS, Anne. *Everyday Life of the Pagan Celts*. Batsford, London: G. P. Putnam's Sons, New York, 1970.

Pagan Celtic Britain. Routledge & Kegan Paul, London. 1967.

SANDARS, N. K. *Prehistoric Art in Europe*. Penguin Books, Harmondsworth. *In print* 1973.

SIEVEKING, A. & G. de G. *The Caves of France and Northern Spain*. Vista, London. 1962.

STONE, J. F. S. *Wessex before the Celts*. Thames & Hudson, London. 1958.

BIRLEY, A. R. *Life in Roman Britain*. Batsford, London: G. P. Putnam's Sons, New York. 1964.

FRERE, S. S. *Britannia: a history of Roman Britain*. Routledge & Kegan Paul, London. 1967.

MEATES, G. W. *Lullingstone Roman Villa*. Heinemann, London. 1955.

RICHMOND, I. A. *Roman Britain*, Penguin Books, Harmondsworth. *In print* 1973.

TACITUS. *On Britain and Germany* (the *Agricola* and the *Germania*), trs. H. Mattingly. Penguin Books, Harmondsworth. *In print* 1973.

TOYNBEE, J. C. M. *Art in Britain under the Romans*. Oxford University Press. 1964.

WEBSTER, G. *The Roman Army*. Grosvenor Museum, Chester. 1956.

BRITISH MUSEUM PUBLICATIONS

BRAILSFORD, J. W. *Guide to the Antiquities of Roman Britain*. 1951.

The Mildenhall Treasure. 1964.

Flint Implements: an account of stone age techniques and cultures. 1968.

JOHNS, Catherine. *Arretine and Samian Pottery*. 1971.

3 Western Asia

ALBRIGHT, W. F. *The Archaeology of Palestine*, rev. ed. Penguin Books, Harmondsworth. 1960.

CAMBRIDGE ANCIENT HISTORY, vol. 1, 2 (revised), 3, 4. Cambridge University Press.

COLE, Sonia M. *The Neolithic Revolution*, 5th ed. British Museum (Natural History), London. 1970.

CONTENAU, G. *Everyday Life in Babylon and Assyria*. Edward Arnold, London. 1954.

DIRINGER, D. *The Alphabet: a Key to the History of Mankind*, 3rd ed. Hutchinson, London. 1968.

FRANKFORT, H. *The Art and Architecture of the Ancient Orient*, rev. ed. Penguin Books, Harmondsworth. 1970.

GHIRSHMAN, R. *Iran*. Penguin Books, Harmondsworth. 1954.

GRAY, J. *The Canaanites*. Thames & Hudson, London. 1964.

GURNEY, O. R. *The Hittites*. Penguin Books, Harmondsworth. *In print* 1973.

HARDEN, D. *The Phoenicians*. Thames & Hudson, London. 1962.

HITTI, P. K. *History of Syria*, 2nd ed. Macmillan, London. 1957.

History of the Arabs, 10th ed. Macmillan, London; St. Martin's Press, New York. 1970.

KENYON, Kathleen M. *Digging up Jericho*. Ernest Benn, London. 1957.

KRAMER, S. N. *History begins at Sumer*, 2nd ed. Thames & Hudson, London. 1962.

LAYARD, A. H. *Discoveries in the Ruins of Nineveh and Babylon*. John Murray, London. 1853.

Nineveh and its Remains. 2 vol. John Murray, London, 1849.

LLOYD, S. H. F. *The Art of the Ancient Near East*. Thames & Hudson, London. 1961.

Foundations in the Dust. Penguin Books, Harmondsworth. 1955.

MALLOWAN, M. E. L. *Early Mesopotamia and Iran*. Thames & Hudson, London. 1965.

MOSCATI, S. *The Face of the Ancient Orient*. Routledge & Kegan Paul and Valentine Mitchell, London. 1960.

PARROT, A. *Nineveh and Babylon*. Thames & Hudson, London. 1961.

SAGGS, H. W. F. *Everyday Life in Babylonia and Assyria*. Batsford, London: G. P. Putnam's Sons, New York. 1965.

The Greatness that was Babylon. Sidgwick & Jackson, London. 1962.

WARMINGTON, B. H. *Carthage*. Penguin Books, Harmondsworth. 1964.

WOOLLEY, C. L. *Excavations at Ur: a record of twelve years' work*. Ernest Benn, London. 1954.

BRITISH MUSEUM PUBLICATIONS

BARNETT, R. D. *Illustrations of Old Testament History*. 1968.

BARNETT, R. D. *The Assyrian Palace Reliefs*. 1970.

BARNETT, R. D. and WISEMAN, D. J. *Fifty Masterpieces of Ancient Near Eastern Art*. 1969.

MITCHELL, T. C. *Sumerian Art Illustrated by Objects from Ur and Al-'Ubaid*. 1969.

RIMMER, Joan. *Ancient Musical Instruments of Western Asia in the Department of Western Asiatic Antiquities in the British Museum*. 1969.

SOLLBERGER, E. *The Babylonian Legend of the Flood*, 3rd ed. 1971.

4 Egypt

ALDRED, C. *Akhenaten, Pharaoh of Egypt*. Thames & Hudson, London. 1968.

The Egyptians. Thames & Hudson, London. 1961.

BEVAN, E. R. *History of Egypt under the Ptolemaic Dynasty*. Methuen, London. 1927.

CAMBRIDGE ANCIENT HISTORY, vol. 1, 2 (revised), 3 *et seq*. Cambridge University Press.

ČERNÝ, J. *Ancient Egyptian Religion*. Hutchinson, London. 1952.

DESROCHES-NOBLECOURT, Christiane. *Tutankhamen: Life and death of a pharaoh*. Penguin Books, Harmondsworth. 1965.

EDWARDS, I. E. S. *The Pyramids of Egypt*. Penguin Books, Harmondsworth. *In print* 1973.

ELGOOD, P. G. *Later Dynasties of Egypt*. Blackwell, Oxford. 1951.

EMERY, W. B. *Archaic Egypt*. Penguin Books, Harmondsworth. *In print* 1973.

ERMAN, A. *Life in Ancient Egypt*. Blackman, London. 1894.

GARDINER, A. H. *Egypt of the Pharaohs*. Clarendon Press, Oxford. 1961.

GLANVILLE, S. R. K. *Life in Ancient Egypt*. Routledge, London. 1930.

HARRIS, J. R. (ed.). *The Legacy of Egypt*. Clarendon Press, Oxford. 1971.

JAMES, T. G. H. *Egyptian Sculptures*. Collins in association with UNESCO, London. 1967.

KEES, H. *Ancient Egypt. A cultural topography*. Faber & Faber, London. 1961.

LANGE, C. and HIRMER, M. *Egypt: Architecture, Sculpture, Painting in Three Thousand Years*. Phaidon, London, New York. 1968.

MONTET, P. *Eternal Egypt*. Weidenfeld & Nicolson, London. 1964.

Everyday Life in Egypt in the Days of Ramesses the Great. Edward Arnold, London. 1958.

PENDLEBURY, J. D. S. *Tell El-Amarna*. Dickson & Thompson, London. 1935.

POSENER, G. *A Dictionary of Egyptian Civilisation*. Methuen, London. 1962.

SMITH, W. S. *The Art and Architecture of Ancient Egypt*. Penguin Books, Harmondsworth. *In print* 1973.

WILSON, J. A. *The Burden of Egypt*. University of Chicago Press. 1951.

WINLOCK, H. E. *Models of Daily Life from the Tomb of Meket-Re at Thebes*. Harvard University Press, Cambridge, Mass. 1955.

BRITISH MUSEUM PUBLICATIONS

BUDGE, E. A. Wallis. *The Rosetta Stone*, 1968.

A General Introductory Guide to the Egyptian Collections in the British Museum. 1971.

SHORE, A. F. *Portrait Painting from Roman Egypt*, 1962.

5 Greece and Rome

ANDREWES, A. *Greek Society*. Penguin Books, Harmondsworth. *In print* 1973.

BALDRY, H. C. *Ancient Greek Literature in its Living Context*. Thames & Hudson, London. 1968.

BARROW, R. H. *The Romans*. Penguin Books, Harmondsworth. *In print* 1973.

BOARDMAN, J. *Greek Art*. Thames & Hudson, London. 1973.

The Greeks Overseas. Penguin Books, Harmondsworth. 1964.

BURN, A. R. *The Pelican History of Greece*. Penguin Books, Harmondsworth. *In print* 1973.

CAMBRIDGE ANCIENT HISTORY, Vol. 1, 2 (revised), 3–13. Cambridge University Press.

CARCOPINO, J. *Daily Life in Ancient Rome*. Penguin Books, Harmondsworth. *In print* 1973.

CARY, M. *History of Rome*, 2nd ed. Macmillan, London: St. Martin's Press, New York. 1965.

CHARLESTON, R. J. *Roman Pottery*. Faber & Faber, London. 1955.

COOK, J. M. *The Greeks in Ionia and the East*. Thames & Hudson, London. 1962.

COOK, R. M. *Greek Art*. Weidenfeld, London. 1972.

The Greeks till Alexander. Thames & Hudson, London. 1961.

COWELL, F. R. *Everyday Life in Ancient Rome*. Batsford, London. 1961.

DINSMOOR, W. B. *The Architecture of Ancient Greece*. Batsford, London. 1950.

FARRINGTON, B. *Greek Science*. Penguin Books, Harmondsworth. 1966.

FLACELIÈRE, R. *Daily Life in Greece at the Time of Pericles*. Weidenfeld & Nicolson, London. 1965.

FORSDYKE, E. J. *Greece before Homer*. Max Parrish, London. 1956.

GRANT, M. *The World of Rome*. Weidenfeld & Nicolson, London. 1960.

GROSE-HODGE, H. *Roman Panorama*. Cambridge University Press. 1944.

HATZFELD, J. and AYMARD, A. *A History of Ancient Greece*. Oliver & Boyd, Edinburgh. 1966.

HAYNES, Sybille. *Land of the Chimaera: an archaeological excursion in the south-west of Turkey*. Chatto & Windus, London. *Spring*. 1974.

HIGGINS, R. A. *Minoan and Mycenaean Art*. Thames & Hudson, London. 1967.

HUTCHINSON, R. W. *Prehistoric Crete*. Penguin Books, Harmondsworth. 1962.

LANE, A. *Greek Pottery*, 3rd ed. Faber & Faber, London. 1971.

RICHTER, Gisela M. A. *The Sculpture and Sculptors of the Greeks*, 4th ed. Yale University Press, New Haven and London. 1970.

SCHLIEMANN, H. *Mycenae: a narrative of researches and discoveries at Mycenae and Tiryns*. London. 1877.

STRONG, D. E. *Roman Imperial Sculpture*. Alec Tiranti, London. 1961.

TACITUS. *The Annals of Imperial Rome*. Penguin Books, Harmondsworth. *In print* 1973.

The Histories. Penguin Books, Harmondsworth. *In print* 1973.

TAYLOUR, W. D. *The Mycenaeans*. Thames & Hudson, London. 1964.

WEBSTER, T. B. L. *Everyday Life in Classical Athens*. B. T. Batsford, London: G. P. Putnam's Sons, New York. 1969.

WHEELER, R. E. M. *Roman Art and Architecture*. Thames & Hudson, London. 1964.

WOODHEAD, A. G. *The Greeks in the West*. Thames & Hudson, London. 1962.

BRITISH MUSEUM PUBLICATIONS

BAILEY, D. M. *Greek and Roman Pottery Lamps*, 1963.

HAYNES, D. E. L. *The Portland Vase*. 1964.

HAYNES, Sybille. *Etruscan Bronze Utensils*, 1965.

Etruscan Sculpture. 1971.

HIGGINS, R. A. *The Greek Bronze Age*. 1970.

Greek Terracotta Figures. 1969.

Jewellery from Classical Lands. 1969.

An Historical Guide to the Sculptures of the Parthenon, 1971.

TRENDALL, A. D. *South Italian Vase Painting*. 1966.

Index

Notes